VIRGINIA COOVER

ELLEN DEACON

CHARLES ESSER

CHRISTOPHER MOORE

NEW SOCIETY PRESS

Resource Manual for a Living Revolution

Copies available from:

Resource Manual
Movement for a New Society
4722 Baltimore Ave.
Philadelphia, PA 19143

Preface

This manual is for people who are concerned or angered by the deterioration of our society and who, because they have some sense that their efforts can have an effect for change, are looking for tools to transform it. It is a working reference for those who are prepared to act to create a better life for themselves and others.

People can and want to change their environment so that human needs can be more adequately met. This manual illustrates that the process can be learned and that people working together can assume leadership and make changes.

While developing courses in nonviolent social change for schools and offering workshops for people already involved in social organizing, we found ourselves repeatedly in a dilemma. We wanted participants to become responsible for their own learning/training, but many of the skills and resources usable by others were in our collective experience and not in print. Thus, it was necessary for students, teachers and workshop participants to rely heavily on us for input.

In order to make these training and organizing resources more available and at the same time to free ourselves to work on our own projects and growth, we decided to write this manual.

This manual's gestation over more than five years has resulted in an inevitable problem. Since its basic text was gathered, our work has moved into new areas. With these new experiences our thinking and our resourcesfulness have (thank goodness!) continued to expand. We would like to include these ideas and resources, some of which seem even more exciting to us right now, but to do so would postpone the publication by several months (or years). We make no apologies for their exclusion: a living revolution must bring continuous changes or it is not what it claims to be. The ideas and tools in this book are, in our judgment, of real use, and we want to make them available to people, now.

The manual is a reflection of ourselves in process. The tools in this manual are ones which we have used in our own organizing and growth efforts. We have tried to convey throughout the book that the building of a fully human society is complex and will be long and demanding, but that it can be done by people working together and supporting each other. The writing and editing itself has been long and challenging, but through it we have grown in our own ability to work together and in an appreciation of the diversity of interest and activities which made it possible.

The problem of sexism in language troubled us throughout. Our attempts to remove sexism from wording and content may be somewhat awkward, but they reflect our best thinking at this time. We have found it difficult to remove sexism and still maintain fluency of expression.

There is one major point, that is not always given clear or sufficient emphasis in the manual, which we would like to emphasize here. *All the theorizing and training in the world are of no use unless they find their expression in concrete, determined action in our daily lives*. Learning skills in this manual is only a first step towards accomplishing change. It is essential to use such resources *to act*, to continue *to reflect* on our actions, refine our thinking and *proceed with further action*. We are excited and proud to be involved with other people working in the world, to make it ours, to make it more human.

Gini Coover
Ellen Deacon
Chuck Esser
Chris Moore

Note on Second Edition: For this new edition we have updated "Part Ten: Groups to Contact" including the addition of groups outside the United States. We have also corrected errors and checked prices and addresses of many of the resources listed. If you find additional errors we would appreciate being notified at the address on the back cover.

Acknowledgements

We would like to express our appreciation to the faculty, staff and students at George School and Westtown School for welcoming us onto their campuses in 1972 to experiment with sharing skills, tools, and information which empower people to make changes in their lives. Special appreciation goes to Kay Edstene, faculty member, who opened the way for us to come to George School and worked closely with us the entire time. We learned as much from her as she did from us.

Janet Hartsough shared in those early experiments and the first year of work on the manual. Her decision to move to California terminated her participation as a member of the writing team but not her support of our efforts.

The Friends Peace Committee of Philadelphia Yearly Meeting, with the special encouragement of George Hardin, gave us a grant to begin preparation of the manual, and it continued to support us as we expanded our vision of what the manual should contain.

The Meeting for Sharing of Quaker Street Half Yearly Meeting, New York, gave us a grant to write sections we decided to add and to help cover printing costs.

As usual in a project of this sort, our projections on costs were inaccurate, and Ellen and Chuck offered loans from their personal funds to cover the final costs of editing and printing.

Several people freely contributed writing time and materials to this project. Bill Moyer offered information used in the preparation of Part Seven "Organizing for Change," and the section on "Analysis." Through his work with the Philadelphia Macro-Analysis Collective (MNS), he helped develop several tools included in the manual. Lynne Shivers contributed several pieces of writing, credited to her in the text, and was repeatedly available to discuss problems. Charles Walker offered many of the written materials used to compile "The Direct Action Campaign." George Willoughby shared with us materials developed and used in courses in social change he co-taught at the Martin Luther King School of Social Change, Crozer, Pa., and at Pendle Hill, Wallingford, Pa. In addition to Christopher,

vii

members of the Training/Action Affinity Group (MNS) who developed, refined and wrote up several of the tools are Susanne Gowan, Stephen Parker, Peter Woodrow and Berit Lakey.

William Coleman, Susanne Gowan, Pam Haines, David Hartsough, Janet Hartsough, Berit Lakey, Gail Pressberg, Jim Schrag, Lynne Shivers, Pam Solo, Marjorie Swann, Charles Walker, and Kirk Wattles reviewed our manuscript and offered extensive suggestions included in the final revision.

Scott Beadenkopf helped edit the manuscript. Scott's suggestions on restructuring and presentation and his careful writing were extremely valuable. Bob Irwin provided general moral support and consultation during the last six months of editing. He expanded and edited the bibliographical materials and wrote much of the information on existing political theories in Part One. He did a general editing of the entire book for accuracy of content.

Jennifer Tiffany, at the *Friends Journal*, typeset the manual for us. Her ability to take corrected and heavily marked up copy and turn it into neatly set type was remarkable. Her suggestions on set up and type choice were extremely helpful, and her patience with the large number of authors' alterations was deeply appreciated.

David Perry did much of the initial layout work and made several helpful suggestions on design.

Chuck Esser contributed the photographs on pages 42, 100, and 114; Ted Hetzel, those on pages xv, 6, 128, 152, 202, 248, 298 and 320. The photograph on page 5 is by J.C. Stockwell and the one on page 334 is from the American Friends Service Committee files. David Willoughby drew the monster.

Cynthia Arvio read the entire manuscript before it went to the typesetter and made numerous grammatical and editorial suggestions which have made the manual more consistent and readable. She proofread most of the galleys and corrections. When David left for Ireland Cynthia oversaw the completion of the layout and did the paste up. Sarah Arvio helped with paste up when last minute pressures became heavy.

George Willoughby assisted us in our decisions about size and style of the finished product and located a printer and binder who did quick, high quality work at a price we could afford to pay.

It is not possible to thank by name all those who developed and improved tools or provided information used or referred to in this manual. It is, in fact, not possible even to know most of the people, past and present, who have made contributions incorporated here. Where these people are known, we have acknowledged their work in the body of the manual. To those of you we are not able to name—the results of your work have been extremely helpful to our own social and personal change efforts, and the information included here was selected because we saw it could contribute to the efforts of others.

Special acknowledgement must go to the entire Movement for a New Society/Life Center community in West Philadelphia for supporting and encouraging the authors in our long and often-delayed efforts. Individuals have cooperated with requests for information, read drafts, made helpful suggestions for revision and inclusion, and done much of the final editing, proofreading and layout work. Most importantly, the people in this community have created a vital training/organizing environment where materials in this manual are being tested, improved, and incorporated into the basic fabric of our social, political, economic, and personal lives.

We wish to thank the Philadelphia War Tax Resistance Fund and the Brandywine Peace Community and Alternative Fund for making loans to help with the printing of the second edition. These two funds, comprised of refused war taxes, personal savings and group deposits, make interest-free loans to social change and service groups. They are two excellent examples of alternative institutions that recycle money to support progressive community projects.

How to Use the Manual

The manual offers tools of empowerment, tools which help people regain control over their own learning and decision making, and make changes in their everyday lives and in the institutions which affect them. It provides information for developing skills in managing and resolving social and interpersonal conflicts creatively. Materials have been selected because they are usable in a variety of situations, by people from a wide range of skill and experience levels. Many of these skills are not taught in traditional educational institutions yet are useful for people to function creatively, independently and cooperatively.

New tools and skills frequently feel awkward the first time they are tried. The process used to learn them often contradicts ingrained patterns of behavior, such as domination, competition, withdrawal, criticism, and cynicism. Many of the tools in this manual are specifically designed to shake us out of stereotypic roles in which we have functioned for a long time, such as leader, follower, expert, teacher and student. These learned roles and behavior patterns have been useful in the society in which we live, but they get in our way when we try to create more flexible alternatives.

To help you locate resources, there are a detailed *Table of Contents* and an *Index* which lists all exercises, skills and major topic areas in the manual.

Tools with specific uses are usually located where general information appears on the same topic. Part Eight includes tools which may be used in a variety of training and action situations.

Wherever a tool that is explained in the manual is referred to, its name appears in boldface italic type. To locate the tool's description, check its name in the Index; to find the location of groups of tools, see the Index under "Exercises."

Bibliographical materials have been integrated into the manual where they are most relevant. A specific resource is usually noted in the general text with information on how to obtain it. Resources which are useful in several ways are listed in the short annotated bibliographies which appear at the end of most parts. When books are referred to in the text, publication information is either there or in the bibliography at the end of the part. For the location of bibliographies, check the Index under "Bibliographies."

Part One of the manual, "The Theoretical Basis for Change," contains resources that help people develop their own analysis, vision, and strategy. Part Two, "How to Work in Groups," presents both a theoretical background for understanding how groups function and a wide variety of practical skills and exercises for improving group process. Part Three, "Developing Community Support," will be useful in maintaining a supportive community base for training and organizing efforts.

In the section on "Personal Growth" (Part Four) are resources which help individuals change and grow both through their own disciplined efforts and through valuable support and feedback from others. "Consciousness Raising" (Part Five) contains ideas, exercises and information on the theory of Paulo Freire useful in raising consciousness. "Training and Education" (Part Six) includes basic information helpful in developing workshops, courses and other training experiences. There are sample workshops and information on efforts to use training methods in both formal and informal educational structures. Training as presented here can be used to learn a specific skill or to raise consciousness. It can also be a form of organizing, a way to build organizational strength, or preparation for people involved in a common project or a campaign.

"Organizing for Change" (Part Seven) contains a wealth of practical information accumulated as we and others developed constructive programs, experimented with alternative institutions, organized for changes in our neighborhoods and carried out nonviolent action campaigns. In Parts Eight and Nine are tools and skills with a variety of uses.

The section on "Groups to Contact" (Part Ten) contains a brief description of resources offered by a number of groups. Not meant to be a complete list of groups involved in social change, it includes those of which we are aware that offer resources supportive to the training/organizing approach presented in this manual.

As much as possible we have tried to avoid "jargon." But when new ideas, experiences and resources are generated, it is unavoidable that words are used in new ways and that new terms are developed. When we have used terms we feel may be new to many of you, or when we have used words differently from current usage, we have defined them in the place where they are explained most fully.

We have not tried to be exhaustive in any area. Since our intention has been to spark ideas and give enough information for a creative beginning, seed ideas and lists have often been used. Where additional resources are known to be available, references are given in the text or in footnotes.

We hope you will use these tools, improve them, develop new ones and in turn share with others those which empower you to make positive changes in your own lives and environment. If you have resources you would like to share with us, you can reach us through Ellen Deacon, 4501 Spruce, Philadelphia, PA 19139.

Contents

Resource Manual

for a

Living

Revolution

Introduction

The Need for Training in Organizing

Our appreciation of the need for training grew out of our involvement with others in the 1960's in efforts to end racial discrimination, poverty, and the Vietnam war and to provide jobs and education to all who wanted them. Our actions, often confusing and threatening to others, sometimes placed us in very tense situations. Periodically we found ourselves in violent or potentially explosive situations as the result of repressive measures by police or military personnel or provocative behavior from fellow organizers and demonstrators.

At that time we learned a style of preparation for action which had been used by SNCC and CORE* workers to cope with violent situations they encountered during attempts to desegregate public facilities. This preparation, called "non-violence training" (more accurately referred to in this manual as "training for nonviolent action") prepared people for a type of aggressive action which excluded the use of violence. Instead it used a commitment to truth and reason as its power and encouraged participants to develop their own resourcefulness to respond positively to people in violent or potentially violent situations. Through training for nonviolent action participants were able to re-train themselves out of rigid, customary ways of looking at and dealing with the problems they confronted. As a result people were able to be more flexible in new situations and respond more positively to people of different beliefs and actions.

Broadening the Uses of Training

In time, efforts to oppose war and injustice expanded to include a number of specific social/political/economic changes.

*Student Nonviolent Coordinating Committee and Congress of Racial Equality.

1

As people's focuses broadened, the experimental and cooperative process learned while training for nonviolent action became useful for the new tasks on which they were working.

Training in a wide range of skills (in a fashion that encourages initiative) is important in helping individuals and groups

—to develop an analysis, vision and strategy, tailored to the exact circumstances in which they find themselves;

—to understand how groups function, how decisions are made, and how they can work in more effective and satisfying ways;

—to face and resolve conflicts and problems arising as they live and work together;

—to develop more egalitarian, decentralized and cooperative learning structures and to use them in developing support communities, long-range campaigns and new economic alternatives.

This manual contains materials for the development of a training program which can be used in these and other areas.

Developing an Analysis, Vision and Strategy

We discovered that agreement on a particular theory was not necessary for people to use the cooperative training style explained here. Where members of a group had different theories, they could explore differences, discover similarities and often find a common basis for working together.

In order to make sense of escalating problems, we found it necessary to understand their causes. We looked particularly closely at economic and political causes and examined the implications of limited resources and environmental problems to potential solutions. We also examined a number of analyses by others, both historic and contemporary. Though this increased our understanding of past and present, we concluded that we are facing a unique time in history, deserving of unique responses. Changing economic, political and environmental realities require us to make a fresh analysis, and compel us to project bold new strategies. We discovered that creating a vision of the kind of society in which we want to live is very important to us in developing these strategies.

Using resources in the manual, people can develop a group analysis, vision and strategy and move toward cooperative action for change. An analysis, vision and strategy need to remain *flexible*, always open to questions and new information. But without an analysis based on *structural causes* of problems, a vision of the kind of world in which we want to live, and a

2

strategy which focuses on *structural changes*, efforts for change are likely to flounder.

Choosing Organizational Structures and Processes

The structures and methods people use help to determine the results achieved. Consensus is a method of decision making which can help create trust and cooperation among group members and help maintain a high level of participation. Processes that make it possible for people to release feelings are needed to free people from old distress and clear their minds for present thinking. Structure and content of meetings developed with the consent and participation of all; processes that make it possible for people to resolve conflicts without "winning" or "losing" at another's expense; evaluations that give people the opportunity to express their satisfaction or dissatisfaction with elements of the meeting—all these are forms which help, we believe, to move people toward the long-range goals of a society based on mutual trust and acceptance.

This manual describes a variety of processes and structures that can be used by groups to help accomplish their goals. We have most frequently used them in small groups of 4-30 people, but many can be used in larger groups by adapting them or by breaking a large group into smaller ones to accomplish specific tasks.

Our experience indicates that small face-to-face groups (usually 3-12 people) provide individuals with the support and challenge necessary to work effectively together. When groups become large, they can divide into smaller units to maintain close working relationships, to simplify internal decision making, to include new members, or to work on different aspects of the same problem. A network of such groups can provide the benefits of a large organization while protecting the autonomy of the local unit and encouraging fuller participation by the individual.

Developing Support Communities

Working in earlier years as isolated individuals, we found we were quickly "burning out": we often felt lonely, overwhelmed and discouraged. Realizing that we needed more support and encouragement from each other, we began exploring with others more cooperative ways to live and work together. We looked for opportunities to face the inconsistencies between our vision and our private lives and to experiment with new institutions and working and living arrangements which incorporated our values.

3

As a result several communal households and working and action collectives were organized, mostly made up of people active in nonviolent social change efforts. Many of the collectives are part of the Movement for a New Society, and many individuals in the households are part of the Life Center Association. The authors have been actively involved in several of these collectives and households. Because these two organizations are referred to frequently in this book, a brief introduction to them is appropriate here for clarity.

The *Movement for a New Society* (MNS) is a network of autonomous small groups, located in the U.S. but with transnational contacts. Because MNS believes that the goals of a movement for radical social change must be incorporated in the way it is organized, the small groups which are the basic units of the MNS network seek to be egalitarian and decentralized. They are in agreement on strategic nonviolence and participation in developing an analysis of the present system and in projecting revolutionary goals. (See section in Part Seven on "Building Organizational Strength" for more detail on how the network and individual groups can function.)

The *Life Center Association* (LCA) is a group of adults and children of diverse ages and backgrounds, living together in about 16 households in West Philadelphia, while working for social and personal change. It owns two of the buildings used by LCA and MNS members.

Many LCA members are working in the approximately fifteen MNS "collectives" located in West Philadelphia and share a commitment to nonviolent social change. Though the overlap is not complete, the interaction between the Life Center Association and MNS membership in West Philadelphia is so regular that it is appropriate (and more convenient) to refer to them in this manual as the Movement for a New Society/Life Center (MNS/LC) community.

Connecting with People

Today numerous individuals and groups are working for change in our society, using a wide variety of methods of organizing to do so. We believe it is important for these groups to maintain contact with each other, sharing skills and information and, from time to time, uniting in ad hoc coalitions around important issues.

Part One

The Theoretical Basis for Change

People working for social change need to understand the context of their labors. Such an understanding can be sharpened by (1) evaluating the success or failure of other efforts, historical or contemporary, (2) developing a theory for change, (3) examining present political, economic and environmental realities, (4) projecting a vision of the kinds of changes wanted, and (5) developing a strategy to accomplish specific goals.

In the past, discussions of theory and strategy tended to be dominated by an elite who planned campaigns and informed the majority about them. We believe that an understanding of the theoretical basis for change needs to be spread widely among participants, to encourage a democratic, decentralized movement for change.

At the same time, it is necessary to avoid a "paralysis of analysis," the feeling that one must understand perfectly all aspects of the situation before acting. It is necessary to learn from action. The study of theory and history and the development of an analysis, vision, and strategy can be combined in small groups where participants support each other in moving from theory to action. A study/action process called a *Macro-Analysis Seminar* has been developed to help people examine problems, project solutions, and act to bring changes. A brief description of it concludes Part One.

There are a variety of theories which have motivated people to bring about needed changes. It is important to scrutinize social change theories carefully (even those that worked else-

7

where) and develop one that fits your own unique time and situation.

The authors' own work for change has been based on a theory which includes a form of nonviolent action, a concept shaped by the examples of Mahatma Gandhi's campaign for Indian independence from Britain, the Norwegian resistance to Nazi occupation during World War II, and the actions of SCLC, CORE, and SNCC * during the civil rights movement in the United States. Because of our bias in this direction, case studies in the sections on "History" and "Theory" focus heavily on nonviolent action campaigns.

But new information makes periodic examination of a theoretical framework necessary. Our own theory has been affected by participation in a variety of personal growth disciplines, and our analysis, vision and strategy are being altered by a reassessment of the ecological limits of the environment and a growing understanding of the economic causes of oppression. Regardless of your political perspective, much of the information in this part can be useful to you as you develop or reassess your own theoretical basis for change.

I
Developing a Theory

A thoughtfully developed theory for change is of key importance for effective action. When the going gets rough it is those with a theory and vision who tend to stay with the struggle and keep their actions consistent with their original intentions. This is especially true of those struggling for change through nonviolent action.

ASPECTS OF A THEORY OF CHANGE

When examining a theory of change the following aspects should be considered:
- the nature of human beings;
- the nature and sources of power;
- the nature and sources of truth and authority;
- the analysis of the causes of social problems;
- the role of individuals and institutions in social change;

* Southern Christian Leadership Conference (SCLC), Congress of Racial Equality (CORE), and Student Nonviolent Coordinating Committee (SNCC).

8

- the vision of the way it can or should be;
- the mechanisms of change, existing or potential.

HOW TO DEVELOP A THEORY FOR CHANGE

1. Write Down Your Own Theory of Change:

Whether you are conscious of it or not you have the beginnings of a theory of change. Using the list of "Aspects of a Theory of Change" above, write down your present beliefs about each and pull these thoughts together. The important questions to consider are *not* whether anyone else agrees with you, but:

- Does your theory make sense to you?
- Is it consistent with your present observations of reality?
- Is it flexible and comprehensive enough to deal with the unknown?
- Can it be tested?

Do this with a group; note the agreements and conflicts between theories. Resolve the conflicts.

2. Investigate an Actual Project or Campaign:

Select a project or campaign in which you have been involved or about which you have read. If you have none in mind, see the "Studying Case Histories" section. Using the chart of the Stages of a Nonviolent Action Campaign or Lakey's Five Stages in a Strategy of Nonviolent Revolution, evaluate the campaign.

- What was the theory for change underlying the campaign?
- Did all the actions reflect this theory?
- Was the theory flexible yet comprehensive enough to give a sound basis for dealing with the unexpected?
- Has the theory of social change been altered or expanded during the campaign? If so, how?
- In what specific ways was the campaign affected by the theory underlying it?

3. Read About Existing Theories:

Not all political activity is based on a consciously-held theory, but it is possible to classify most, if not all, political work as being based at least implicitly on one of the following perspectives. None of these do we perceive to be the "right" theory. But all are the results of efforts to understand social-political-economic reality, and some acquaintance with each of the following can be valuable to you in developing your own theory.

Marxism. Marxism has been the most influential school of

9

thought in the socialist tradition. Developing in the latter half of the 1800's, it has been the major philosophy for many successful 20th century revolutionary movements such as those in the U.S.S.R., China, Yugoslavia, and Vietnam; as well as being the guiding theory for numerous revolutionary parties and social change groups around the world.

At the base of the Marxist analysis is the contradiction between production, which is done socially, and the appropriation of the socially produced wealth by a small group of people, the ruling class, who own the factories. Marxists, or "scientific socialists," would replace the system of private ownership, where profit goes to the few, with a system in which: (1) production was based upon people's needs, (2) the wealth that was produced socially would be more evenly divided among the people who produced it, and (3) the means of production (raw materials, tools, and factories) would be socially owned. This condition in which the means of production would be socially owned is known as socialism or communism.

Marx felt that society was moving toward socialism because of the internal conflict within capitalism between the workers and the owners of the means of production. This clash is known as the class struggle. The class struggle, in which working people come into direct conflict with the owners of the means of production, is the process by which society moves forward toward positive social change and is also the process by which people make history.

Class conflict is believed to move the economic system from capitalism to socialism and eventually to communism. Socialism is seen as a transition stage in which the state continues to exist. In communism the functions of the state are no longer necessary and it "withers away." Under communism it is claimed that people will be allocated goods according to their needs and not according to their ability to work.

The struggle for socialism, and against class exploitation, is fundamental for positive social change, but the form that that struggle takes is a hotly debated topic among Marxists.

Socialist organization varies from large open mass political parties such as are found in Italy and other Western European countries to small secretive cell groups in nations where there is a higher level of repression. Organizational structure to some extent reflects the diversity of thinking about the role of the masses in making decisions. The large parties generally have a higher degree of participation than the small cell groups which see themselves as the vanguard of the revolution whose purpose is to educate and lead the workers.

Strategy and tactics among Marxists are also very diverse. They include parliamentary cooperation such as that of many Western European socialist parties, nonviolent demonstrations and direct actions, guerrilla warfare, and conventional armed struggle.

There are numerous books written from a Marxist perspective which can be of help to people involved in social change organizing. Some of the basic ones include: Karl Marx, *Wage, Labor, and Capital* (International Pub., 1969); *The Marx-Engels Reader*, Robert C. Tucker, editor (Norton, 1972); Mao Tse-Tung, "On Contradiction," "On Handling Contradictions Among the People," and "On Practice"; V.I. Lenin, *Essential Works of Lenin* (Bantam, 1966). Other Marxist writers of interest include Antonio Gramsci, *The Prince and Other Writings* (International Pub., 1970), and Wilhelm Reich, *Sex-Pol* (Vintage, 1972). C. Wright Mills' *The Marxists* (Dell, 1962) is a helpful critical exposition, brief history, and anthology of classic texts.

Anarchism. Also dating from the 19th century, anarchism, like Marxism, calls for the overthrow of capitalism, but insists further that the abolition of the state (coercive government) must be achieved simultaneously or a new "state-socialist" oppression will be established (as happened in Russia), rather than the free federation of autonomous communities that anarchists want. Their remarkable success in establishing such a society in Spain in the 1930's is recorded in Sam Dolgoff (ed.), *The Anarchist Collectives: Workers' Self-management in the Spanish Revolution 1936-1939* (Free Life Editions, 41 Union Square West, New York, NY 10003, $3.95). Anarchists consider both history and science to bear out their belief in the superior justice and efficiency of voluntary forms of social organization. "Direct action," the "affinity group," concern for the consistency of means with ends, and the effort to integrate personal with social change were anarchist themes rediscovered by the New Left and feminist movements. Daniel Guerin's *Anarchism* (Monthly Review, 1970) is a modern introduction to the movement's ideas and history, while Alexander Berkman's *What is Communist Anarchism?* (1929; Dover 1972) is a classic exposition, thorough and clear. Murray Bookchin's *Post-Scarcity Anarchism* (Ramparts, 1971) is the most impressive recent book; Paul Goodman's works, from *Communitas* (1947; 1960) and *Gestalt Therapy* (Delta, 1951; all others Vintage) to *Drawing the Line* (1962), *People or Personnel* (1965), and *New Reformation* (1970) form the most wide-ranging contemporary body of anarchist writing.

Feminism. * One dictionary calls feminism "the doctrine advocating the social and political rights of women equal to those of men." But to many feminists this definition does not go far enough. Besides struggling for women's civil rights, they seek an end to the systematic cultural, political, social, sexual, psychological and economic servitude of women to men and to patriarchal institutions.

Feminist author, lecturer, and writer Andrea Dworkin, in *Our Blood* (Harper & Row, 1976) describes three elements of feminist struggle. The first, "herstory," is a rediscovery of the past. Women are researching what has been left out of the textbooks—both their governmental, social and artistic accomplishments from matriarchal societies to the present, and the subtle and blatant ways that they have been oppressed. (The existence of the matriarchy is controversial; a scholarly proponent is Evelyn Reed, see *Woman's Evolution*, Pathfinder Press, 1975.) The second is an explanation of the present: What are the contemporary sources of oppression? And how are roles defined—in the workplace, in sexual terms, in marital relationships, in the home and in cultural institutions? The third is a vision of a future based on the values of sisterhood: affirmation of self; control over body and life; refusal to be a victim; justice, and equality.

Issues which concern all women include the need for decent working conditions; passage of the Equal Rights Amendment; affirmative action in employment; good, free day care; safe, legal abortions; an end to sterilization abuse; the establishment of women's health centers and the elimination of hazards to women's health; political office for women. Furthermore, women are engaged in the creation of a women's culture, with feminist bookstores, publishing houses, music, art, and schools.

Many women pursue change through informal consciousness raising groups, or through participation in groups like the National Organization of Women (NOW). NOW continues to struggle with the political implications of its actions, but is viewed by many as primarily a reformist group.

Socialist feminists have developed a more explicit political analysis. They view patriarchy and capitalism as twin power structures, thoroughly intertwined and mutually supportive, that must be analyzed, challenged and overthrown. A new society based on worker ownership and control must emerge in order for women to achieve equality.

Radical feminists see the struggle between the sexes as the

* With thanks to Gail Pressburg and to the Feminist Collective of MNS.

central force in history and capitalism as merely the latest and perhaps most dangerous creation of patriarchy. They see the nuclear family and male domination in the home as the basis of women's oppression. After patriarchy is overthrown, a woman-centered or androgynous society with new egalitarian social and economic structures is to be established.

Lesbian feminists fall predominantly into these last two categories. "Lesbian-feminist politics is a political critique of the institution and ideology of heterosexuality as a primary corner-stone of male supremacy...and extends the analysis of sexual politics into an analysis of sex itself as an institution." (Introduction, *Lesbianism and the Women's Movement*, ed. by Nancy Myron and Charlotte Bunch. Diana Press, 1975.) Its commitment to women as a political group leads to a strategy to gain power for women, not just the establishment of an alternative or separate community.

Some important feminist books are: Juliet Mitchell, *Woman's Estate* (Vintage, 1971); Sheila Rowbotham, *Woman's Consciousness, Man's World* (Pelican, 1973); Shulamith Firestone, *The Dialectic of Sex* (Bantam, 1970); Susan Brown-miller, *Against Our Will: Men, Women and Rape* (Bantam, 1976); Rosalyn Baxandall, Linda Gordon and Susan Reverby, eds., *America's Working Women* (Vintage, 1976). An excellent account of past struggles is contained in Eleanor Flexner's *Century of Struggle* (1958; Atheneum, 1973). Important anthologies are *Masculine/Feminine*, ed. by Betty Roszak and Theodore Roszak (Harper, 1969); and *Sisterhood Is Powerful,* ed. by Robin Morgan (Vintage, 1970).

Fascism. This term is often loosely applied to any repressive and authoritarian regime, but more properly is applied to regimes like those of Mussolini and Hitler. They attained power by mobilizing mass support on a basis that was subjectively revolutionary and anti-establishment, but which in fact involved alliance with the rich to maintain the social hierarchy by disciplining labor. Appeals to national pride and purpose and a spirit of moral regeneration (in opposition to cynicism and corruption in political and cultural life) served to divert attention from fascism's political-economic reality. Two important aspects of the phenomenon are illuminated by Wilhelm Reich's *The Mass Psychology of Fascism* (1933; Noonday, 1970; Touchstone-Clarion, 1974) and Daniel Guerin's *Fascism and Big Business* (Monad Press, 1973). While police murders, frame-ups, and government subversion are real, though usually unacknowledged, parts of U.S. capitalist democracy (see, for example, Nelson Blackstock, *Cointelpro: The FBI's Secret War on Political Freedom,* Vintage, 1976), the U.S. is not a fascist nation, and it could become a police state without ever being fascist.

Gandhian nonviolence (satyagraha). The nonviolence of Mohandas K. Gandhi (1869-1948) attempts to realize Truth through love and right action. Its main elements are: the improvement of one's own life as a prerequisite for social action; constructive work to achieve one's goals (in India the constructive program included education, decentralized economic production, and work among the poor); and campaigns of resistance against evil. Gandhians break laws perceived to be unjust (civil disobedience), but adhere to the principle of non-injury (ahimsa), refusing to hurt, humiliate, or hate another person; they seek to convert, not to conquer, the opponent. A good study of the Gandhian philosophy of conflict is Joan V. Bondurant's *Conquest of Violence* (Berkeley, 1965). Readings on Gandhi's campaigns and those of other practitioners of this type of nonviolence are listed in this manual under "Studying Case Histories." Gene Sharp's "Types of Principled Nonviolence" in A. Paul Hare and Herbert H. Blumberg, eds., *Nonviolent Direct Action* (1968; available from War Resisters League, 339 Lafayette St., New York, N.Y. 10012, $3.00) distinguishes satyagraha from five other kinds of nonviolence.

Social change through personal change. This approach, characteristic of many religious groups and also of some psychotherapy and "human potential" proponents, relies on exhorting or helping people to change themselves, and shies away from collective political efforts. The position's logic does not recognize that just as a biological organ retains its identity and functions while its individual cells die and are replaced, so the organs of society replace defectors and doubters with more reliable agents in a way that sustains their functions; and furthermore, most individuals do not ordinarily participate in the decisions that fundamentally shape public misery or happiness. A popular example of this viewpoint was Charles Reich's *The Greening of America* (Bantam, 1970).

Liberal reform. Liberal reform tries to solve problems without an adequate depth of understanding. A good example is Common Cause, the "citizens' lobby." Problems are explained through vague metaphors: "...our instruments of self-government are in need of repair..." (John Gardner, *In Common Cause,* Norton, 1973). Basic realities, such as the ownership of most corporate wealth and the holding of major executive

14

branch policy-making positions by a small upper class, are given insufficient weight (see G. William Domhoff, *The Higher Circles*, Vintage, 1970). Even an ostensibly radical analysis, if it fails to come to grips with such crucial parts of reality, can be in essence liberal reformist—an example being Michael Harrington's *Socialism* (Bantam, 1972).

Liberalism and conservatism. These two, supposedly the choices our two-party system offers, are no longer distinguishable. Though respectable theories can be associated with these titles, liberalism and conservatism function today as sources of rhetoric through which politicians obscure the fundamental choices to be made. They are convenient banners for the we-they competition for office, but have no meaning for policy, as dismayed principled conservative and liberal voters have repeatedly discovered. (The spectacle of "moderate Republican" Richard Nixon running the largest federal budget deficits in history and imposing wage-price controls, both traditionally anathema to Republicans and conservatives, may suffice as an example.) These ideologies are tending to collapse into a power elite defense of the status quo and to polarize into more principled and coherent radical right-wing and left-wing positions.

Libertarianism. A relatively new approach, though it claims many forebears, libertarianism proclaims the absolute sovereignty of each individual and the limitation of government's role to protecting individuals from force and fraud. This leads them to hold positions seen as "left-wing" (opposition to censorship, foreign interventions, and sex and drug laws) as well as ones seen as "right-wing" (non-intervention by government in the economy, abolition of regulatory agencies, and lowering of taxes). An extensive catalog of libertarian literature is published by Laissez Faire Books (206 Mercer St., New York, NY 10012); they will send "Liberty Against Power," a free introductory pamphlet and reading list, on request. Murray N. Rothbard's *For a New Liberty* (Laissez Faire Books, $8.95) is a recent work by one of the philosophy's most incisive writers.

UNITING THEORY AND PRACTICE

Work for social change is more effective when theory balances practice. Practice is necessary to acquire and test information, while theory is necessary to develop a framework within which data acquires fuller meaning.

It takes time to gather information, to reflect on what is learned and to develop strategies which can be tested. When this process occurs within a group of people committed to fundamental change, the theory developed is likely to be more comprehensive and flexible than when the process occurs individually.

Uniting theory and practice requires time and energy, but the achievement of long-term positive changes is more likely when action and reflection are joined.

For those who are not yet involved in on-going actions for change, the following suggestions are offered to help unite theory with practice.

1. *Get involved* in an existing organization or movement for change. (See Part Ten: "Groups to Contact," or locate a list of organizations involved in social change, if one exists for your area.) Stay involved while you study the group's theory and test it against your own.

2. *Talk* with people involved in social change. To understand the organizer's approach, some of the following questions might be helpful.

• What is your theory of social change?
• What is your strategy for social change?
• How does your program reflect your goals and strategy?
• What kind of personal support do you have for your activities?
• What is your concept of power?

3. *Observe* direct actions. (See *Observation of an Event.*)

4. *Integrate* your exploration of theory with training for nonviolent action (see Part Six). Of particular relevance is the exercise *Nonviolent and Violent Revolution.*

5. Better yet...*begin focusing* on an area where change is needed in your life. Join with others. Apply the theory you're learning to situations of relevance to you and your friends.

INVESTIGATING NONVIOLENCE AS A THEORY FOR ACTION

If you do not already have a comprehensive theory for social action, much can be learned by investigating the practice and meaning of nonviolent action. This can be done (1) by reading about nonviolent actions and campaigns and (2) by getting involved in the type of training and action explained in Parts Six and Seven.

Some people have found nonviolent action useful as one of several tactics. Others have claimed nonviolence as a religious or philosophical doctrine and have lived their whole lives according to its teachings. For the authors, nonviolence theory is particularly attractive because of the continuity it offers as (1) a basis for making strategic choices for action and (2) a flexible framework for making personal choices about work, play and interpersonal relationships on a daily basis. Of all theories for change we have explored, democratic nonviolent social change theory offers the most diverse and creative options.

The following aspects are important to our theory of change and seem to be consistent with our understanding of the theory of nonviolence.

1. The existence of *conflict* must be faced, and differences of opinion and needs recognized. Hidden conflicts must surface before they can be resolved. If the needs of one party are met by the use of force and the other's needs are not met, the conflict is *not* resolved, but only hidden, and will surface again as soon as the weaker party has adequate power to force a change.

2. The amount of *power* available to people in positions of authority depends to a large extent on the amount of cooperation their subjects give to them. Authority may use violence or manipulation to encourage cooperation, but power can be removed from authority through noncooperation.

3. The *causes* of social problems are both personal and systemic. To end injustices both people and institutions must evolve new values and behavior.

4. *People and institutions* have the capacity to do great good and great harm. People whose basic physical and emotional needs are met want to live in harmony with other people. Institutions make no moral choices, but develop a life of their own and have great influence on the condition of people. They shape people's choices as long as people remain unaware of this influence.

5. *Truth* is to be found on all sides of a conflict; therefore it is essential to respect the opponent as a source of truth and as part of the solution to the problem. The nonviolent activist adheres to the truth as s/he sees it, but is open to the possibility that his/her position and goals may change as s/he listens seriously to the opponent.

6. A policy of *non-injury* and non-retaliation tends to disarm the opponent. The goal is not to destroy him/her, but to reveal truth and solve the conflict.

7. Acceptance of *suffering* may be necessary. Because others have often been required by force to suffer, willingness to share suffering will make mutually acceptable solutions more possible.

8. *Openness* in planning and actions must be maintained,

17

both for internal democracy and to present a clear image to outsiders.

9. *Goals* desired as an end product of a campaign for change need to be *built into the process* used to achieve them. For example: to build a cooperative, decentralized society, the processes and institutions developed by activists will need to be cooperative and decentralized.

10. Injustice in our society is deeply rooted, and attempts to remove it will take our *time*, energy, and personal and group discipline, over many years.

11. The *ecological environment* is the basic support system for human life. All activities need to be in harmony with it. When enough actions threaten its delicate balance, human life will cease to be possible.

12. *Social changes* are more likely to persist if they are made by people *voluntarily*. Changes forced on people by violence or intimidation will not last when coercion is decreased or removed.

Resources For Investigating the Meaning and Practice of Nonviolence

1. Involve yourself in training sessions, workshops and actions using resources in the following sections of the manual. Use these tools to solve the problems you are now facing.

2. Read case studies found in Part One: "Studying Case Histories."

3. Books which offer a mixture of case histories and theoretical presentations are listed below.

Civil Disobedience: Theory and Practice, Hugo Adam Bedau, ed., (Pegasus, 1969). Presents a variety of viewpoints pro and con, including articles by Chomsky, King, and Goodman.

Conquest of Violence, Joan Bondurant (Univ. of California Press, 1965). A penetrating analysis of nonviolent theory and action. Includes a number of case studies of nonviolent campaigns in India during the career of Gandhi. Explains satyagraha as an instrument of struggle for fundamental change.

Ends and Means, Aldous Huxley (Harper, 1937). Major theoretical analysis of the dynamics of ends and means for nonviolent theorists. Considered a benchmark in the development of nonviolence theory and still relevant.

The Essays of A. J. Muste, Nat Hentoff, ed. (Simon and Schuster, 1967). A collection of writings of this lifelong activist in labor and peace.

Gandhi's Truth: On the Origins of Militant Nonviolence, Erik Erikson (W.W. Norton and Co., 1969). An astute psychological perspective on Gandhi and his nonviolence.

King: A Critical Bibliography, David L. Lewis (Praeger, 1970). Very good descriptions of the ground work necessary for and actual process of building direct action campaigns.

More Power Than We Know, Dave Dellinger (Anchor, 1975). A memoir of the anti-war and social change movement that discusses its strengths and weaknesses and tries to identify its lessons for the future. Stresses the need to hold fast to both human values and to clear-headed radicalism.

Nonviolence in America: A Documentary History, Staughton Lynd, ed. (Bobbs-Merrill, 1966). Selections confirming that nonviolence is a part of the American tradition. Contains examples of nonviolence demonstrated by Quakers, abolitionists, labor unionists, progressives, civil rights workers, etc.

Nonviolent Direct Action: American Cases: Social-Psychological Analyses, A. Paul Hare and Herbert H. Blumberg (Washington, D.C.: Corpus Books, 1968). A good selection of civil rights and anti-war action narratives followed by important analytic essays. Includes Sharp's "Types of Principled Nonviolence," Lakey's "Mechanisms of Nonviolent Action," and excerpts from Bondurant, Gregg, and Erikson.

Peace Agitator: The Story of A. J. Muste, Nat Hentoff (Macmillan, 1963). Biography of the labor activist and peace movement leader (1885-1967) whose shrewdness and integrity inspired radical action from World War I to Vietnam.

The Politics of Nonviolent Action, Gene Sharp (Porter Sargent, 1973). "The most comprehensive attempt thus far to examine the nature of nonviolent struggle as a social and political technique, including its view of power, its specific methods of action, its dynamics in conflict and the conditions for success or failure in its use" (preface).

The Power of Nonviolence, Richard Gregg (Schocken, 1966). A standard work on the philosophy and practice of nonviolence, particularly as related to Gandhi's movement. Focuses on the individual in struggle and on nonviolence on the personal level. A classic.

The Quiet Battle: Writings on the Theory and Practice of Nonviolent Resistance, Mulford Q. Sibley, ed. (Beacon Press, 1963). Covers a wide scope of issues and geography. Selections both historical and contemporary.

Revolution and Equilibrium, Barbara Deming (Grossman, 1971). Meticulous reporting and eloquent essays ranging from early 1960's peace action to material from the author's involvement in the civil rights and anti-war movements.

Revolutionary Nonviolence, Dave Dellinger (Anchor, 1970). An outstanding record of involvement in the issues of our time from World War II, civil rights, and the Cuban revolution to the anti-Vietnam War movement. Includes valuable assessments of the fate of nonviolence in the civil rights movement and "where things stand now" after the 1968 convention in Chicago.

Strategy for a Living Revolution, George Lakey (W.H. Freeman, 1973). Outlines a five-stage model for organizing radical change and examines how the strategy for nonviolent revolution in the U.S. relates to struggles in other countries, particularly those of the Third World.

The Urban Guerrilla, Martin Oppenheimer (Quadrangle Books, 1969). A consideration of the internal dynamics of revolutionary movements and insurrections. Compares violence and nonviolence as means of achieving radical change.

4. Films can be used to stimulate a group to explore questions of theory. The following four films were selected from an annotated bibliography of "Films for Social Change" by Ken Henke and George Willoughby, June, 1971. The full bibliography can be requested for 25 cents plus postage from Lynne Shivers, at the Philadelphia Life Center.

Gandhi's India, 58 min. blk and wht, Indiana University, Bloomington, Indiana (NET). BBC documentary on Gandhi's life and influence. Gandhi's ideas and strategy of civil disobedience; footage of Gandhi and interviews with his associates, followers and others.

Huelga! 54 min. color, 1967 film of United Farmworkers' grape strike. Interviews with Chavez and strike organizers as well as grape growers, examples of the Theatro Campesino, working conditions in the field, and the Delano to Sacramento march of 1967. More current films are available by contacting your nearest United Farmworkers organizing office. Films vary on price and availability at different offices.

King: A Filmed Record...Montgomery to Memphis, order from BFA Educational Media, 221 Michigan Ave., Santa Monica, CA 90404. An artistically well-done documentary of the Black struggle for equality and justice from 1955 to 1968: Montgomery, sit-ins, freedom rides, 1963 March on Washington, Birmingham, Selma, Chicago, Poor People's Campaign, Memphis, Dr. King's funeral.

Sit-in, 54 min. blk and wht, order from McGraw-Hill Text Films, 1221 Ave. of the Americas, NYC, NY 10020. An NBC documentary on the Nashville sit-in in 1961 showing progress of the campaign, footage of training and lunch counter incidents, and economic boycott. Well done.

II
Studying Case Histories*

Familiarity with historical examples gives a valuable framework for exploring the theory of social change movements. It also allows for a strategic examination of the way different tactics are used and of the construction of campaigns. It is possible to compare actions, get a sense of one's own cultural heritage, and to further a long term outlook on the whole process of social change.

Because of our own involvement in training for nonviolent action, we have selected from actions which do *not* depend on violence for their source of power. Some of the campaigns suggested for study had clear commitments to nonviolent action, but many did not. In some cases violence erupted through confusion or in spite of plans to the contrary. They all provide good material to examine those forces which make for constructive change.

Social change movements that include the use of violence as one source of their power should be studied, especially where these have brought about large economic and cultural changes (as in the socialist revolutions of this century). We have *not* included such movements here, but they are available through most libraries and history departments.

SUGGESTIONS FOR STUDYING CASE HISTORIES

Case studies of nonviolent actions are not always available through traditional sources. The most complete list is in *Exploring Nonviolent Alternatives* (Porter Sargent, 1970) by Gene Sharp. For areas of interest not included in the bibliography you can develop case studies of your own.

To aid in the examination of case histories the following guidelines may be useful:

1. Familiarize yourself with model case studies found in

---

* Special appreciation to George Willoughby and Ken Henke, whose bibliographies prepared for the course in nonviolent social change at Pendle Hill in 1970-71 provided the basis for the bulk of this section.

books like *Conquest of Violence* by Joan Bondurant. Note particularly Bondurant's Analysis of Five Campaigns, including her 10 point outline on pages 45-46. (For a derivative of these 10 points as used by the authors see *Combining A Case Study with Strategy Game*).

2. If you are developing an account of a case study not already documented, use the analytic framework developed by Bondurant, or think about including these broad areas:

Context (political, economic, historical)
Preparation
Organization
Action
Reaction
Consequences

3. Studies can be made by individuals, co-learners, or a group, using a process similar to that developed for *Macro-Analysis Seminars*.

4. For short term workshops, case studies of specific incidents or campaigns provide a good, non-lecture approach for learning about the history of nonviolence. Determine the degree to which the case involves nonviolent action. A mixture may be present.

BIBLIOGRAPHY ON CASE STUDIES OF ACTIONS AND CAMPAIGNS

1. General Reading on Nonviolent Actions

Conquest of Violence: The Gandhian Philosophy of Conflict, Joan Bondurant (above).

Nonviolence in America: A Documentary History, Staughton Lynd, ed. (above).

Nonviolent Direct Action, A. Paul Hare and Herbert H. Blumberg, eds. (above).

Passive Resistance in South Africa, Leo Kuper (Yale Univ. Press, 1957).

The Politics of Nonviolent Action, Gene Sharp (above).

The Quiet Battle, Mulford Sibley (above).

2. Gandhian Nonviolent Actions

A. *Conquest of Violence* (above).

B. *Gandhi,* Geoffrey Ashe (Stein and Day, 1968).

C. *Mahatma Gandhi,* B.R. Nanda (Beacon, 1958).

D. *Mahatma*, D.G. Tendulkar (Bombay: Jhaveri and Tendulkar, 1954).

E. *Nonviolent Resistance,* M.K. Gandhi (Schocken, 1962).

Books A-E can be used to read about the following campaigns:

Satyagraha in South Africa (1906-1914)
#B pp 96-125; #C pp 90-120; #D pp 76-151.
Champaran Indigo Campaign (1917)
#B pp 157-66; #C pp 156-62; #D vol. 1, pp 199-213.
Ahmedabad Labor Satyagraha (1918)
#A pp 65-73; #B pp 167-71; #C pp 162-65; #D vol. 1, pp 219-221.
Satyagraha Against the Rowlatt Bills (1919)
#A pp 73-88; #B pp 184-95, 198, 200; #D vol. 1, pp 240-264; #E pp 102-103.
Vykom Temple Road Satyagraha (1924-1925)
#A pp 46-52; #B p. 275; #D vol. 2, pp 180-182; #E pp 177-203.
Bardoli Campaign (1928)
#A pp 53-64; #B pp 275-76; #C pp 269-271; #D vol. 2, pp 327-330; #E pp 209-19.
Salt Satyagraha (1930-1931)
#A pp 88-104; #B pp 279-302; #C pp 290-309; #E pp 220-290.

3. Civil Rights Movement—Black Struggle for Freedom in the U.S.

Montgomery Bus Boycott (1955-1956)
King: A Critical Biography, David Lewis (Praeger, 1970), pp 46-84.
"Montgomery Diary," Bayard Rustin, *Liberation*, April, 1956.
"Our Struggle," Martin Luther King, Jr., *Liberation*, April, 1956.
"We Are Still Walking," Martin Luther King, Jr., *Liberation*, December, 1956.
Nonviolence: A Christian Interpretation, William R. Miller (Schocken, 1966), pp 298-305.
Stride Toward Freedom: The Montgomery Story, Martin Luther King, Jr. (Ballantine, 1958).

Birmingham, Alabama (1963)
King: A Critical Biography (above), pp 179-209.
Nonviolence: A Christian Interpretation (above), pp 329-343.
Nonviolence in America: A Documentary History (above), pp 458-481.
Why We Can't Wait, Martin Luther King, Jr. (Signet, 1964).

Additional readings for case studies on the Black struggle for freedom in the U.S., including sit-ins, Mississippi voter registration and freedom schools, freedom rides, and actions in Selma, AL; Albany, GA; Chicago; Memphis; and Washington, D.C.:
The Angry Black South, Mitches and Peace (Corinth, 1962).
Black Protest: History Documents and Analyses 1619 to the

Present, Joan Grant, ed. (Fawcett, 1968), pp 218-323, 329-349, 393-402.

Freedom Now: The Civil Rights Struggle in America, Alan F. Westing, ed. (Basic Books, 1964), pp 87-103, 271-74.

Freedom Ride, Jim Peck (Simon and Schuster, 1962).

King: A Critical Biography (above), pp 140-70, 214-31, 264-96, 313-53.

Nonviolence: A Christian Interpretation (above), pp 306-28.

Nonviolence in America (above), pp 415-58, 482-85.

Why We Can't Wait (above), pp 42-43.

4. Quakers in Colonial Pennsylvania (1681-1756)

Pacifism in the United States, Peter Brock (Princeton Univ. Press, 1968), pp 81-158.

The Quiet Battle (above), pp 210-230.

5. Women's Movement

Century of Struggle: Woman's Rights Movement in the U.S., Eleanor Flexner (Harvard Univ. Press, 1959). The best comprehensive history.

Everyone Was Brave: The Rise and Fall of Feminism in America, William O'Neill (Quadrangle, 1969). See Chapter 5.

Jailed for Freedom, Doris Stevens (Boni and Liverwright, 1920). Full of human interest stories, by one of the key organizers and inmates.

Living My Life, Emma Goldman (Dover, 1970). A record more of incidents than planned actions, but an important historical account.

Rebirth of Feminism, Judith Hole and Ellen Levine (Quadrangle, 1971). Contains a chronological listing of events from 1961 plus documents of this time.

Story of the Woman's Party, Inez Haynes Irwin (Harcourt, Brace and Co., 1921). About the militants.

6. Labor Movement

Delano: The Story of the California Grape Strike, John G. Dunne (Farrar, Strauss and Giroux, 1967).

The Essays of A. J. Muste, Nat Hentoff, ed. (Simon and Schuster, 1970).

Living My Life (above).

The Politics of Nonviolent Action, Gene Sharp. See Chapter 6. Also check index under Labor, Strikes, etc. (above).

The Wobblies: The Story of Syndicalism in the U.S., Patrick Renshaw (Doubleday Anchor, 1967).

7. Latin America

Resistance in Latin America: The Pentagon, the Oligarchies and Nonviolent Action, A Quaker Action Group (MNS, 4722

Baltimore Ave., Phila., PA 19143, 50¢ postpaid).
Strategy for a Living Revolution, George Lakey (W. H. Freeman, 1973).
Helder Camara's Latin America, Betty Richardson Nute (London: Friends Peace and International Relations Comm.; available from Peace Education Division, AFSC, 1501 Cherry, Phila., PA 19102, $.85).

8. Europe

Norwegian Resistance Against the German Occupation (1940-45)

Civilian Resistance as a National Defence, Adam Roberts (Penguin, 1969), pp 136-53.
Nonviolence: A Christian Interpretation (above), pp 253-9.
The Power of Nonviolence, Richard Gregg (Schocken, 1966), pp. 30-5.
The Quiet Battle (above), pp 156-86.
Tyranny Could Not Quell Them, Gene Sharp (WRL, 339 Lafayette, New York, NY 10012).

Czechoslovakia (1968)

Czechoslovakia, 1968, Adam Roberts and Philip Windsor (Columbia Press, 1969).

Danilo Dolci's Direct Action in Sicily (1952-present)

The Man Who Plays Alone, Danilo Dolci (Pantheon, 1968).
A Passion for Sicilians, Jerre Mangione (Morrow, 1968).

9. Recent U.S. Actions

"Culebra: Nonviolent Action and the U.S. Navy," Charles C. Walker (Haverford Monograph, sections available from Gandhi Institute, Box 92, Cheyney, PA 19319).
"The Edgewood Arsenal and Fort Detrick Projects: An Exchange Analysis," Waldman, Richards, and Walker (Nonviolent Action Research Project, also available from Gandhi Institute, $2.00 postpaid).

III
Analysis of the Political Economy

Increasingly, people working on social change are recognizing the need to distinguish between the symptoms of social problems and their structural causes. The assumption that social problems in the U.S. are accidents in a basically sound and humanitarian political-economic system is being seriously questioned. To understand the causes of war, poverty, injustice, and the ecological crisis in the U.S. and abroad, basic realities need scrutiny. Some of these are:

• the finite nature of the world's resources;
• the effects of pollutants on life support systems;
• the political and economic causes of war;
• the flow of wealth and protein from poor, hungry nations to rich, over-fed ones;
• the role of U.S. aid and investment in distorting poor countries' economic development;
• continued economic and military support by the U.S. to dictatorial regimes which torture and abuse their own citizens;
• the relationship between the structure of the economic system and the continuation of domestic problems, such as racism, sexism and crime;
• the role of the U.S. government in redistributing wealth and income in this country disproportionately to the rich.

People seeking long-term, meaningful solutions to these and other global problems need to begin with a sufficient understanding of the workings of our social, political and economic system. Otherwise their proposals and actions may go wide of the mark, and may even aggravate the problems.

DEVELOPING AN ANALYSIS: THE BASIC PROCESS

1. Collect written materials on the political-economic system. Annotated reading lists are available from many social change organizations and traditional university departments of political science and economics.

2. If you are unfamilar with political and economic materials you may want to begin with readings that provide basic information on the functioning of political and economic systems. Talking with people well-read in these areas may help you decide the best way to begin.

3. When you have a general understanding, select areas you perceive to be important and focus in on them.

4. Whenever possible find a few other people who are interested in reading similar materials. Reflect on information with others and relate what you are reading to the realities you see around you.

5. Use resources in this manual to facilitate your learning process. Note especially Part Two: "Working In Groups."

One study/action seminar used to help groups develop an analysis and apply it to their social change efforts is the *Macro-Analysis Seminar*. This seminar has process suggestions and reading lists available. A brief description of it is included later in this part.

IV
Visions for a New Society

An understanding of the root causes of social problems is essential in directing the energies of social activists, but it is not enough. A vision of a healthy society is also necessary—to guide their actions and to enable them to develop a coherent strategy for change. It is all too easy to become caught up in the day-to-day battle against a particular social evil, and to lose sight of long-range goals.

A well-articulated vision for a new society can:
• allow organizers to talk about alternatives in concrete terms;
• provide a basis for developing an action strategy with long, middle, and short-range goals;
• serve as a model against which organizers can evaluate the structure of the movement itself;
• enable people to work for the creation of positive alternatives as well as fight against existing injustices.

You can begin developing your own vision for a new society through some of the following:

1. Seminars on developing a vision using a format similar to the *Macro-Analysis Seminar* (note particularly variation #2).

2. Visit or read about other societies. These may be historical, contemporary or future projections. By studying alternative societies we can:
• learn from other people's successes and failures.
• see theoretical ideas in operation.
• excite our vision of what might be.
• build a sense of community with other people engaged in building a better world.

3. Pick a specific problem which affects you and your friends, e.g., poor medical care. Use any of the following tools to project a vision of how things should or can be. Be as concrete as possible.
Brainstorming visions of a good alternative
Vision Gallery
Scenario Writing

Personal Liberations Web Chart
Visionary Personal Preferences

V
Planning a Strategy

A strategy is a broad plan which combines separate actions in such a way as to reach the objectives sought. It is concerned with the method by which the overall struggle is conducted. A long-range strategy for change is the product of a coherent social analysis and of a realistic vision. It develops a theory for change into an action program that can suggest immediate action projects, as well as long-range perspectives that will carry a group through years of hard work, setbacks and short-term successes.

A good strategy will:
- provide a long-range framework for short-term actions;
- consider results likely to follow from proposed tactics;
- provide a method to be used for each tactic; such as nonviolence, guerrilla warfare, limited violence as defined, or silent worship;
- use tactics which are consistent with its basic goals;
- use success and repression to its advantage;
- help in making decisions about the best use of people's energies and skills;
- help to measure whether offers of "help" from local groups, foundations or government bodies would restrict or cripple the program for change;
- provide a framework for action which can be continually evaluated during action and modified by experience when necessary;
- relate efforts for change on local issues to larger national and transnational movements for change;
- suggest creative ways for people to live, work and relate to each other supportive of its basic goals;
- help resolve tensions between personal lifestyle and protracted involvement in political and economic change.

The most extensive and valuable discussion of these issues is found in "The Dynamics of Nonviolent Action," Part III of Gene Sharp's *The Politics of Nonviolent Action*.

STRUCTURAL CHANGE VS SOCIAL IMPROVEMENT

We are discovering that major social problems in our society result from serious structural problems in political and economic institutions, not from isolated flaws in an otherwise fine society. To bring widespread and lasting changes it is essential to make changes at structural levels. In planning a strategy it is important to distinguish between efforts made solely to improve the immediate condition of people and those designed to include structural changes in the political, economic and cultural systems.

One way to think about this problem is in terms of Revolutionary Reforms and Reformist Reforms. * Any major change in a society is the result of a series of changes which build on each other and which may in themselves be perceived as reforms.

Revolutionary reforms (1) arise out of an analysis which understands the structural causes of social problems, (2) are a part of a long-term program to bring structural changes to the political-economic-cultural system, (3) use means of working and organizing which are consistent with the long term program for change, (4) are initiated by grass-roots organizations and (5) are perceived by the public as a people's victory.

Reformist reforms may bring some tangible improvements in the welfare of people but do not challenge political-economic structures in their goals or in their means. As a result no structural changes occur in the political-economic system and basic social problems continue. Improvements are usually limited to small numbers of people and may not last long.

Revolutionary reforms produce a whole series of major changes in the structure of the political-economic system in a short period of time. This is often perceived as a break-through because it seriously affects the lives of many people.

* Appreciation goes to George Lakey and William Moyer, whose thinking about these concepts was helpful to us. The terms Revolutionary Reform and Reformist Reform are from Andre Gorz, Strategy for Labor (1964; Beacon, 1967).

The long-term effects of revolutionary and reformist reforms on the structure of the political-economic system can be presented schematically as:

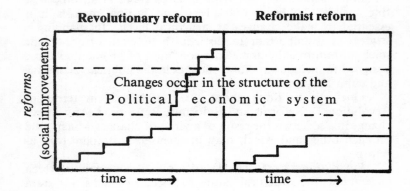

Earlier reforms may be less visible, but they are an essential part of the groundwork for structural changes still to come. The degree to which structural changes can be made and maintained depends on how well people have been prepared to work and live with them through earlier activities.

Reasons for pursuing earlier reforms might be:
• to raise consciousness among a large number of people, spread a radical analysis, and involve others in thinking about alternatives;
• to involve neighbors, workers or consumers in an actual shift of decision-making power to the local level;
• to test the ability and willingness of established institutions to make important changes (for example, the legitimacy of a government cannot be effectively challenged until it is clear that it is no longer able to change to meet people's needs);
• to improve group morale through limited successes;
• to offer selected opportunities for people to practice noncooperation with the illegitimate demands of established institutions, to develop skills and to train others for long-term efforts in social change.

Examples of limited reforms are national health insurance, limits on electoral campaign expenditures, increased day care facilities, and restrictions on false claims in advertising. Where these are government-sponsored reforms designed to prove "the system works," they become reformist reforms. But when these activities are part of a careful strategy for structural change in the political, economic and cultural system, they can become revolutionary reforms in the way they are organized and in the consciousness-raising effect they have on others who come in contact with them.

TOOLS TO DEVELOP, TEST AND RE-EVALUATE A STRATEGY

It is helpful to develop a long-term strategy for change and to test it before spending major amounts of money and time on any one social activity. Once efforts are underway, new information will be discovered, some of which may make re-evaluation of the strategy necessary. Tools which may be useful to develop, test or re-evaluate a strategy for change are listed below:

Force Field Analysis
Decision-Making Structure
Developing Strategies
Scenario Writing
Nonviolent and Violent Revolution
Strategy Game
Combining a Case Study With Strategy Game

A STRATEGY FOR A LIVING REVOLUTION

To develop and test out your own strategy it can be helpful to read or talk about the strategic thinking of others. Because we have found George Lakey's five-stage model of revolutionary change helpful to our thinking, we are including it here. These stages are developed at length in his book, *Strategy for a Living Revolution*.

1. Cultural Preparation—"People begin in this stage to achieve a common identity strong enough to support them in the struggle. Individuals see that frustration and misery are not simply their own lot, but that they are oppressed as a group." (p. 50)
Activities: Consciousness-raising; changing the way people look at themselves; changing their image of the system through direct experience, movies, readings, and training; developing a community of support; clarifying the illegitimacy of dominant institutions; developing a constructive theory of change and rough indication of goals (long and short term); promoting the growth of a collective consciousness to undergird a mass movement.

31

Methods: Consciousness-raising groups, macro-analysis seminars, training, leaflets, guerrilla theater, street speaking, meetings, marches, etc.

2. Building an Organization—"As the consciousness of oppression spreads, more people are ready to organize themselves for revolutionary change. Organization is essential for a struggle movement, for only through organization is it possible to generate enough force to slough off the old order and create new institutions. Isolated, spontaneous incidents can no more accomplish substantial change than can occasional rioting—each is a witness which can be appreciated in symbolic terms but does not change structures." (p. 66)

Activities: Radical caucuses, radical political parties, affinity groups, resistance communities, alternative institutions, transnational organizing. Must be radical in the following ways: Insist on fundamental change; make connections between concrete issues and fundamental causes; emphasize brother/sisterhood and community; prepare for a mass movement, being careful to act with, not for, the people; internationalize the program; act with consistent openness, even in the face of repression.

Methods: As aids to preparation—flow charts, strategy games, scenario writing, web chart, etc.; as well as building institutions and a network of cooperating small groups; continuation of methods from the first stage.

3. Propaganda of the Deed—Direct Action—Dilemma demonstrations: "One which puts the opponent in a dilemma: whichever response he makes helps the movement. If he allows the demonstration to proceed, the movement gains that opportunity to educate the people. If he represses the demonstration, the people are awakened further to the underlying nature of the regime." (p. 103)

Activities: Attempting to act out the future in the present, such as sit-ins and heal-ins; fraternization with soldiers and police; acts that speak for themselves regardless of the news media's attitudes, such as diverting war tax resistance funds to community organizations. Many methods of nonviolent action are applicable.

4. Political and Economic Noncooperation—The population ceases to support the old order.

Activities: Draft resistance, tax resistance, boycotts of consumer goods, strikes for worker control, civil disobedience, unreliability of troops and police.

5. Intervention and Parallel Institutions—Parallel Institutions such as workers' councils or other coordinating bodies are improvised in a crisis situation and win the allegiance of the people, displacing the old order when repression fails.

Activities: What were formerly "counter-institutions" now become institutions. "Coordinating councils on local, regional, national, and transnational levels help to smooth a transfer of power from the corporations and government to the people's institutions." (p. 199)

VI
Macro-Analysis Seminars*

Macro-Analysis is both a collection of processes for learning, thinking, and sharing and a structured list of books and articles which develop a radical critique of the present social order and consider a variety of visions of a better society and strategies for achieving revolutionary change. Macro-analysis seminars developed with a particular concern for helping people to move from ideas to action. The information given here is intended to encourage you to start one. For more detail we recommend the macro-analysis manual (see below). Its process and readings are the result of several years of experience and the feedback from over 200 seminar groups in the United States and in some other countries as well.

The only basic requirements are: copies of the manual, a set of the reading materials it describes, and a group of people willing to give 3 hours of time and energy to each session, plus additional reading time every two or three sessions. The standard seminar runs for about 24 three-hour sessions, usually one session each week. The manual also describes how to do a 12-session seminar.

1. Purpose:
To help activists:
  • see social problems within the context of political-economic forces and examine their interconnections and systemic causes;
  • understand the dynamics of power relationships and the role of power in effective action for social change;

* Thanks to the Philadelphia Macro-Analysis Collective (MNS) for its assistance in the preparation of this section.

- develop a frame of reference out of which clear values arise (for better evaluation of assumptions and goals for action, to improve judgment on concrete programs);
- apply their analysis and insights to social change efforts and find actions which they can undertake;
- connect their social concerns with their personal needs and energies;
- discover new questions that need asking;
- take active responsibility for their own learning, decrease their reliance on experts, and think independently and critically about important issues.

2. Content:

Each of the major sections of the seminar is briefly described below:

Introduction: It is particularly important for groups whose members don't know each other well to spend some time at the beginning sharing basic assumptions, goals, visions for a new society, and personal expectations of the seminar. This is also a time for the group to deal with housekeeping details: meeting time and place, duration of seminar, finances, child-care, etc.

Analysis: This section, the longest part of the seminar, is planned to provide people with basic information about the social and economic problems we face, with an emphasis on the interrelationships among problems and their basic causes. Reports and discussion on materials from the three topic areas (ecology, U.S. relations to third world countries, and U.S. domestic problems) are combined with group time to think through their implications for social action and personal change.

a. Ecology—includes: "limits to growth," food, population, environment and pollution, role of corporations, energy, economic and political implications, lifestyle, liberatory and intermediate technology, current events and action.

b. U.S. Relations with the Third World—includes: historical and present-day perspectives; the loans business; foreign aid, hunger and the philanthropists; OPEC and the North/South conflict; the development crusade; the multinationals; militarism and the maintenance of oppression; the struggle for self-reliant development; and facets of underdevelopment at home.

c. United States Domestic Problems—includes: power in the U.S.; role of corporations; militarism; the economy and inequality; the oppression of women; feminist perspectives; men's liberation; gay liberation; classism; work and alienation; economics of everyday life; poverty; racism; crime, justice and prisons; farming, food and agribusiness; historical perspective; possible solutions.

Visions of a Better Society—includes: the need for visionary thinking; utopian novels; means of livelihood and way of life; contemporary socialist perspectives; two anarchist perspectives; toward a participatory society; a nonviolent revolutionary vision; historical alternatives: China, Spain, Yugoslavia, Czechoslovakia; a libertarian socialist vision; reform under capitalism; a feminist vision.

Strategy—includes: social change history; electoral and third party approach; who will make the revolution; anarchist strategy; workers' control as a strategy; strategy and tactics; building a movement; nonviolent movement approach; direct action; violence and nonviolence; feminist strategy and organizing; building alternatives; living the revolution; personal change and community.

In both the Vision and Strategy sections participants devote time to developing their own visions and strategies, in addition to the reading and report format.

Action: This section provides tools and suggestions to help move a seminar from study to actual social change work.

3. Activities

Each topic area usually includes three to four three-hour sessions, each with the following typical format:

1. Excitement sharing (10 min)
2. Agenda review (2-10 min)
3. Choice of facilitator or assistant facilitator for the next session (1-5 min)
4. Brainstorm of questions which group members would like to answer in the topic area (5-10 min)
5. Reports on readings. Four to six short reports on different readings, prepared in advance by members of the group. Each report is followed by a time for clarifying questions and comments. (See *Timed Report or Presentation*.) (5 min report and 5 min for questions times number of reports = 40-60 min)
6. Break (10-15 min)
7. Relating it to social change. Group develops new goals and projects for change based on information gained from all reports in a topic area. Many tools listed in "Exercises and Tools" could be used here. (20-120 min)
8. Evaluation of session (10-15 min)
9. Plan next session. Choose readings. (10-20 min)

In a five-minute report, the reporter presents only a few key points or points that were personally important, along with a few facts for each point; a criticism of the reliability of the article, if necessary; and implications of the reading for social change. During each report, a recorder can list on a wall chart the points in the report under the headings: PROBLEMS, SOLUTIONS, PROJECTS.

4. Process:

The macro-analysis seminar handbook suggests the use of many of the group process techniques included in this manual, such as use of facilitators and timed agendas. (See Part Two: "Working in Groups.") We quote their explanation:

"Many study and seminar groups have great difficulties with their manner and style of functioning. Many groups which are organized around exciting topics and have attracted interested people seem to get bogged down in poor 'process.' Some groups lack a shared time discipline and find that they don't cover the material they had wanted to. Some groups are unable to focus on one topic, and wander all over the map. In some groups particularly verbal people tend to dominate the discussion.

"We have worked hard to break these kinds of patterns. The process which we suggest in this manual attempts to be democratic, honest, and encouraging of real sharing. At the same time it allows the group to focus its attention and successfully grapple with the topic at hand...."

5. Group Responsibilities:

All members are responsible for the success of the seminar. Specific roles or tasks are shared, often rotated, among as many of the group as possible:

a. *Convenor*—arranges meeting time and place, refreshments; at beginning of seminar, orders reading materials.

b. *Facilitator*—starts meeting, oversees the process, serves as chairperson. (An assistant facilitator is often helpful in sharing responsibility for planning and tending the meeting. S/he assumes the facilitator role at the next meeting.)

c. *Recorder*—writes essential ideas on a board visible to all.

d. *Timekeeper*—helps group move through agenda by noting when agreed-on times are up.

See the section on "How to Facilitate a Meeting" for additional information.

6. Materials Needed

a. Large pads of newsprint for wall charts, and crayons or markers; or large chalkboard.

b. Reading materials.

c. Macro-analysis manuals. Groups proposing to undertake a seminar may send for *Organizing Macro-Analysis Seminars: A Manual* from which the preceding description was summarized. The manual provides a theoretical framework as well as specific information on how to gather a group, order materials, start the seminar, and run the meeting. It includes a detailed suggested reading list and an annotated bibliography. Some of the basic books are listed at the end of this section.

7. Resources Available:

The macro-analysis manual is available from the Philadelphia Macro-Analysis Collective (MNS), 4722 Baltimore Ave., Phila., PA 19143. Cost is $1.00 for the manual, 25¢ for the current reading list, and 50¢ for postage postpaid. Inquire about special bulk rates.

Members of the collective are glad to help groups starting seminars, or to direct them to experienced people in their local areas. A quarterly newsletter is published through which people in seminars share ideas, new reading suggestions, and enthusiasm.

8. Variations on Macro-Analysis Seminars:

Variation #1: Issue-Oriented Seminars on important topics such as racism or nuclear power that are not extensively covered by the macro-analysis manual can be researched and presented using the same or a similar process and format. In addition, groups are encouraged to incorporate current events and their own learning materials into the seminar.

Variation #2: Vision or Strategy Seminars. The macro-analysis seminar includes major sections on vision and strategy, in which participants not only discuss readings on a broad range of visions and strategies, but also develop their own. Some groups may prefer a short seminar, based on the macro-analysis format, but focusing primarily on visions and alternative societies or strategies. Such a seminar could go into more depth than the corresponding sections of the introductory macro-analysis seminar.

Variation #3: Seminars adapted to other countries and cultures. A manual, *Organising Macro-Analysis Seminars*, by Jenny Jacobs, Sheila Rose and Jim Schrag, is available (Macro-Analysis Working Group, Friends Peace and International Relations Committee, Friends House, Euston Road, London, NW1 2BJ, England, about 75¢). A Canadian-oriented reading list for seminars is available from Dick Renshaw, Coady House, 60 Grant St., Toronto, Canada, for $.35 plus postage.

If your group develops a seminar in a new subject area or with successful variations in process, the Philadelphia Macro-Analysis Collective would love to hear about it.

VII
Selected Bibliography

General Resources on Analysis, Vision, and Strategy

The Capitalist System, edited by Richard C. Edwards, Michael Reich, and Thomas E. Weisskopf (Prentice-Hall, 1972; new ed. forthcoming 1977). An excellent anthology analyzing a range of foreign and domestic problems and relating them to the political economy.

Moving Toward a New Society, by Susanne Gowan, et al. (New Society Press, 4722 Baltimore Ave., Phila., PA 19143, 1976, $3.75 postpaid). A cogent analysis of the problems facing society today, visions of a good society, and practical discussions of ways to get there. Recommended reading.

Post-Scarcity Anarchism, by Murray Bookchin (Ramparts Press, 1971). Stimulating essays on ecology and revolutionary thought, liberatory technology, Marxism, France 1968, and other topics by an influential contemporary anarchist. He emphasizes what is new in the possibilities of our time.

Analysis: Ecology

The Closing Circle, by Barry Commoner (Bantam, 1971). A readable overview of the ecological crisis, discussing the roles of population, technology, and profit and the social and economic implications.

Toward a Steady-State Economy, edited by Herman E. Daly (W.H. Freeman, 1973). Essays that put political-economic thought in a context of biophysical and moral constraints, aiming to promote a new way of looking at the subject.

Analysis: U.S. Relations with the Third World

Global Reach: The Power of the Multinational Corporations, by Richard J. Barnet and Ronald E. Mueller (Simon and Schuster, 1974). A well-researched study of the MNCs' influence both abroad and at home.

The Trojan Horse, by Steve Weissman et al. (Ramparts Press, 1975). A good collection of essays on the history, purpose, and effects on both poor and rich countries of "foreign aid."

Analysis: U.S. Domestic Problems

America's Working Women, edited by Rosalyn Baxandall, et

al. (Vintage, 1976). A documentary history offering an analysis of the conditions and struggles of working women, paid and unpaid, through all of U.S. history. Essential background for the situation of women today.

Common Sense for Hard Times, by Jeremy Brecher and Tim Costello (Common Sense, Institute for Policy Studies, 1901 Q St., NW, Washington, DC 20009, 1976; $3.95 plus .55 postage). Subtitled "The Power of the Powerless to Cope With Everyday Life and Transform Society in the Nineteen Seventies." Talking with people around the country, the authors describe the resistance of working people to the system's efforts to keep them divided and resigned to accepting hard times. They find in this capacity for solidarity and co-operation reason to believe we can collectively take charge of our lives.

The Higher Circles: The Governing Class in America, by G. William Domhoff (Vintage, 1970). A calm, clear, and systematic presentation of what the upper class is and how it rules. His concluding "Critiques of Other Views" successfully argues his case via contrasts with conspiracy theories and liberal pluralism.

Underhanded History of the U.S., by Nick Thorkelson and Jim O'Brien (New England Free Press, 60 Union Square, Somerville, MA 02143, 1974, $1.20 postpaid). From the colonial period to the present, a witty but serious challenge in comic book form to standard history. Sound history and inspired cartooning.

Why Do We Spend So Much Money? and *What's Happening to Our Jobs?,* by Steve Babson and Nancy Brigham (Popular Economics Press, Box 221, Somerville, MA 02143, 1975 and 1976, $1.00 and $1.45). Readable, well illustrated booklets in a question-and-answer format explaining the reasons for high living costs, unemployment, and other everyday economic problems—with thoughts on possible solutions. Factual and enlightening.

Visions of a Better Society

The Anarchist Collectives: Workers' Self-Management in the Spanish Revolution 1936-1939, ed. by Sam Dolgoff (Free Life Editions, 41 Union Square West, New York, NY 10003, 1974, $3.95, postage .50). How anarchist principles worked in practice. Historical background plus eyewitness accounts of the libertarian economic and social organization created behind the lines of the civil war.

The Chinese Road to Socialism, by E. L. Wheelwright and B. McFarlane (Monthly Review, 1970). The Maoist strategy for economic development, presented and analyzed by two economists. Contrasts with the Soviet model of socialism are highlighted.

Communitas: Means of Livelihood and Ways of Life, by Paul and Percival Goodman (1947; Vintage, 1960). A classic of social thought: analyzes a wide variety of community plans and societal models, shows their implications for the people's way of life, and proposes imaginative new models.

Ecotopia, by Ernest Callenbach (Banyan Tree Books, c/o 2940 Seventh, Berkeley, CA 94710, 1975, $2.75). Oregon, Washington, and northern California secede from the U.S. in 1980 and create a new society. The first American journalist permitted inside, twenty years later, reports on their strange ways. Well conceived and written.

Fields, Factories and Workshops Tomorrow, by Peter Kropotkin, edited by Colin Ward (1899; Harper Torchbook, 1974). An updated version of Kropotkin's case for decentralization of industry, local self-sufficiency, and the integration of manual and intellectual work—a book that influenced both Gandhi and Mao.

Small is Beautiful: Economics as if People Mattered, by E. F. Schumacher (Harper, 1973). The pioneer of "intermediate technology" discusses economics from a human-scale, ethical perspective that Theodore Roszak's introduction links to an organic and decentralist tradition.

Socialist Alternatives for America: A Bibliography, by James Campen (second edition forthcoming from Union for Radical Political Economics, 41 Union Square West, New York, NY 10003). The out-of-print first edition featured nearly 600 annotated items covering theories of the new society, relevant experiences of various countries, aspects of socialist alternatives (like economics, ecology, sex roles, etc.), and useful complementary material. A superb, extremely helpful guide to thought and study.

Workers' Councils and the Economics of a Self-Managed Society, by Paul Cardan (1957; Phila. Solidarity, GPO 13011, Phila., PA 19101, 1974, $1.25 postpaid). Historically-based speculation by a major European theorist on the possible practical meaning of socialism; concise, sharp thinking. Illustrated with amusing drawings.

Strategy

The Case for Participatory Democracy, edited by C. George Benello and Dimitrios Roussopoulos (Viking, 1971). Essays in analysis by anarchist and libertarian socialist authors; good essays on strategy by Lens, Lynd, Roussopoulos, and Calvert.

Socialism and Revolution, by Andre Gorz (1967; Anchor/ Doubleday, 1973). An effort to define socialist strategy for advanced industrial countries; includes thoughts on reform and revolution and the tasks of a party.

Strategy and Program, by Staughton Lynd and Gar Alperovitz (Beacon, 1973). Reflections on the old and new lefts, a model of a "pluralist commonwealth," and a list of programmatic ideas.

Strategy for a Living Revolution, by George Lakey (W. H. Freeman, 1973; Movement for a New Society, 4722 Baltimore Ave., Phila., PA 19143, $7.50 postpaid). Good thinking on many aspects of political strategy (such as the limits of civilian insurrection, organizing in a police state, choosing tactics, and the role of counter-institutions) in the context of a model for nonviolent revolution. Combines well-grounded historical analysis with imaginative projection of future possibilities.

Strike! by Jeremy Brecher (Fawcett, 1972). Narration of six periods of mass strikes in U.S. history, when workers challenged capital, the state, and trade union leadership; how struggle continues today, and the chances for moving "from mass strike to new society."

What is Class Consciousness?, by Wilhelm Reich (1934; Liberation. P.O. Box 1267, Peter Stuyvesant Sta., New York, NY 10009, $1.00; or reprinted in *Sex-Pol*, Vintage, 1972). The powerful classic pleading the need for revolutionary strategy to connect with the everyday concerns of people and to recognize our own fears and potential confidence as political data.

A MOVEMENT SONG

Do what the song says. (Play *very* slowly the first time, then faster and faster.)

Words and music by Susanne Terry Gowan

Part Two

Working In Groups

Working in groups, whether in our own families, at workshops, or in continuing organizations, is one of the most basic social activities and is a large part of work for social change. Therefore, it is important that groups working for change develop effective, satisfying, democratic methods of doing necessary tasks both for their own use and to share with others.

The elimination of authoritarian and hierarchical structures is important for democratizing groups, but does not mean the rejection of *all* structures. Groups that have taken the latter course have generally become ineffective, or else have reverted to the same, but no longer explicit, authoritarian leadership as before. Good group functioning is a product of *cooperative* structures and the intelligent, responsible participation of the group's members.

"Working in Groups" contains practical suggestions for the creation of cooperative group structures and for the development of personal group skills. It also presents a theoretical framework for understanding how groups function and exercises and games that help make this theory concrete.

Part Two includes five major sections:

    I. Group Dynamics
    II. How to Facilitate a Meeting
    III. Tools Used to Improve Group Process
    IV. Conflict Resolution—Some Useful Processes
    V. Bibliographies

I
Group Dynamics*

Group dynamics is the study of forces acting within a group of people. It is also a major field of study from which we have gained valuable insights. As we have studied group dynamics we have selected information which has been useful to our particular focus on social change.

Good internal dynamics do not happen by accident. They come from an awareness of how the group functions, aspects that need to be modified, and dynamics that need to be built upon to improve group efficiency and personal satisfaction among participants.

In this section we include information on four areas which have helped us examine the way groups function and improve the way we work together: (1) some general characteristics of groups, (2) task and maintenance functions, (3) leadership, and (4) decision making. The exercises explained and illustrated at the end of this section can help make your learning practical as well as theoretical. Two approaches for developing a workshop in group dynamics are included with other sample workshops in Part Six.

For those who want an overview of group dynamics we recommend *Dynamics of Groups at Work*, by Herbert A. Thelen. This book and several others are annotated in the bibliography at the end of Part Two.

SOME GENERAL CHARACTERISTICS OF GROUPS

Cohesiveness: The degree to which the members of a group like and support each other. Depends on how much there is agreement on basic goals and values, how many good experiences members have had with each other. This is described later on as a sense of "community," to be enhanced by "community building exercises."

Climate: The psychological tone of a meeting. How much attention do the members have for the issue at hand? Do participants feel easy with expressing their feelings? Is the spirit joyful, tense? The climate is affected very much by the physcial arrangement of the meeting place. Is it too warm or cool; too crowded or noisy? Other factors affecting climate might be time

---

* Taken in part from an earlier draft by Lynne Shivers.

pressure and uncertainty over goals. The climate is often set by the perceived leaders.

Pressures: Compelling influences. What are they? Time? Money? Are they external or internal pressures? To what extent do they help the group reach its goals; make members act in rigid ways?

Goals: Ends the group strives to attain. Goals can be long and/or short-range. If goals are clear, little leadership is needed. If goals are not clear and/or members are unclear how to accomplish the goals, leadership functions need to be filled. Have individuals clarified their own goals to the extent that group goals are possible?

Structure: Interrelationship of all the aspects of a group, such as: the decision-making process, different roles, membership, goals, styles and processes of communication. Structure may be formal, in that it is defined and deliberately followed by the group, or it may be informal.

Standards: Expectations regarding behavior in the group, e.g., amount of involvement, or being on time. It makes a difference whether standards are set by "leaders" or all the members, and whether or not standards are conscious.

Control: Regulation of the group. How does a group insure its own continuation and the completion of its long term tasks? How are new members included or excluded? Controls of some sort are essential to the life of a group. Are controls used flexibly as needed? Do they work against the goals of the group?

TASK AND MAINTENANCE FUNCTIONS

The activities necessary for effective group operation can be divided into "task" functions, needed to help the group achieve its goals, and "maintenance" functions, needed to build and maintain the group. These functions are explained in Charts A, B and C.

Ability to perform these functions is not hereditary, but is learned. When people take on a group function they are commonly said to take on a role. The term "role" conveys to many a rigidity of behavior not intended here. Because we wish to stress the importance of roles being filled by different group members as needed, we will often use the term "function" to emphasize the distinction between the person and the behavior. Please note that when referring to task and maintenance activities we use the terms "role" and "function" interchangeably.

Understanding these roles will help your group discover and use its resources more fully. Interpersonal tensions may decrease as group members perceive many group problems not as

CHART A—Group Task Functions *

This chart describes behavior needed to help a group achieve its long or short range goals. A skilled member will assume these roles as they are needed.

Function/Role	Purpose	Technique
Initiator	Give direction and purpose to the group	Proposing tasks, goals, defining problems, suggesting procedures and solutions
Information-seeking	Make group aware of need for information	Requesting relevant facts, clarification
Information-giving	Provide group information relevant to its work	Offering relevant facts, avoiding reliance on opinion when facts are needed
Opinion-seeking	Test for consensus, find out group opinion	Asking for feelings or opinions about something
Opinion-giving	Provide basis for group decision	Stating feelings or beliefs, evaluating a suggestion
Clarifying	Eliminate confusion	Defining terms, interpreting ideas, indicating issues and alternatives
Elaborating	Reduce ambiguity, show consequences of plans and positions	Giving examples, developing meanings, explaining
Coordinating	Adjust issues or harmonize issues that may conflict	Suggesting ways that different issues can be handled
Procedure-developing	Establish an order to the meeting	Suggesting agenda, order of business, where to go next
Summarizing	Show how ideas are related; draw ideas together	Pulling together related issues, showing contradictions, restating suggestions, offering conclusions
Philosopher-critic	Show that a particular issue is not unique; bring in insights from similar experience	Drawing general statements from specific ones; critically examining assumptions and ideas (*not* people)

* Charts on Task and Maintenance Functions were developed primarily from materials used in a course on group dynamics at Temple University led by Professor Erma Jones, and the training experiences of Friends Peace Committee and Life Center training groups, c/o Lynne Shivers, 4722 Baltimore Ave., Phila., PA 19143.

CHART B—Group Maintenance Functions

This chart describes behavior needed to build and maintain the group as a working unit. A skilled member will assume these roles/functions as they are needed to keep the group working together harmoniously.

Function/Role	Purpose	Technique
Encouraging	Bring out others' opinions and give others recognition	Being friendly, warm and responsive to others. Accepting others' contributions.
Expressing feelings	Call group attention to reactions to ideas and suggestions made	Expressing own feelings and restating others' feelings and opinions
Relieving tension	Reduce tension, allow group to express feelings	Joking, clowning, attention expanders, breaks, etc.
Compromising	Maintain group cohesion	Offering or accepting compromises; yielding status, admitting error
Facilitate communication	Maintain open discussion, keep channels open	Drawing out silent members, suggesting procedures for discussions
Setting standards and goals	Make group aware of direction and progress	Expressing the group concern, suggesting tasks, stating standards for group to achieve
Interpreting	Explain, interpret what someone has already said	Paraphrasing initial speaker
Listening, following	Provide stimulating, interested audience for others	Accepting ideas of others; going along with the group

CHART C—Task and Maintenance Functions

The following functions contribute both to the maintenance of a group and to the accomplishment of its tasks. This is, of course, true of all the functions listed above, to some extent. Group maintenance is vital to group achievement, and, in most cases, group achievement is important to group maintenance.

Function/Role	Purpose	Technique
Harmonizing, mediating	Reconcile disagreements, reduce tension	Conciliating differences, offering compromises
Testing agreement	Find out how close group is to agreement	Noting progress, stating areas of agreement, making tentative proposals for group reaction, asking if agreement is possible
Evaluating	Keep group in line with goals, provide sense of progress	Measuring accomplishments against goals, noting progress and blocks

47

people's "faults," but as unfilled roles. Experience with task and maintenance roles is also an important foundation for understanding complex but vital processes such as leadership, decision making, and prevention of group problems.

The important skill to be learned here is *the ability to identify and fill unfilled roles*. But remember, the key to effective use of these roles is an understanding of their appropriateness, and this requires a knowledge of membership roles as a whole. Below is a list of suggestions on how you can learn to identify the roles and practice filling them.

Suggestions for Learning Task and Maintenance Roles

1. Use the *Fishbowl Exercise* format to observe task and maintenance roles and to become familiar with them. Evaluate your own and others' ability to fill these roles.

2. Put roles with their purposes and sample techniques on index cards. Shuffle and pass them out to the group. In an assigned task or in the group's normal activity, participants assume the role(s) they have been dealt. In a small group a person may need to fill two or more roles. Discuss and evaluate. What could people have done to better fill the roles they were assigned? Variation: Let people volunteer to take roles they normally find difficult.

3. Take task and maintenance role charts (A, B and C) to meetings that you normally attend and identify the roles as they are filled. Are there important roles not being filled? Practice filling them.

LEADERSHIP

Questions of leadership have presented endless problems to people seeking social change. Leadership has become confused with authoritarianism and the wielding of undemocratic economic and political power in our society. As a result people often refuse to take on leadership responsibilities or do so by emulating the style of leadership they have observed. Neither has resulted in the emergence of viable political and social alternatives for our society.

Our experience has taught us that leadership can best be understood as a set of functions rather than as a personal trait. Dominating leadership is fulfillment by one person of many group functions and roles of leadership at the expense of, and *with the cooperation of,* other members. In group-centered leadership all members take on responsibilities that often would fall to one person. The result is a less centralized leadership, not vulnerable to the loss of one or two individuals. When all group members share leadership responsibilities the group's cohesion and durability tend to increase.

Leadership is a composite of learnable skills through which the efforts of individuals are coordinated to accomplish group goals. These skills are used as is appropriate in a given situation.

To exercise group leadership means:
- to accept and clarify feelings of another without threat;
- to aid the group's insight into its feelings and attitudes;
- to relate emotions/feelings to the demands of the present situation;
- to state all sides of a controversy fairly and objectively;
- to summarize group discussion;
- to bring a group to a point for decision making without threat;
- to recognize and interpret forces operating in a group;
- to recognize and articulate themes noticed in discussion;
- to sense the development of tension;
- to coordinate the questions and steps a group needs to consider in order to reach a decision;
- to collect thinking and restate it for group acceptance and action;
- to encourage others to gain experience in and learn skills of leadership.

To the degree to which participants recognize and learn these skills, they are in a position to decide to what extent they want to formalize leadership roles, to share and rotate them among the members, or to experiment with a variety of structures.

Exercises can be used to help people examine their own attitudes toward leadership, understand the skills involved, and begin to share the leadership function. Some we have used are:

Brainstorm on the question "What do you associate with leadership?"

Statements Exercise using: A good leader needs to...; The problem I see in leadership...; What I mean by a leader is ....

Take the list of leadership skills above to meetings. Observe how others function. Is there a leadership skill not being provided? Try to fill it.

Needs for leadership are closely related to the clarity of the group's goals, as well as to its structures. When the goal and/or structure are confused or in disagreement, there is a corresponding need for greater initiative and the presence of leadership.

These relationships can be explored by using the *Fishbowl Exercise* modified in the following way:

• Trainer will decide the topic for discussion using a sentence or topic which is very confusing. Ex: "Given the intricate relationship of nonviolent philosophy with compatible and valuable strategy and tactics, which of them is most necessary to the most essential leaders, members, constituents, and opponents in a social change campaign?"

• Possible evaluation questions: Was the goal of the group clear? If not, why not? If so, how was it clarified? How was leadership exercised and by whom? Were attempts to fill leadership functions accepted in the group? Why or why not? Could leadership functions have been handled better?

DECISION MAKING

When faced with the difficult decisions of building a new society a group needs to take advantage of the resources of all of its members. As we take control over our decision-making process we are learning several things:

1. *We need to understand the decision-making process to have control over it.* There are a number of ways to acquire a better understanding.

• Take a few minutes to evaluate the decision-making process of any group session. Some questions to raise to make the process visible are:

How was the leader selected?

What did the group want to accomplish? Does everyone in the group agree?

How and when were decisions being made?

What steps or structures were used to make decisions? How did they work?

Have individuals clarified their own goals, so that group goals can be clarified?

• Recognize when the process breaks down and review task and maintenance functions to see which ones are not being performed. Continue the meeting with people trying to fill the missing roles.

• Use the *Fishbowl Exercise*. If a fictitious topic is used, be particularly certain that (1) the decision to be made is a difficult one AND (2) that there is a pressure of time to make the decision. Time pressure will expose the decision-making process and problems will surface more quickly.

It may be useful to use the Fishbowl format for a portion of a regular meeting. Divide the group into "fish" and "bowl" and proceed with the original agenda. After an agreed-upon time, period, evaluate and ask "fish" and "bowl" to exchange places.

• Try the NASA Game. An excellent game, used to explore a number of processes, including how groups make decisions, especially through consensus. Also used to examine the relationships of knowledge to influence, and of openness of the group to individual initiative. (Found in *A Handbook of Structured Experiences for Human Relations Training,* Vol. 1, pp 52-57.)

• Practice designing steps or structures which facilitate decision making.

• Do the Broken Squares Game. This is used to examine cooperation and personal obstructive behavior in solving group problems. Focuses well on feelings. (*A Handbook of Structured Experiences for Human Relations Training,* Vol. 1, pp 24-29.)

2. It is helpful to explore different theoretical processes of decision making, e.g., totalitarian, voting, consensus, and to understand the advantages and disadvantages of each. To learn more about these processes read *Roads to Agreement* by Stuart Chase.

Experiment with different decision-making processes: consensus, majority vote, central director, hierarchy. This can be done in a regular meeting of your group, in a *Fishbowl* format, or in the Broken Squares game. Evaluate the advantages and disadvantages of each structure, taking into account your own feelings and the morale of the group.

Typical communication patterns for the different decision-making processes can be illustrated as:

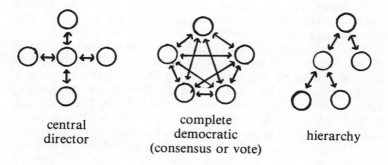

central
director

complete
democratic
(consensus or vote)

hierarchy

3. It is important to demystify the abilities of some people to facilitate decision making.

Following each meeting evaluate contributions of the facilitator in moving the group toward decisions and in dealing with the agenda. Also note areas where improvement is needed. By articulating the functions that need to be filled, such as summarizing, coordinating, etc., more people can learn about these functions and specific ways of carrying them out. In addition, both experienced and inexperienced facilitators take turns facilitating in most of our regular meetings, so that the skills are learned and practiced by all. (Large or difficult meetings, of course, require experienced facilitators.)

CONSENSUS DECISION MAKING AND WHY WE PREFER IT

Consensus is a process for making group decisions without voting. Agreement is reached through a process of gathering information and viewpoints, discussion, persuasion, a combination of synthesis of proposals and/or the development of totally new ones. The goal of the consensus process is to reach a decision with which everyone can agree. Consensus at its best relies upon persuasion rather than pressure for reaching group unity.

Consensus does not necessarily mean unanimity. A group can proceed with an action without having total agreement. In the event that an individual or small group cannot agree with a given proposal and is blocking consensus, the facilitator may ask if the individual(s) are willing to "stand aside" and allow the group to act, or if they feel so strongly about the issue that they are unwilling for the group to act. If the individual(s) agree to stand aside, their disagreements can be noted in the minute of the meeting, and the group is free to act on the decision. If the individual(s) are not willing to stand aside, action is blocked unless a compromise or substitute agreement can be found. The group may agree to postpone the decision until a later time so that more information can be gathered, people have a chance to discuss the issues in more detail, tempers can cool, participants have a chance to reflect on the options before them, or a compromise can be worked out by the major disagreeing factions. Some large groups (with several hundred attending) use a modified consensus technique in which two or three persons are not enough to block consensus unless they object strongly.

The consensus method is an effort to achieve a balance between task and maintenance needs in the decision-making process, and is most suitable for groups whose members value their association highly. Many small groups actually use a kind of consensus process even if officially they take votes. In order to preserve the unity and spirit of the group, they take votes only when they feel sure that the group is nearly in complete agreement, and they take time to reconsider close votes.

Consensus decision-making sometimes requires a great deal of patience. It is necessary to listen carefully to opposing viewpoints to reach the best decision. In spite of this drawback, the consensus method has the following advantages over a voting method:

• It produces more intelligent decisions, by incorporating the best thinking of everyone.

• It keeps people from getting into adversary attitudes where individual egos are tied to a proposal that will win or lose.

• It increases the likelihood of new and better ideas being thought up.

• Everyone has a stake in implementing a decision, because all have participated in its formation. Participants have more energy for working on projects with which they are fully in agreement.

• It lessens significantly the possibility that a minority will feel that an unacceptable decision has been imposed on them.

An example of consensus: We have seen a single person, whose voice had not adequately been listened to at first by the group of fifty people, use the attention focused on him by the process of testing for consensus to persuade the whole group (which had been on the point of agreeing to a proposal) to decide differently. All agreed that the new decision was wiser. In a voting situation, a person outnumbered so heavily is more likely to feel that the situation is hopeless.

EXERCISES AND GAMES
FOR LEARNING ABOUT GROUP DYNAMICS

Group dynamics learning is most effective through an experimental and experiential self-training approach to solving your own group's problems. The central purpose for any exercise should be to increase people's awareness of how groups function and of their own participation in groups. Below are exercises which may be used in a variety of circumstances and with a variety of topics. Exercises should be chosen for their relevance. A number of excellent texts on group dynamics are listed at the end of Part Two.

We encourage groups to design their own learning structures for particular issues for which we have not included exercises. Remember that when a topic for discussion is used in an exercise, it needs to be brief, clear, and relevant.

1. *Fishbowl Exercise*   (60-90 min)

Purpose: To examine an issue in group process through observation of a group at work. To allow people to learn through guided observation. We have most frequently used the fishbowl structure to examine task and maintenance roles.

Description:

1. Participants volunteer to be in one of two groups of about equal size: the task group ("fish") or observer group ("bowl"). The exercise gets its name because it works best when the task group sits close together inside an outer circle of observers.

2. The observers should decide or be told beforehand what and how to observe. Observation check sheets or written instructions are helpful to point out what behavior or problems to look for. When studying task and maintenance roles, charts similar to Charts A and B can be used.

3. It may be useful to give the task group special instructions, depending on the goal of the exercise. For instance, some people might be assigned specific roles or given special information.

4. The facilitator needs to make the task clear to the group before the exercise starts. Writing the task on a chalkboard may be useful.

When a group is examining maintenance roles it is helpful to choose a topic with which participants have some familiarity, e.g., "How have the women's and men's liberation movements affected our lives over the last few years?"

When a group is examining task roles, decision-making processes, leadership skills or conflict resolution issues, it is helpful to choose a topic which requires the group to reach a decision, e.g., "Come to consensus on the three most important ways the women's and men's liberation movements have affected this group since we began meeting."

5. The facilitator needs to ask the task group before starting if there are any questions, and to tell both groups how much time they will have. It's usually not good to interrupt the group once time has started, even for informational questions. Interruptions will make evaluation more complicated and destroy the sense of "reality" that the task group needs. Laughter or discussion among the observers will also be disruptive to the task group.

6. Issues and problems in decision making may surface more quickly if time pressure is added.

7. The facilitator calls time (s/he can give the group a

54

warning if desired) and asks for evaluative comments—first from observers and then from the task group. Once the important issues have been brought out, the evaluation is ended.

8. Often it's helpful to repeat the Fishbowl with a similar problem, reversing the roles of "fish" and "bowl." Everyone then has a chance to observe, and some participants get an immediate opportunity to put their new insights to use. Note: The observers learn most about group process, while the task group provides the raw material for them to examine.

2. *The Graveyard Exercise** (2-3 hrs)

Purpose: To help individuals evaluate their participation in groups and ask for group help in participating more creatively. To create intimacy in a group. To increase awareness of roadblocks that interfere with group process.

Materials: Large sheets of paper and pencils for each participant.

Description:

1. Ask people for their consent to do an exercise that will examine their personal participation and look at the help they need from this group.

2. Pass out large sheets of paper. Ask people to take from 10 to 40 minutes to list on one half of the paper how they see themselves functioning in this group. Give examples: as quiet, as needing approval, as posing questions, as a clown, etc. On the other half have people list what they need from this group to function most efficiently and creatively in helping the group to reach its goals.

3. After people finish writing have them think about a few things they have listed that are most important. Then give each person 2 to 5 minutes to share those points—without discussion.

4. After the sharing, have people examine how they can meet the needs they have expressed. Reach agreement on areas where people are willing to try. This can be the end of the exercise or the goals can be written down and checked back on later.

5. The exercise can be continued by posing a group task, something that the group wants to do, and examining the group process after a period of working on it. How were the members' needs met? How were the group's goals achieved?

---

* Thought up in a graveyard by Susanne Gowan.

55

Special Instructions: This exercise helps group members set real goals for themselves and the group to change on-going group process. Keep a positive tone and prevent individuals from dumping their irritations on each other. Remind individuals that everyone has been doing the best s/he could up till now. It can be useful to begin or end by brainstorming group accomplishments or strong points, so that individuals don't get depressed.

3. *Elephant Game* (1½-2 hrs—includes 30 min for evaluation)

Purpose: To help groups examine how to function cooperatively, how group decisions are made, how leadership is selected and how to solve simple tasks. The exercise also introduces some of the basic elements in nonviolent action and builds a strong sense of community in the group.

Materials: Two large rooms, minimum, one of which has lots of tables, boxes, chairs, etc.

Description:

1. At least two trainers are needed. Trainers begin by telling the group the purpose of the game and a brief outline of its stages. The group will have two chances to go through the maze. The first time will be short—an opportunity to test out its process and signals. There will be a short caucus time between the first and second maze when it will be able to correct or improve its signals. The second maze will be longer, more difficult, and have some unexpected obstacles. Before proceeding, ask the group if it is willing to try the game.

2. Inform participants that: (1) they will have 10 minutes (12 minutes if there are over fifteen participants) to develop a process to get through the maze, (2) while in the maze only one person, "the eyes," may have his/her eyes open, and "the eyes" may not touch or speak to the other group members in any known language. "The eyes" will know the route of the maze. (3) The rest of the group may touch and speak, but everyone except "the eyes" must keep his/her eyes closed.

Note: Trainers should avoid calling the person with his/her eyes open "the leader." Everyone may speak and participate during the 10 min. decision-making period prior to going into the maze.

3. Pause to answer questions.

4. Give the group its first 10 min. planning time. One of the trainers should observe the group process and periodically inform the group how much time it has left. The trainer should look for: how "the eyes" was selected, how the people at

the front and back of the line were selected, the group's criteria for "leadership," how signals were developed, how the group approached the task, participation levels of group members, participation and roles of men and women, how agreements were reached, etc.

5. One trainer should go to the unoccupied room and set up a physical maze of tables, chairs, etc. The first maze should be short, three or four obstacles, and might involve crawling under a table, going around several chairs, and then over another table. It should take 10 or 15 minutes for the group to go through the first maze.

6. At the end of the 10 minute planning time the trainers should show "the eyes" the maze. The best way to do this is to walk him/her through it.

7. The trainer and "the eyes" should return to the group. Participants should be told to "line up," if that is the tactic they have chosen, and to close their eyes. Remind them that the game will be more effective if they keep their eyes closed and that the entire group should go through the maze.

8. The group should *always* be allowed to complete the first maze or it may become demoralized. If the group failed to develop an adequate process and is in total chaos, encourage it to go back to the first room and correct its signals, choose new "eyes" or restructure the line. Move to step #5.

9. After the participants have successfully finished the first maze, give them five minutes to polish their signals. Everyone can talk and see during this period. One trainer should observe group dynamics while the other sets up the second maze, about six or seven obstacles.

10. At the end of five minutes, "the eyes" should be shown the second maze. Remind the group that it will encounter some unusual obstacles this time.

11. The group should begin the maze as before. The trainers, however, will hassle people, subtly at first and more aggressively later. The purpose of this harassment is to make the task more difficult, to increase stress, and to simulate the element of surprise and new information. Facilitators should make the task increasingly more difficult to complete, *but not impossible*. Completion should take no longer than 15 minutes or boredom will set in.

Early harassment might include whispering to one of the people in the line, "Will you please come with me. It's part of the game," and then leading a portion of the group away from the task at hand; blowing in people's ears, mild tickling, etc. Later harassment might include bodily breaking the line apart, kidnapping members of the line (or "the eyes"), and aggressive tickling. Toward the end of the maze trainers should decrease or stop harassment so that the task can be completed.

Facilitators need to watch out for the bodily health of themselves and participants. Sudden jerking around while being tickled or lashing out in anger or irritation should be expected. Be creative in harassing people, but don't provoke dangerous situations.

12. After participants have completed the maze they will need 5 to 7 min. to blow off steam, share excitement, etc. This time should not be structured. Facilitators might ask, "What happened...?" and then let people talk or move about.

13. After the initial excitement has been shared the facilitators should help the group evaluate three areas: (a) how the group made its decisions prior to going into the maze; (b) how the group functioned going through the maze) and (c) the relation to components of nonviolent action.

(a) In evaluating the pre-maze planning session the trainer should ask questions about group participation, leadership selection, how the group approached the task, etc. (see step #4 for other topics around which to develop questions).

(b) To evaluate functioning in the maze, ask questions like: How did you feel in your role as a member of the line? How did the people with special roles—"the eyes," the persons at the head of the line and at the end—feel and perform? Where did you get your support? What communication system was developed and how did it work? Did you have all the information you needed to perform the task? How did the group handle unexpected new experiences? What questions does this exercise raise about leadership? about participation? How did you deal with boredom? attacks?

(c) To identify and discuss the components of nonviolent action, ask the group members to apply the insights from the game to real life. Some of the questions might include: How important is it for all the group members to participate in decision making? to have all the information? How important is diversified or collective leadership? How and why is it important to build support groups for nonviolent actions? What roles does sexism play in building nonviolent actions? Who was harassed most? What responses made human contact with the hasslers? What made harassment stop? How does this relate to how you should respond in a demonstration? What did this exercise say about the need for planning and preparation?

Facilitators may need to push participants to transfer information they learned in the exercise to real-life experiences.

Avoid lecturing about nonviolent theory, but give case studies re: leadership, support groups, communication systems, strategy, etc., where applicable.

Special Instructions: This exercise can lead to some distrust of the trainers, and should not be used early in a workshop. Whenever it is used, participants need a chance to vent their hostile feelings toward the trainers. Group affirmation also helps to rebuild trust. Trainers should acknowledge that it was a difficult task and tell the group specific things that it did well.

Note: This game is called the Elephant Game because participants usually hold each other's hands as they go through the maze, thus resembling circus elephants holding on to each other's trunks and tails.

For further reading: "Some Conditions of Obedience and Disobedience to Authority," Stanley Milgram, pp. 243-262 in *Current Studies in Social Psychology*, Ivan Steiner and Martin Fishbein, eds.

4. *Tinkertoy Dog (Moose, Cow, etc.) Game*   (1½-2 hrs)

Purpose: To explore group dynamics in a tightly defined problem situation. To explore competition. To examine through analogy how groups work. To explore feelings related to tasks and roles. To study roles in relationship to task performance.

Materials: Two medium size sets of Tinkertoys. (Tinkertoys are a children's play product sold in the U.S. and some other countries in sets containing a number of standard small building components: e.g., short sticks, long sticks, wheels, connectors, etc. Any similar standard product or homemade components will work.) Two to three rooms or screen partitions. Fairly simple dog or other animal constructed by trainers from tinkertoys and placed in a separate room before the game begins.

Description:
1. Divide the group into small groups of 6 to 8 people. (Do *not* use the word *team* for these small groups.) Explain that there is a model of a tinkertoy dog in another place that participants cannot see. The job of each group is to duplicate perfectly the prototype of the dog in the other room using the tinkertoys supplied by the trainers.

2. Roles to be filled by the group members are:

Looker—Sees the original dog and talks only to the messenger.

Messenger—Sees neither the original dog nor the model

59

being built. Can talk with the looker, builders, and other messengers.

Builders—One to three people build the dog with the tinkertoys supplied. Can talk with each other and the Messenger and ask the Feedbacker questions.

Feedbacker—Can see both the original and the group model. Can talk with anyone, BUT only in response to questions AND can only respond by "that's right" or "that's wrong." Volunteered messages and nonverbal signals are out.

Supplier—Has the set of tinker toys and can distribute them to the group. Must see that the group has no more than 6 unattached tinkertoys at any one time. Supply is set apart from the group. *Note:* role of Supplier can be doubled with that of a Builder or eliminated if group is small. Greater alienation occurs if the role is left separate. See #6, evaluation, below.

3. After instructions are given, each group gets a set of tinkertoys and ten minutes to select people for each role and to develop a system of communication.

4. The trainer should tell the groups that at any time during the game they can call for a group meeting to discuss communication or process of construction. Actual description of the dog and its construction cannot be discussed, nor may the Looker see the Builders' dog. Meetings may be called by any member of the group.

5. Time limits are usually not set for the construction. A moderately complicated dog takes about 45 minutes.

After the first group has completed a model, the trainers can stop the game or allow the other groups to complete the task.

6. Evaluation: (may take 30 min.)

The following questions will bring out useful information:

• How were the roles selected? Were any specific qualifications considered? What roles did men and women play? Any sex-role patterns? How did people feel in their roles?

• Did the two groups work together? compete with each other? Why? Nothing in the directions except physical placement of the groups and possibly time limits would indicate that they could not work together.

• What kinds of internal support systems existed for the various members?

• Did the group call meetings? Was communication smooth? What systems of communication were used? Did people get feedback on how they performed their roles?

• What analogies can be made about how groups with right role definitions function? What insights have participants gained about roles? roles and task completion? roles and personal satisfaction? (People who do meaningless or isolated work burn out, lose loyalty to the group, and will refuse to work on or may actually sabotage group process and goals.)

• The relationships in and between the construction groups are frequently analogous to the way movement or church groups work. What are some parallels?

5. For additional exercises in group dynamics see: *A Handbook of Structured Experiences for Human Relations Training*, by William Pfeiffer and John E. Jones, in four volumes.

II
Facilitation of Meetings*

Meetings are an important part of work for social change. They are times in which we share information, give each other support, and accomplish mutually agreed upon tasks. They are increasingly times of creativity, fun and challenge, and are an integral part of our efforts to build a better society.

This section focuses on the practical aspects of facilitating meetings. The tools and suggestions presented here are intended for use in formal meetings, whether of a small living group, a large organization, or a working collective. Some suggestions may also be useful for informal gatherings or planning sessions. Many of the resources were developed for groups that make decisions using consensus (see Consensus Decision Making) but most can be used by groups using other decision-making methods.

Facilitation skills are most thoroughly learned through observation and experience, and you will learn from mistakes and bad meetings as well as good ones. But these notes can be useful for people without a model to observe, and for reflecting on the experience you acquire.

Before any meeting that you facilitate, be certain that the goals of the group and members' expectations of the facilitator are clear. Then it will be possible to use our suggestions for facilitation as they are appropriate.

A good meeting will exhibit some of the following qualities,

---

* This section draws substantially from Berit Lakey's article "Meeting Facilitation, The No Magic Method."

all of which can be encouraged by good facilitation:
- commonly understood goals
- a clear process for reaching those goals
- a sense of involvement and empowerment (the participants feel that the decisions are *their* decisions; that they are able
to do what needs doing)
- a high level of energy and enthusiasm
- a sense that it is a meeting of real people, not just of roles
or recorded messages.

WHAT IS A FACILITATOR?

A facilitator fills a role similar to that of a "chairperson,"
but never directs the group without its consent. S/he helps the
members of a group decide what they want to accomplish in a
meeting and helps them carry it out. S/he takes responsibility for
reminding the group of its task, tests for consensus, and in
general makes sure that the task and maintenance roles discussed
in the last section are being filled. The facilitator initiates process
suggestions which the group may accept or reject, but at no time
does s/he make decisions for the group or take on functions
which are the responsibility of the group as a whole. A good
facilitator helps participants be aware that *they* are in charge,
that it is *their* business that is being conducted, and that each
person has contributions to make to the group. It is to emphasize
the mutual responsibility of the group and the democratic nature
of the process that we use the word "facilitator" rather than
"chairperson," "secretary," or "president."

SELECTING A FACILITATOR

In small groups which meet regularly the function of
facilitation may be shared or rotated informally, but in large
meetings or meetings which are anticipated to be difficult, a
clearly designated facilitator (or co-facilitators) is (are) needed.
Co-facilitators are able to take turns facilitating and giving
support to each other. The person not actively facilitating can
pay more attention to the emotional atmosphere of the meeting.

When choosing a facilitator or co-facilitators, try to get a
good balance of the following:
- little (or less) emotional investment in the meeting
- ability to encourage others to participate
- a general overview of the task or goal of the group for
that meeting.
- energy and attention for the job at hand and courage to
push the meeting along to meet time limits.

PREPARATION FOR MEETINGS

1. Be aware of the physical arrangements—e.g., temperature, arrangement and comfort of chairs, ability to hear.

2. Make sure that everyone is informed about the meeting time and place and has pre-meeting materials if necessary.

3. Think about how late-comers can be up-dated so meeting can continue uninterrupted. Should someone take them aside? Who? Can the agenda be clear enough to inform them as to what has happened?

4. Arrange in advance for someone to present each agenda item, preferably the person who submitted the item. Be prepared to give background information as to why the item is on the agenda, if necessary.

5. If an item is expected to be complicated or produce tension, consider ahead of time processes for its discussion. Breaking the item into several parts, which can be discussed one at a time, may be helpful.

6. Gather necessary materials such as written presentations, paper, pencils, marking pens, blackboard, chalk, and chairs.

7. Have an alternate ready to facilitate in case of an emergency, or if the facilitator becomes tired or needs to participate actively in the discussion.

8. For most meetings it will be necessary to collect agenda items and plan a tentative agenda beforehand. Write a proposed agenda on a large wall chart or blackboard that will be visible to everyone, or distribute individual copies to participants. This will be helpful both during the meeting and in democratizing the process of agenda formation.

TIPS ON AGENDA FORMATION

1. Select a process to gather the group. Are *Introductions* or *Excitement Sharing* necessary? Singing or a brief game might be appropriate.

2. Make tentative judgments about priorities for the agenda. What could be held over to the next meeting if necessary? How should the meeting end? When should difficult items be discussed? If possible, create a balance of long and short items. Deal with difficult items after the group is warmed up, but before it is tired.

3. Estimate the time needed for each item and put it on the agenda chart. This will give participants an idea of the relative importance of each item; help participants tailor their participation to the time available; allow realistic decisions about which items to include and when to end the meeting; and give a sense of progress to the meeting.

4. If formation of the agenda will need to occur at the meeting, try *Agenda Formation in the Whole Group*. Advance thinking about the group is still important. A gathering process should be used before agenda formation.

5. Think about what breaks or *Attention Expanders* the group might need.

6. Plan an evaluation of the meeting near the end.

FACILITATING THE MEETING—BEGINNING TO END

1. *Excitement Sharing* or other introductory activity. Can be started while waiting for latecomers.

2. Get group agreement on who should facilitate and for how long.

3. Agenda review and approval: (a) Show the group the agenda and give an idea of what is to be covered and how. You may need to explain why each item has been included and how it fits the group's needs. Go through the whole agenda before asking for comments. (b) Ask for approval, corrections, or additions. If there are several additions or changes, take them all down before trying to make decisions about ordering them. (c) Determine the ending time for the meeting, if not already fixed.

4. Make sure someone is taking notes, if appropriate (see *Taking Notes*). Select a timekeeper, if appropriate, and clarify expectations about sticking to time.

5. Use short agenda items, fun items, announcements, and breaks throughout the agenda to provide rest and relief from more emotionally taxing items.

6. Go through the agenda item by item. Applause, a few deep breaths, mutual congratulations, and dramatically crossing the item off the agenda chart are useful tension relievers and indicators of accomplishment between items.

7. Before the end of the meeting select a convenor, facilitator(s) or planner(s), subject matter and process if appropriate, and time and place for the next meeting. This should be done before participants begin to leave.

8. Evaluate the meeting. Start with the good or positive aspects, then things that were not good. Insist on getting concrete suggestions for improvement of negative aspects. Try not to end on a negative note. Don't get caught up in further discussion of agenda items. (For further information see *Brief Evaluation of a Meeting*.)

9. Try to end the meeting with a feeling of togetherness—a song, shaking hands, some silence, standing in a circle and

saying things we like about each other—anything that affirms the group and puts a sense of closure to the time spent together.

10. End the meeting on time. If the agenda is taking longer than anticipated, renegotiate it. Get group agreement that the time be extended or items be held for the next meeting.

FACILITATING GROUP MAINTENANCE

1. Stay aware of the group maintenance functions listed in the "Group Dynamics" section.

2. Remember to use *Affirmation* and appreciation. Comment on special contributions of members and accomplishments of the group.

3. Try to maintain an atmosphere in which people take each other seriously, though without eliminating humor. Help to make it safe for people to share the feeling behind their opinions.

4. Suggest an unscheduled break if people are fidgeting, falling asleep, or too depressed to function. Likewise, a group that is full of energy and charging ahead may want to postpone a scheduled break.

5. In tense or tiring situations try humor, *Affirmation*, *Attention Expanders*, changing seats, silence, a group nap, etc. Some groups might rebel at the suggestion of "wasting time" on a game, but will welcome a stretch break or informal hilarity.

GENERAL SUGGESTIONS FOR FACILITATION

1. Bring out opinions:
   • Encourage the expression of various viewpoints—the more important the decision, the more important it is to have all pertinent information (facts, feelings, and opinions).
   • Call attention to strong disagreements. When handled forthrightly, differences of opinion yield creative solutions.
   • Ask people to speak for themselves and to be specific. Don't allow statements like, "Some people seem to feel. . ." or "What s/he is trying to say is. . ."

2. Help everyone to participate:
   • Don't let two or three people monopolize the discussion. Ask for comment from others.
   • Some people might need to be asked to speak more briefly or less frequently.
   • When there is a need for a lot of discussion or clarification involving everyone, small groups may be used to increase participation and to bring back proposals for further discussion and decision. (See *Breaking Into Small Groups*.)

65

3. Keep the role of facilitator neutral:
   • If you have personal opinions to offer, do so outside of your role as facilitator. For example, say, "Stepping out of my role as facilitator, I think..."
   • If you find yourself drawn into the discussion in support of a particular position, it would be preferable to step aside as facilitator until the next agenda item. If you have no replacement already planned for, ask for a volunteer.

4. Keep discussion relevant. Point out to the group when discussion is drifting off the topic or becoming trivial. Cut off discussion when repetition occurs or when people become weary.

5. Keep track of time and remind the group before time is up. If a timekeeper has been selected, be certain that s/he is alert.

6. Encourage individuals to pursue on their own, projects or ideas in which they have strong interest, but in which the group does not.

FACILITATION WHEN CONSENSUS IS SOUGHT

1. Encourage presentation of viewpoints, especially when they may be conflicting. Draw out those who do not speak. A real consensus comes only after the open facing of differences. When dealing with complex or controversial decisions, consider using the **Small Group to Large Group Consensus** process.

2. Listen carefully for agreements and hesitations within the group. When a decision cannot be made, state points of agreement and of hesitation. Stating points of agreement helps group morale, may lead to agreement in principle on the issue, and may make possible agreement on new proposals. Stating points of hesitation makes them clearer and makes resolution possible. Often hesitations are based on misunderstandings and will quickly end when stated clearly.

3. Testing for Agreement:
   • Test for agreement as soon as a decision seems to be emerging. Periodic testing will help clarify disagreements, making discussion more fruitful.
   • State the tentative consensus in question form, and be specific: "Do we all agree that we'll meet on Tuesday evenings for the next two months, and that a facilitator will be found at each meeting for the next one?" rather than: "Do we all agree that we should do it the way it was just suggested?" If you are not clear how to phrase the decision, ask for help.
   • Insist on a response from the group. Don't take silence

for consent. The participants need to be conscious of making a contract with each other.

• Sometimes stating the perceived agreement in the negative helps to clarify group feeling: "Is there anyone who does not agree that...?" This method is especially useful for groups under time pressure or with a tendency for nit-picking, but it is also important for group members to be fully supportive of the decision. If you have doubts about their commitment, ask them.

• Be suspicious of agreements reached too easily—test to make sure that members really do agree on essential points.

4. *When there is no agreement:*

• Ask those who disagree to offer alternative proposals for discussion and decision.

• If agreement still cannot be reached people may need time to reflect on the feelings behind their opinions. Propose a break or period of silence, or postpone the decision.

• If postponing the decision, try to reach agreement on a process that will happen before the item is brought up again. (See the section on "Conflict Resolution—Some Useful Processes.") It is often productive for representatives of opposing factions to work together to draft a compromise proposal during the interim.

• When one or two people are blocking consensus, ask if they are willing to stand aside, to allow the group to proceed with the proposed action. It may help them stand aside if the group assures them that (1) the lack of unity will be recorded in the minutes, (2) the decision is not precedent-setting, or (3) they are not expected to carry out the decision.

PROBLEMS THAT COMMONLY ARISE IN GROUPS

When group tensions are repeatedly ignored to accomplish tasks, immediate decisions may be made but, in the long run, individual energy and group morale will drop. Investment of valuable time and energy is necessary for a group to accomplish its tasks *and* make working together enjoyable.

Group members should watch for negative behavior, including their own. Braden and Bradenburg, in their book, *Oral Decision-Making,* have identified roles which participants fill to answer their own needs, but which rarely answer the needs of the group. These are: Blocking, Dominating, Special-interest pleading, Playboy, Recognition-seeker, Cynic, Follower, Aggressor, Self-confessor, Help-seeker. None of these roles are problems in themselves, but if they irritate individuals, block group functioning, or discourage participation, they will need to be dealt with.

It is always necessary to take initiative in solving problems. Suggest or try new methods even though they may feel uncomfortable. If problems persist, insist on discussing them to find solutions.

Further discussion of conflict within groups can be found in section IV below.

Some Common Problems and What to Do About Them:

1. Members are doing distracting things, playing with the cat, rattling papers, having a side conversation, etc.

ISSUES: People aren't interested in the discussion, they don't identify with the issues, don't feel they are important, attention is lost. Usually destructive to group morale.

PREVENTION: Get general agreement on the agenda before beginning the meeting. Make sure there aren't more efficient ways of solving the issues besides a full meeting. Schedule a break to revive people. If known to be a regular problem, encourage all members to point out distracting behavior of others and ask for breaks when they need them.

WHAT TO DO NOW: Ask the people involved if they are interested in the discussion, or why they don't seem to be taking part. Take a break.

2. People come in late, or have to leave the meeting early. People wander in and out of the meeting several times.

ISSUES: Members need to feel included, to be brought up to date about what they have missed, without making the meeting drag for others.

PREVENTION: Sometimes not possible. But it helps to start a meeting when you intend to start it, so people will feel more urgency to arrive on time. Ask people to clear their schedules so they won't have to leave a meeting temporarily. End the meeting at the agreed-upon time. If people must leave temporarily to care for children, prepare food, etc., have an agreed-upon procedure to update people when they return.

WHAT TO DO NOW: Briefly summarize the important business the person has missed, or ask someone in the meeting to do that quietly, so as not to disrupt the meeting. Ask what additional expectations people have of leaving early.

3. Someone is dominating the meeting.

ISSUES: People are often not aware of their own

destructive behavior. They may feel that they make better contributions than others.

PREVENTION: All the members could become aware of group dynamics issues, such as task and maintenance roles and climate. Members could agree on a minimal structure to facilitate the participation of all members. A time limit for contributions may be useful.

WHAT TO DO NOW: Ask for contributions from people who have not said anything. Ask the dominator(s) to let others speak. Point out when people repeat themselves. Use a *Participation Equalizer*.

4. Someone consistently brings up one idea, one solution, one issue to most group meetings.

ISSUES: The person may not feel that s/he is being heard, or that the group is acting on his/her suggestion, or that s/he is accepted by the group as a person.

PREVENTION: Not always possible. Rigid behavior is not rational, and a person usually cannot be argued out of irrational behavior.

WHAT TO DO NOW: A group member can state to the person that s/he has been heard, and try to explain why his/her ideas have not been accepted or acted upon. Waiting until after the meeting may be better. The person deserves honest feedback, even if it is painful. Alternatively, the group may offer to schedule a special meeting for the purpose of listening to the person and dealing with the issue.

5. Non-participating members.

ISSUES: Members may not feel they have anything to contribute, climate may not be conducive to allowing more timid members to participate, or other members may dominate. When members do not participate, they usually do not identify with decisions made, and may not abide by decisions.

PREVENTION: Facilitator can encourage others who have not spoken to contribute their information or opinions. If men speak more often than women or adults more often than children, etc., these roles can be revealed if one person keeps a record of the number of contributions from each participant, and shares the results with the group.

WHAT TO DO NOW: A *Participation Equalizer* may be appropriate.

6. "Bad vibrations"—tension in the meeting.

ISSUES: Caused by a variety of poor group processes: domination, nonparticipation, unresolved conflicts from earlier meetings, poor facilitation, etc.

PREVENTION: Members can educate themselves about group dynamics and thus be able to spot problems before they pile up. Choose a facilitator able to handle the meeting.

WHAT TO DO NOW: Take a short break. Deal concretely with the most difficult cause of the tension by raising it for discussion. Adjourn the meeting to allow individuals or small groups to work on the problems. When reconvening, begin with a unifying or easy item, or *Attention Expander*.

7. Strong opinions or feelings prevent constructive discussion.

ISSUES: People may not be able to listen to "opponents" because they feel defensive. A dialogue develops between opposing sides which excludes alternatives.

PREVENTION: Catch conflicts early. On sensitive issues, begin with sharing of personal experiences rather than opinion. State areas of agreement. Introduce topic with humor. Break topic into component parts.

WHAT TO DO NOW: Switch to a non-discussion format, where each person shares briefly his/her opinions or feelings. This helps people listen to each other and know that they are being heard. Break into pairs to release feelings or seek new ideas. Use one of the methods in the section "Conflict Resolution—Some Useful Processes."

8. Someone walks out, upset.

ISSUES: Possible wide variety of causes. Deeply felt disagreement with process or decisions. A walk-out is a final gesture. It can be an attempt to communicate with the group or to get away from the group.

PREVENTION: Not always possible, since the person may be unwilling to compromise a firmly-held position. But a walk-out may be prevented if the person is asked in a non-judgmental way what his/her disagreement or disapproval is, and what s/he would rather see happening.

WHAT TO DO NOW: Depends on a lot of variables. If the person left on principle and cannot be reached, the meeting could decide to continue or wait until the next meeting to decide on the issue involved. If the person left because s/he was upset, the group could ask one or more persons to talk with him/her, and ask him/her to rejoin the group if appropriate.

9. Group is not able to make a decision.

ISSUES: No one is taking on the role of summarizer and facilitator. Goals may not be clear.

PREVENTION: People can be aware of membership roles, covering both task and maintenance functions. Goals and

70

agenda can be discussed and agreed upon before the meeting begins.

WHAT TO DO NOW: Summarize the discussion up to that point. Ask for redefinition of goals. Re-state the issue or question. Ask if the group is ready to make a decision. Take a break. Decide not to decide until the next meeting.

10. People are discussing many issues at once.

ISSUES: An agenda has not been set and agreed upon. The meeting has not yet focused. (Or, see #9 above.)

PREVENTION: Set a clear agenda beforehand, so people know issues they are most concerned with will be covered. Use flip charts so people have a visual reminder of the issue. As other issues come up, they can be recorded on another chart for future attention. Make sure there is a facilitator.

WHAT TO DO NOW: Ask if a contribution is on the issue being discussed at the moment. Also, same points as in prevention.

11. Group is having difficulty focusing or setting priorities.

ISSUES: Process and/or issues have not been clarified or agreed upon. Issue taken is too complex.

PREVENTION: Before meeting have one or two members plan a way to break down issues into manageable pieces. Use *Priority Setting Tools*.

WHAT TO DO NOW: State what you see as separate issues. Ask group to list issues or add to ones you have stated. Ask group to set priorities and take them one at a time.

12. Low morale.

ISSUES: Group has no short-range goals or successes. Goals are too hard to achieve or results are not visible. Group work is not satisfying or enjoyable. People lack sleep, food, or exercise!

PREVENTION: Set short, medium and long-term goals. Choose realistic goals. Find ways of evaluating progress.

WHAT TO DO NOW: List concrete achievements or positive aspects of group. Check if individual and group goals match. (See *Identification and Ranking of Individual, Small Group and Whole Group Goals or Priorities*. Break so people can eat, sleep or exercise.

TOOLS USED FREQUENTLY AT MEETINGS

The following pages give descriptions of tools we use frequently at meetings, presented in roughly the order in which they are used. Most meetings begin with excitement sharing, introductions, or another warm-up, followed by some review of the agenda for the meeting. Before proceeding, the facilitator checks to see that someone is taking notes and keeping track of time, if appropriate. Brainstorming and breaking into small groups are basic techniques used in many variations in business meetings and workshops. Attention expanders or breaks are necessary for most meetings. An evaluation invariably concludes the formal agenda of the smallest and largest meetings.

The general facilitation of a meeting incorporating these processes is reviewed earlier in this section, and tools less frequently used are presented in the section "Tools for Specific Purposes."

1. *Introduction Tools*

Purpose/Uses: Help people get acquainted; set positive, human tone for the meeting. Give people some personal knowledge of other group members on which to build a level of trust necessary for efficient and satisfying group functioning. Help people learn people's names.

Description:
METHOD 1—*Personal Introductions:* Each person gives name, where s/he is from, and one other fact about him/herself. Facilitator should suggest what this third fact might be: something positive, like recent accomplishment or excitement; something relevant to the theme of a workshop, like a vision for the new society; etc. Avoid using a question that could be answered by a long list of accomplishments or organizations that a person belongs to.

METHOD 2—*Pair Introductions:*
1. Ask people to pair up with people they do not know or know less well than others in the group.
2. Person A listens to or "interviews" person B, and then B listens to A, for five minutes each way.
3. Drawing on what was heard in the five minute periods, A and B then introduce each other to the group. The facilitator can make specific suggestions for things to include in the introductions.

Example:
Affirmation Exercise to Introduce Each Other (20 min)
Divide group into pairs. Each person takes three minutes to share things that s/he likes about him/herself. One person is the speaker and the other is the listener. At the end of three minutes the roles are reversed. When both people have had a turn to talk,

the whole group re-forms and pairs introduce each other, noting something they like about each other.

Variation: At introducing time person A introduces her/himself as though s/he were person B, and vice versa. This is good for producing laughter and helping people reduce self-consciousness in front of the group.

METHOD 3—*"Hello A, I'm B"*

Purpose: Helps participants remember the name of everyone in the group. Acts as an icebreaker. (Not practical in groups over about 15 people.)

Description:

1. Participants sit in a circle, and one person begins by saying, ''Hello, I'm A_____'' (his/her first name).

2. The next person in the circle says, ''Hello, A_____. I'm B_____.''

3. The third person says, ''Hello, A_____ and B_____. I'm C_____.''

4. Each person, in turn, greets all the preceding participants, and the last person greets everyone else in the circle. By the end of the exercise, almost everyone can remember the names of all the participants.

5. The group may help anyone who has difficulty recalling names. These are not meant to be competitive games.

Variation: *"I'm So-and-So, the Whatever."*

1. With the group sitting in a circle one person says, ''I'm _____, the _____,'' giving his/her name and an imaginary occupation, or at least an occupation or job that the person doesn't do. When the occupation or whatever is stated, it can be accompanied by a small dramatic gesture or action describing the job, which of course everyone following repeats. Example: ''I'm Mari, the lion-tamer.''

2. The next person in the circle says, ''S/he is _____ the _____ (Mari the lion-tamer) and I'm _____ the _____,'' giving his/her name and another occupation.

3. Each person says the names and jobs of everyone before him/her in the circle; the last person in the circle says them all.

2. *Excitement Sharing*

Purpose/Uses: To create a positive atmosphere at the beginning of a meeting, group session, or class. To put people more in touch with each other's lives and activities. Used in place of introductions, where group members already know each other.

Description:

Participants share something good or exciting that they

73

have done or that has happened to them since the last time they got together. If the group is small, encourage everyone to share at least one thing. If the group is large and time limited, only a few people may share excitements.

If groups of people are represented (households, project groups, etc.) groups can be asked to meet briefly and come up with a collective excitement which one member of the group can share.

Discourage protracted comments, questions, and discussion. Do *not* confuse excitements with announcements.

3. *Agenda Formation in the Whole Group*

Purpose/Uses: To help a group plan its activities. To commit a group to following a common process.

Materials: Flip chart or chalkboard and writing implements.

Description: There are many agenda formation processes, ranging from formation before the meeting by a committee or an individual to the formation of the agenda by the whole group upon its arrival at the meeting. Where the group is small and/or meets regularly, the latter is practical; otherwise, we recommend some degree of advance planning.

1. The group brainstorms items that people would like to see covered in the given period of time. The question to be brainstormed can be phrased: "What things would you feel badly about if they weren't covered by the time we leave?"

2. Group items that have common properties.

3. Set priorities by ranking on the basis of importance, length of time they will take, or whether they can be left until future meetings.

4. If projected times total more than is available, it will be necessary to use another process of removing or postponing items or reducing time limitations.

5. Always allow for breaks, warm-up exercises, etc. for long meetings.

Variation #1: In large groups participation can be maximized by breaking into smaller groups. Do steps 1-4 and return to whole group. Post priorities of each small group and do steps 2-5 in the whole group.

Variation #2: Do step #1 in large group. Ask for a few volunteers to do steps 2-5. Feed back all information to the whole group to check for accuracy and decide time allocations.

Variation #3: When the agenda has been planned before the meeting, it is necessary to review the proposed agenda and

74

obtain the group's verbal approval or approval of changes before the business of the meeting begins.

4. *Time Limits*

Purpose/Uses: To increase consciousness about the amount of time people use. To allow people to control the amount of time they wish to spend on certain tasks. To stop activity that the group does not agree it wants to continue. To indicate how long business will take so people can make choices about what they want to accomplish at a particular meeting. To simulate real experiences where response time is limited. To designate the period of time for which a group has contracted to work together. To encourage people to think rapidly and concisely. To give a sense of accomplishment and progress.

Description:

    1. People assign times to each item on the agenda.

    2. Someone volunteers to watch the time and calls "time's up" and in some cases also gives early warnings of a few minutes.

    3. When time is up, if the group continues on the item, the time keeper continues to remind the group that time is up and the facilitator asks the group if it wants to spend more time on the item. If so, an amount is agreed upon. In some cases to spend more time on the item will mean other items will need to be shortened or dropped, or the meeting time lengthened.

Variations: Time limits can be set and the whole group asked to watch the time. (A clock should be available.) Or a time keeper can be asked to simply give a warning ____ minutes before the end of the meeting so last-minute details can be taken care of. Variations are unlimited if time limits are used flexibly as needed.

Note: The role of time keeper can be alienating, but it is very important. It should be rotated often. If time is allowed to slip by unconsciously, the end of the meeting will arrive with important business unfinished, creating tension and frustration among members. As people in groups become more aware of their use of time and more skillful in their own facilitation, strict time limits will become less necessary.

5. *Taking Notes*

Purpose/Uses: To record decisions. To remind members of responsibilities. To inform absent members. Reading back the minutes after a decision or at the end of a meeting can add to the group's sense of clarity.

75

Description:
1. Select a note-taker at the start of the meeting. Rotate the job. If individuals don't share in this function, discuss the problem.

2. Be clear as to the purpose of note-taking. To record decisions only or to reflect different opinions? To be typed or distributed? If so, by whom?

3. At small meetings (two to six people), the note-taker can take notes on lined paper with carbon copies. Each person can then have a copy of the minutes at the end of the meeting.

4. For larger meetings, the notes can be re-copied or typed, duplicated, and distributed.

5. Minutes may be presented in chronological order, or by categories such as (a) decisions, (b) discussions, (c) reports, (d) all other, and (e) next meeting time, place and purpose.

Things for note-taker to remember:
- Record facilitator, note-taker, all people present.
- Record the date.
- Underline decisions made. *"We agreed..." "It was approved..."*
- Headline. It isn't important to record every word. It is usually best to be brief.
- Read back minutes on important decisions to be sure that they are correct.
- Record the date, place, time, and facilitator of the next meeting.

- Note who will do what between meetings, who will follow through on decisions.
- The date, place, time, and facilitator of the next meeting.

Example: A sample page might look like this:

NEWSLETTER: After discussion of the relative costs of xeroxing and offset printing, *it was agreed* that Mary will have the newsletter xeroxed at a place she knows.

6. *Brainstorming*
Purpose/Uses: To get out as many ideas as possible in a limited amount of time. It frees the imagination to come up with new ideas about goals, projects, whatever.

Description:
1. The group decides on a specific question, such as "What do you hope to get out of this training workshop?" or "What should be included in our next newsletter?" Set a time limit for brainstorming and stick to it.

2. Each person tosses out every idea which occurs to him/her. *No one is allowed to criticize or discuss the ideas until time for brainstorming is up.* A recorder (or two) should be appointed to list all the ideas on a flipchart or chalkboard. Encourage creative thinking. Bizarre ideas can lead to creative new approaches.

3. After the list is made, discussion and evaluation of the list can take place. The list is refined and some ideas are eliminated or combined. Depending on the use for which the items are intended, the group could go on to set priorities, pick one suggestion as a topic for another brainstorm, and so forth.

7. *Breaking into Small Groups*

Breaking into small groups is one of the most basic discussion tools that we know, yet it is often overlooked. It can be planned for or "resorted to" when a "simple" agenda item turns out to be much harder to dispose of than expected. It can give participants in a large group the chance to speak without making meetings drag on for hours. Yet some time must be spent dividing up and reporting back. Sometimes it will be important for everyone to be heard by the whole group. In each case the advantages and disadvantages will need to be weighed.

Purpose/Uses: To enable everyone in a large group to try out ideas and express opinions. To get out information and help people get "heard."

Materials: One very large room or several small rooms.

Description:

1. Item for discussion is introduced in the large group, and the task of the small groups is clarified. If factual information is required it should be given before the group breaks up. The facilitator states time limits, location of meeting places, and whether reports will be expected from each small group.

2. Large group breaks into small groups. This can be done informally, but it is often quicker to count off or use some other method. In some cases groups may need to be balanced by age, sex, opinion, etc. Our concept of small group ranges from three to about fifteen. The more trust needed for the discussion, the smaller the group should be. For consensus decision making under time pressure, ten people is probably a maximum, and six to eight is better.

3. Small groups meet for a clearly specified period of time. Each group should select a recorder, reporter, and facilitator, if needed.

4. Small groups report back to the plenary (large group). If it is not a decision-making discussion, the reports can be limited to a few minutes and the two or three most exciting points that came up in each group. Proposals from the small groups will need sufficient time for clear presentation and questions.

Variation: Instead of reporting back to the plenary, everyone reshuffles into another small group composed of one representative from each of the original small groups. Everyone is a "representative" and reports in the new small groups. Discussion follows in the new small groups. Participants can then return to their old small groups for further working on their proposals if necessary.

8. *Attention Expanders* (Light and Livelies)

Purpose/Uses: Lift the spirits or ease tensions in a group. Give people a break so that they can better tackle difficult or tedious tasks. Can also be used as trust building exercises.

Attention expanders can be songs, nursery rhymes, "children's" games, or physical exercises. They grab attention away from analyzing, reminiscing, worrying or brooding about a problem, and focus attention on a simple, enjoyable activity. When the group resumes its agenda people have more energy and attention for the task at hand.

Once you have seen what works, make up your own attention expanders. Use some of the games you remember from childhood. Many other exercises can be used as attention expanders; see also "Community Building Exercises." A good resource for games is *For the Fun of It*, by Marta Harrison and the Nonviolence and Children Program (Friends Peace Committee, 1501 Cherry, Phila., PA 19102, 1976. $1.25 plus $.40 postage and handling).

Examples:

1. The *Hokey Pokey*: This is the old favorite: "Put your right foot in, put your right foot out, put your right foot in and shake it all about. Do the hokey pokey as you turn yourself around. That's what it's all about." (Sing it to your own tune if you don't know it.)

2. *Touch Blue*: Have everyone touch something blue on someone else, something yellow, a knee, some glasses, etc. Call the next thing just as soon as people touch whatever has been named.

3. The *Magic Glob*: Take out of your pocket an imaginary magic glob. Pantomime making something out of it, then shape it back into a ball or pass it on to the next person. S/he makes a

new object and passes it on again. It can be divided into two parts and sent both ways around a circle.

4. *Waking up in the Jungle:* Ask people to think of their favorite jungle animal and its noise, and to pretend that they are that animal waking up. As they wake up, the noises should get louder and louder. A good quick game for sleepy groups.

5. *Three-person Machine*: Form groups of three. Each group designs and acts out a machine, such as a sewing machine, washing machine or pencil sharpener, for the whole group to guess.

9. *Brief Evaluation of a Meeting*

The tool described here is for brief evaluation of a single meeting. For an extensive discussion of purpose, guidelines, and structures for evaluation of conferences, actions, campaign, etc., see Evaluation under Part Eight.

Purpose/Uses: To help a group learn from its mistakes and accomplishments. To give feedback to people who have held specific roles, e.g., facilitator, reporters. To provide a sense of closure to a meeting.

Description:

1. After explaining the format, the facilitator asks, "What went well in the meeting?" People respond, trying to be as specific as possible, but without getting into discussion.

2. The facilitator then asks, "What went poorly, and how could it be improved?" S/he should make sure that each negative idea is followed by suggestions for improvement.

3. During the evaluation one person writes the comments on a flipchart or chalkboard in three columns: GOOD, PROBLEMS, IMPROVEMENTS.

4. Time should be taken at the end, if necessary, to discuss implementation of ideas for improvement.

Comments: We have found that the evaluation works best if people feel that it is safe for them to say anything, therefore we discourage discussion or comments on what other people say. This rule is not as strict as in brainstorming though care should be taken *NOT* to get back into old discussions.

A minimum time for evaluation of a meeting is five minutes. In a large group, the facilitator needs to be firm about moving on or to set time limits on people's contributions.

For additional information see *A Manual for Group Facilitators*, by the Center for Conflict Resolution in Madison, Wisconsin.

III
Special Tools

The tools for groups presented here may sometimes appear quite complex and elaborate. They are, however, generally based on fairly simple techniques. In many cases, we have presented both the basic technique and elaborations which were developed for specific situations.

Probably the most common error and source of dissatisfaction in the use of the tools explained below is their inappropriate application. This most often happens when a group or facilitator attempts to apply the tool in a cookbook fashion, without adapting it to meet the special needs of the group. Of course, inexperienced groups must expect to learn to a certain extent through trial and error.

Some of the basic group techniques like Brainstorming, Breaking into Small Groups, and sharing in turn without discussion are often used in combination with other specific processes. Sometimes these combinations are used in a unique situation not likely to be repeated, or the combination is not very successful, and is not remembered. In other cases the combinations are so successful that they are recorded, used again, and gradually achieve the designation of "new tool." Once you are familiar with the basic tools, you can create "new tools," which will often meet your needs better than tools in the manual.

DECISION-MAKING TOOLS

The line between decision-making and conflict resolution is a fine one, where disagreement and emotion are involved. *Resolution of Conflicts Preventing Consensus, Decision-making Method Used by the Re-evaluation Counseling Communities,* and the *"No-lose" Problem Solving Process* are other techniques applicable to decision making.

1. *Determine Goals and Expectations*   (20-30 min)

Purpose/Uses: To include full group in determining goals for a session or workshop. To give a small group sufficient information on which to design a proposed agenda for the larger group's consideration.

Description:
  1. Large group divides into groups of 5-6 people each.

2. Participants **Brainstorm** their goals and expectations for the session or workshop.   (10 min)

3. Each small group selects the five most important goals or issues to be covered. Use Priority Setting Tools.

4. Priorities are presented to the whole group.

5. Goals and expectations are then given to the trainers/ facilitators who will use them to design additional sessions. (Optional: The whole group can attempt to select the 5 most important goals before they are given to trainers.)

2. *Small Group to Large Group Consensus*

Purpose/Uses: To help a large group make a decision. To facilitate total membership participation in the decision-making process.

Description:

1. Problem or issue is defined by the whole group.

2. Whole group **Brainstorms** possible solutions to the problem.

3. Large group breaks into small groups of 6-8 people to discuss the problem, review possible solutions, and develop a proposal for a solution that they will present to the whole group.

4. Proposals from the small groups are presented tot he large group and are recorded on flip charts.

5. Discussion by the large group. Facilitators should look for common conclusions in all the reports and call for a consensus decision on these points. Disagreements should be identified.

6. Small groups work on contested points and try to develop new proposals.

7. Small groups present new proposals to large group. Facilitators try to find a consensus. Steps 6 and 7 can be repeated as many times as necessary.

8. Once consensus is reached, facilitators need to help the group define the steps needed to implement the decision.

Note: It is very helpful for the group to set and abide by time limits for each step of this process. Groups will use all the time they are given, but can work faster with a forceful facilitator and timekeeper. Holding to the time limits while solving a complex problem can increase the group's accomplishment and progress.

3. *Discussion Format for Distressing Topics*

Purpose/Uses: To avoid the pattern of debate where both sides defend a fixed position without listening to the merits of the other side or seeking a third way. To deal with negative opinions in a positive way. To allow everyone a chance to participate.

Description: The basic format: All participants share their feelings, opinions, or ideas for two to four minutes apiece, *without discussion*. (When people know that they will have a chance to speak but cannot respond immediately, they are better able to listen to differing opinions and ideas.)

There are many variations possible on this basic format. For example, participants could begin a discussion by sharing personal experiences related to the topic, or by sharing opinions and ideas on a specific proposal. The following format was used by a communal household in a meeting on "a more ecologically/economically sound kitchen/house."

Variation:

1. Person states what s/he is angry, bothered, frustrated about as a concern. Example: "I'm concerned that we waste so much water in the house." S/he makes a proposal on how to correct the problem. Example: "Draw a bowl or sink full of water for washing, rinsing, shaving, etc."

2. Other persons respond by stating what they do *and* do not agree with. They make additional suggestions on how to correct the problem, or a counter proposal.

Each person should have a chance to respond once before anyone speaks twice. All people should be brief!

3. The person who stated the concern originally should have a chance to restate the concern, withdraw it, or alter it whenever s/he has new insight or needs to clarify it.

4. Each time a new proposal is made by the person who originally stated the concern, the process starts over again until consensus is arrived at, or the proposal is withdrawn.

4. *Method for Decision Making and Development of Program**

Purpose/Uses: To deal with a matter too complicated or tension-laden to be handled easily in a large group. To save the time of the whole group. This approach can also be used for collective writing.

Description:

1. Participants in a large group *Brainstorm* approaches, issues, possibilities, goals, solutions.

2. Individuals reflect on the brainstormed lists to synthesize, order priorities, sort out personal reactions or ideas.

3. Results of personal thinking are shared.

* Pam Haines, Phila. Macro-Analysis Collective (MNS), 4722 Baltimore Ave., Phila., PA 19143.

4. Group discusses issues which need to be taken into consideration, might be difficult, need further thought, etc.

5. A smaller group is appointed to develop a proposal based on the input from 1-4.

6. Small group presents proposal.

7. Large group accepts proposal in substance, suggests minor changes, and returns to small group for revisions. If there is substantial disagreement or serious limitation, as much of the process as necessary is repeated. Another person can be added to the small group if necessary.

8. Small group checks revisions informally with a few people or with whole group if necessary.

9. People act on it.

5. *Finding the Least Common Denominator* *

Purpose/Uses: To solve a group problem. Often used in classroom situations.

Description:

1. Facilitator defines problem and states it to the satisfaction of the group. (E.g., "For many of the games we play, we need to designate a person who is 'it.' We need a way of choosing that person with which everyone agrees.")

2. Group **Brainstorms** ways to solve the problem.

3. Facilitator has people indicate by a **Straw Vote** if there is any disagreement with each suggested solution. If one (or more) solution(s) meet with no disagreement, the one which generates the most excitement is selected. If only one or two people object to the best solution, their opinions are stated and worked through.

4. If no solution meets with near agreement, choose the best two, three, or four and get agreement to try each for a set period of time. If the situation does not allow for such experimentation, repeat the process beginning with Brainstorming. New options may surface. Other methods for dealing with minority dissension can be tried. The group can then consider a permanent solution.

Note: Flexibility is essential in moving from the information generated by Brainstorming and Straw Vote to the finding of a solution. An objective attitude on the part of the facilitator will enhance trust and cooperative attitudes within the group.

* Developed by members of the Nonviolence and Children Collective, Friends Peace Committee, 1515 Cherry, Phila., PA 19102.

TOOLS FOR BETTER LISTENING

Structured Speaking (Re-statement Technique)

Purpose/Uses: To ensure that "opponents" in a discussion listen to each other and understand the other's position. Can be used as training exercises as well as in actual meeting situations. Can also be used as a method for beginning discussion of an emotion-laden topic.

Description: The following variations employ the basic format:

1. Person A states a position, opinion, or conflict while person B just listens. (2 min)

2. B re-states or summarizes A's position, while A listens. (1 min)

3. A corrects or clarifies. (1 min)

4. Steps 2 and 3 are repeated until A agrees with B's restatement.

Variation #1: *5-2-1 Exercise* (30 min)

1. (When using this as an exercise, decide on a topic before beginning.) Explain the purpose of the exercise and its structure. Write topic on the board or wall chart. It is important to choose a topic that can elicit personal response rather than theory: thus, better than "What is noncooperation?" might be "What is my interpretation of noncooperation?" or "How have I stopped cooperating with unfair demands made on me?"

2. Have people divide into pairs of person A and person B. During the exercise no discussion is allowed. Pairs should be far enough apart so that they don't bother each other.

3. For 5 minutes A talks, B listens (no discussion)
   For 2 minutes B summarizes, A listens (no discussion)
   For 1 minute A corrects, B listens (no discussion)

4. The facilitator calls time at each change and restates the next step *briefly*. At the end of the 8 minute sequence, time is called and a restatement of the next segment is made.

5. Following the second time the trainer might want to lead a brief (10-15 min) discussion about the process of listening and what people learned about their ability to listen. Best responses come when trainer just listens and occasionally agrees.

Variation #2: *Listening In Threes*

1. For 5 minutes A talks, B and C listen.
   For 2 minutes B summarizes, A and C listen.
   For 1-2 minutes C gives reactions, A and B listen.

2. People rotate roles and repeat the process.

Variation #3: *Listening In Pairs*

Purpose/Uses: To discover differences and sources of tension. Also as above.

Description:

1. The basic Structured Speaking format is used until B can summarize or re-state what A said to A's satisfaction.

2. B then states agreements and disagreements (in that order) with A's position.

3. A re-states B's agreements and disagreements until B is satisfied with A's re-statement.

4. A can then agree and disagree with B's position, etc., until the time runs out, until the conflict is resolved, or until the areas of agreement and disagreement are clear to both.

5. In an ongoing group more tensions may exist than those between A and B. Therefore after #4 this process may need to be repeated with other pairs (C and D, or C and A, etc.) focusing on a new tension.

PARTICIPATION EQUALIZERS

1. *Matchstick Discussion*

Purpose/Uses: To place limits on dominant or over-eager speakers. To encourage shy speakers to contribute.

Description: Each participant is given one, two, or three matches (same number each). Each time someone speaks s/he throws a matchstick into the center of the group. When one person's matchsticks are all gone, s/he may not speak again until all matchsticks have been used and matches are redistributed, or a new process is agreed upon. People may *not* give their matches to other members of the group.

2. *Conch Shell Discussion*

Purpose/Uses: To make people conscious of when they interrupt others. To help people break habit of interrupting each other. To make clearer to the group who speaks most.

Materials needed: One conch shell—or almost any object that is distinctive and won't be lost or forgotten. (The conch shell was suggested by Golding in his novel *Lord of the Flies*.)

Description: Members of the group may speak only when they hold the conch shell. Speaker passes shell to next person who wants to speak. A group may wish to exempt a trainer or facilitator from this rule.

3. *Timed Report or Presentation* *   (5-20 min per report)

Purpose/Uses: To give information to the group. To encourage all participants to share in the responsibilities of research and information giving.

This tool is grouped with participation equalizers because it represents a clear departure from the traditional methods of presenting information, relying on one expert who lectures for an hour or more at a time.

Description: Members of the group prepare and give presentations on agreed-upon topics.

1. Preparation: At the preceding meeting of the group, individuals volunteer to report on specific topics of interest to the group. Number of reports and time allotted to them should be decided tentatively at this time. Between meetings, the individuals prepare their reports, timing them if necessary.

2. Reports are incorporated into the agenda for the meeting, generally with a brief period following each report for clarifying questions and comment, and a longer period for general discussion following the last report. With sufficient preparation, important information from many books or articles can be presented in this format. Rarely are more than fifteen minutes required if the report is well prepared.

PRIORITY SETTING TOOLS

Groups frequently have to sort information, separate extraneous material from what is important, and identify individual goals as opposed to group goals, before they can proceed to act. The following tools facilitate this process.

1. *Straw Vote*

Purpose/Uses: To identify questions or problems blocking consensus. To raise group consciousness about the positions the members of the group are taking. To identify which way the group is leaning on a particular question.

Note: This tool should not be used by a majority to coerce a minority into accepting the majority viewpoint. It is a tool for clarification only.

Description: A straw vote is taken by the same process as normal voting. The facilitator asks for a show of hands to indicate how the participants feel about a particular issue. The difference between a straw and a regular vote is that the straw vote does not represent a group decision. Once the issues and

---

* Developed by the Phila. Macro-Analysis Collective.

people with concerns are identified, modifications of the proposal are considered, and the group can proceed to a decision through consensus.

2. Identification and Ranking of Individual, Small Group, and Whole Group Goals and Priorities

Purpose/Uses: To identify the individual, small group, and whole group concerns, and discover which issues everyone is willing to accept and deal with.

Description:

1. Whole group brainstorms list of goals and expectations or solutions for problems.

2. Group breaks into small groups which identify individual concerns and concerns of the small group.

3. Where appropriate, individuals or small groups rank their preferences by indicating their first and second choice, etc.

4. Small groups report back to whole group. Whole group goals or solutions are identified and agreed upon. Structure may be set up for individuals and small groups to pursue their concerns at a later time.

3. 2/4/8...

Purpose/Uses: To help a group identify its top priorities. To allow total group participation in the decision.

Description:

1. Facilitator asks group to define its problem. For example: "What should the top two priorities be for our peace group during the next year?"

2. Group *Brainstorms* a list of possible priorities.

3. Large group breaks into pairs. Each pair selects and agrees on two priorities.   (5 min)

4. Pairs join together to form groups of four persons. Each quad selects two priorities from the four possible priorities that the pairs brought with them.   (8 min)

5. The quads then join to form groups of eight and again reach consensus on the two top priorities.   (12 min)

6. The process can continue until the whole group has merged and agreed upon common priorities, or it could be combined with another decision format, like *Small Group to Large Group Consensus*.

Note: People should be held to time limits as much as possible, or the exercise will drag. Time limits may need to be enlarged if the issue is particularly complex.

4. *Most Disappointing*

Purpose/Uses: To identify the top priorities of an individual or group when items need to be cut from an over-full agenda.

Description: Facilitator asks participants to identify agenda items that they would be disappointed about if they were not covered in the meeting. These items are handled before less important items.

5. Other Tools Useful in Setting Priorities
Small Group to Large Group Consensus
Time Line

IV
Conflict Resolution

Inevitably in group work, conflicts will arise for which there seems to be no quick and easy solution. The conflict may be between two participants or may involve a larger number of people. By using a variety of processes we are discovering that conflicts can be clarified and resolved in a way that allows all members of the group to continue to work together cooperatively and creatively.

The use of these conflict resolution techniques assumes the desire of both parties to resolve the conflict in a mutually acceptable way, and therefore must be distinguished from conflicts with the government or an employer, or any conflicts where one party may choose to exercise legal authority and/or force to have its way rather than negotiate a solution satisfactory to both.

While we have used these techniques most often in ongoing groups, the principles and many of the techniques are applicable outside of meetings, in neighborhoods, and in places of work.

For successful conflict resolution the following elements seem to be necessary:
- to allow enough time to deal with the conflict;
- to define the problem in terms that are clear and acceptable to all parties in the conflict;
- to deal with negative feelings in positive ways;
- to help people identify in concrete terms what makes them unhappy with the situation; distinguishing between feelings and reality;

- for each member of the conflict to identify his/her real needs;
- to allow an opportunity for individuals to unload feelings of hurt, fear, etc. in the presence of accepting people;
- to have at least one person give special attention to the process, someone uninvolved, if possible.

PROCESSES FOR CONFLICT CLARIFICATION AND RESOLUTION

1. *Clarification of Conflicts Preventing Consensus*

Purpose: To give a fair hearing to differences. To encourage unloading of feelings that prevent people from stating or hearing information accurately.

Description:

1. When consensus is forming and one person displays consistent and firm opposition, the decision is postponed long enough to allow that person to explore his/her feelings about the decision with a friend or someone "safe."

2. The person then tries to put into writing his/her thoughts as clarified by giving attention to the feelings involved. S/he also tries to formulate a proposal, in writing, for solving the problem, and returns with it to the next meeting. As a result, the person is either more able to find unity with others on the decision or is more able to articulate disagreement. Either way the group is better able to return to seek together for a consensus decision.

3. Step 2 can be repeated as many times and by as many different people as necessary.

2. *Decision-making Method Proposed for Use by the Re-evaluation Counseling Communities*

This method employs the process of emotional discharge (unloading hurts and other feelings by crying, laughing, raging, etc.) to deal with feelings that may be blocking clear thinking about the decision (see Re-evaluation Counseling). This method assumes that when sufficient information is available for consideration by minds unconfused by old distresses, a workable solution, acceptable by all, will emerge clearly. It also assumes that in cases where consensus is blocked, it may be necessary to begin carrying out an interim decision, and that feedback from the results of that decision can clearly show whether the decision needs to be modified.

The whole group affected by the decision, or a committee chosen from the group, can pursue this process. Proponents of opposing viewpoints should, of course, be represented in the decision-making process.

Purpose: To reduce tension through discharge of feelings, so that people on either side of a disagreement can think more clearly about the problem. To provide a way for the group to choose a course of action, even when disagreement remains.

Description:

1. Facilitator begins with a clear statement of the situation and goals of the group.

2. If there is a difference of opinion, each of the people involved has a counseling session (a one-to-one process where the "counselor" listens attentively and unjudgmentally while the "client" unloads feelings blocking thinking about the decision).

3. If this does not resolve the conflict, they then arrange a session in a group where they switch viewpoints. Each one alternately tries to argue for the other's viewpoint and listens.

4. If this does not resolve the differences, a debate is arranged between the conflicting points of view, in which only issues are dealt with, not personalities.

5. If conflict persists, the group tries to determine, in a general discussion, which of the conflicting points of view to put into practice.

6. If the difference is still unresolved, the group tries to decide which set of assumptions leads to the most interesting developments (e.g., projected consequences that provide the most opportunities for further learning and growth), then comes to a judgment rather than allow vacillation to continue. It then puts the judgement into effect, modifying or changing the decision as new data come in.

3. *"No-lose" Problem Solving Process*

This process is derived from the "no-lose" method for resolving conflicts taught in Parent (and Teacher) Effectiveness Training courses. It is designed for parents and children, but we feel it is applicable to adult-adult and child-child conflicts. This method relies on the skills of Active Listening and sending "I-Messages," briefly described following a description of the conflict resolution process.

This process is designed to resolve conflicts in which real needs are being frustrated. It is NOT recommended as a method of resolving conflicts based on differences in beliefs, values, or philosophy of life, unless such differences can be demonstrated to have tangible effects on the needs of others. Example: Children wanting to go barefooted into a restaurant may have a collision of values with their parents over the properness of the action. Unless sufficient evidence can be submitted by parents that such dress (or undress) will deny other members of the family accommodation at the restaurant, it is unlikely that children will change their minds.

Fundamental to the success of this process is the willingness of all participants to give up the use of power over others to resolve conflicts. For solutions to work they *must* be truly acceptable to all persons expected to carry them out.

For further information on Active Listening, "I-Messages," and the "No-lose" Method of resolving conflict, read *Parent Effectiveness Training,* by Thomas Gordon (Wyden Press, 1970,), or write P.E.T. Information for the nearest 8-week course (531 Stevens Ave., Solano Beach, CA 92075).

Description:

The first time the process is used it should be explained briefly, listing the steps.

It is *important to note* that during steps 1-7 other problems may arise that need to be solved. Do not try to solve them at this time. Write them down on a separate list and save them for later problem-solving.

1. *Define the problem in terms of both people's needs.* Each person should identify the conflict in terms of his/her own needs in a format like: "When _____, I (feeling), because _____." (See explanation of *"I-Messages"* below.) *Example*: "*When* the dishes are left unwashed following lunch *I* am irritated *because* I have to cook supper, and I don't have time to wash the pans and move the dirty dishes out of the way." Avoid making statements of blame like: "When you don't wash the dishes after lunch, you are irresponsible and insensitive to my needs."

2. *Restate the problem* in such a way as to include both person's needs. *Example*: "The problem is—person A needs to be at the next place on time and person B needs clean space." Both persons A and B must agree with the definition of their needs. If difficulty occurs in reaching agreement, rotate attempts to state the problem. Until agreement can be reached as to the nature of the problem, solution is unlikely.

3. *Brainstorm alternative solutions.* Think creatively. All parties to the conflict should participate. All suggestions are listed. Use a sheet of paper large enough for all participants to see. No discussion, acceptance, rejection, or evaluation of solutions should happen at this stage. Brainstorming should continue until each person sees on the list several solutions with which s/he is willing to work.

91

4. *Evaluate alternative solutions.* Each person in turn evaluates the list of solutions. Solutions which are unacceptable for any reason to any participant should be eliminated. It is essential that participants continue to be honest about their own feelings and needs throughout this process. Trust and encourage others to state their own feelings and needs. *Never* try to tell another person what his/her needs are, though use of *Active Listening* (see below) is effective and appropriate. The result of this step is a list of possible solutions which are acceptable to both (or all) parties.

5. *Decide on the best solution, acceptable to everyone.* Usually one solution will appear to be much better than the rest, but don't jump in relief to one solution without at least evaluating each of the other possibilities. Choose the best solution and make a mutual commitment to try it.

6. *Implement the solution.* Think through together the implications of the chosen solution. Who will do and not do what, when? How will things be different? How will things be better? Set up a time when participants will evaluate how well the solution is working.

7. *Evaluate how it is working.* Find out how each person feels about the solution. If solution needs adjustments, try to make them. Check to see that all persons still agree with the statement of the problem. The problem may have become clearer or disappeared, or new problems may have arisen. If anyone is unhappy with the solution or feels it is unfair or won't work, repeat the process from the beginning.

4. Active Listening

This is a way of helping another person solve his/her own problems by listening for the feelings behind his/her statements and reflecting them back.

For example:

Friend: Boy, was that a terrible meeting. I don't know who those big shots think they are.

Active Listener: You are feeling very frustrated about the meeting.

Friend: Yes, they talk all the time and repeat themselves so many times.

Active Listener: You get tired of hearing them talk all the time.

Friend: Well, they say some good things, but yes, they talk too much.

Active Listener: You feel you have something to say, too.

Friend: Yes. I had a fine proposal I wanted to share, but I didn't get a chance.

Active Listener: You feel you should be able to make your contributions.

Friend: Yes, maybe some process suggestions at the beginning would make it easier for everyone to get a chance to share ideas. I have some ideas to suggest.

Active listening helped the friend move from feeling frustrated and angry to finding the specific cause of the frustration (denial of the opportunity to share his/her own creative ideas) and to begin to generate possible ways to avoid the problem next time as well as improve the meeting for others. Active listening will work only if the Active Listener can concentrate on feeding back the feelings and refrain entirely from judging the friend, belittling the problem, or trying to suggest solutions of his/her own. If the feelings are not fed back correctly the Friend will either correct the Active Listener or get frustrated (eventually) and quit talking. (For additional information see 3 above.)

5. *"I-Messages"*

When people are unhappy, frustrated, or disturbed by the effects of another's behavior on them, too often the response is a negative statement of blame which increases the conflict and usually leads to no satisfactory solution for either party. When the statement is converted into an "I-Message," including: *"When*...(unacceptable behavior) *I* (speaker's feeling), *because* (consequences of the behavior to the speaker)," then a more positive resolution of the problem is possible. *Ex:* "People never get here on time. They must not care," should be changed to *"When* meetings don't start on time, *I* get irritated, *because* I have a limited amount of time to complete our business." (For additional information see 3 above.)

6. Other Tools Useful for Conflict Clarification and Resolution
    Listening in Pairs
    Discussion Format for Distressing Topics

USING CONFLICT RESOLUTION IN THE NEIGHBORHOOD

The following story is an account of an incident in which both conflict resolution and facilitation tools/skills were used with positive results. The names and location have been changed to protect the privacy of the people involved. We want to thank Nina Huizinga for sharing with us an account of this incident, which she mediated.

An Anecdote

The 1300 block of Park Ave. had a problem. Thomas, who lived on the block, liked to repair cars. In the process he was training young people, like the Smith's son Greg, in a valuable skill, and he was earning extra cash. It was getting to be a business. However, other neighbors on the block were annoyed. They complained that the noise, the cars left up on jacks, and the parking spaces continually occupied by cars waiting to be repaired were a nuisance and a hazard and made the block look messy.

Mrs. Jones, Thomas' next door neighbor, was especially upset because she was most affected by the noise, parked cars in front of her garage and the fact that Thomas did not seem willing to listen to her when she complained to him about the problem. She had invested money into fixing up two houses on the block and felt that Thomas was "running the block down." There had been some unpleasant confrontations between the two and some apparent retaliation from Thomas (garbage on Mrs. Jones' porch and slashed tires). Feelings were especially high after the police towed away two of Thomas' cars, taking them to be abandoned, which Thomas mistakenly interpreted as being caused by Mrs. Jones.

Mrs. Jones finally complained to the block leader, Martha. Martha, together with another woman on the block, tried to talk to Thomas about the problem, but neither side was really willing to listen to the other. There was talk of calling in the police. Martha called in Carolyn for help, because she had once lived on the block, knew the people involved, and yet was a neutral person to whom both sides might listen.

Carolyn talked with Thomas and heard his side of the story. He felt that he was being harassed by his neighbors and that it was essentially none of their business. He was not harming anyone; as a matter of fact, he was doing a good thing by saving the people on the block money by repairing their cars, while also sharing his skills with others. He was annoyed that his cars had been towed away and that he had had to get them and pay a fine. He was insulted at the idea that people accused him of slashing Mrs. Jones' tires. The possibility was discussed of trying to get permission to use a vacant gas station for his work, perhaps having this be the start of a skills sharing community workshop. Nothing was decided.

At this point a small delegation from the block went to the

police station, intending to find out what rights they had in the situation. Unexpectedly, the police responded by sending out several cars to the block and by verbally intimidating and threatening Thomas and Greg, who were working on cars. The block was immediately polarized as a result. Greg's family, the Smiths, were angry. Martha, Sue, and Stephen, who made up the delegation, were embarrassed and upset at the police's reaction and fearful of the block being torn apart by the incident. Since they were all white and Thomas and Greg were black, there were racial feelings also stirring on the block.

With the block leaders, Carolyn set up a time and a place for a meeting to which all of the parties in the conflict were invited. She talked with all of them, listened to their stories, and assured them that the meeting would be strictly structured and that she would remain impartial but would allow them to work out the problem.

The meeting happened, but neither Thomas nor Mrs. Jones showed up. Both had good reasons, but their absence meant that the personal conflict between them was never solved. Nevertheless, the meeting worked well for those who took part, and as a result the block is still a cohesive organization.

At the meeting Carolyn first introduced the techniques of conflict resolution. The people present agreed to follow the rules and to stay to the end of the allotted time. Two hours were set aside for the process. A timekeeper and note taker were chosen from neutral block members present, and Carolyn facilitated the process.

Each involved party then got five minutes to tell his/her story (no interruptions were allowed). After each story, the note taker repeated what had been said, and the story teller had to agree or make corrections until it was changed to his/her satisfaction. Then the next person got a chance. Each person was held strictly to five minutes, with two and one minute warnings.

Following the accounts, the conflictees were allowed to ask questions of each other. Before a person answered a question, however, s/he had to repeat the question, to be sure that s/he had heard it correctly. Sometimes the participants slipped away from this structure, but Carolyn would then briefly summarize the points made and get agreement on those points from the conflictees before continuing. This question/discussion time took about a half hour.

The group then listed the grievances of each side on wall charts. Referring to these, they then answered in turn the question, "What can I do to help solve this conflict?"

The meeting finished with an evaluation in which important

insights were shared. Greg felt that he had really been listened to, something he had not expected. He offered to tell Thomas how the meeting had gone. Martha, Sue and Stephen learned not to be so naive about the police. They also learned that if Mrs. Jones had a complaint she should bring it to a block meeting, that they shouldn't try to deal with it as a separate group. Marilyn, who was a neutral party and had not been attending block meetings, learned that her absence had made a difference, since she had had considerable experience working on police abuse cases. The people at the meeting acknowledged that although it had at first seemed as if racial conflict were involved, the original quarrel was between two neighbors, Thomas and Mrs. Jones, who were both black. People also agreed that their skepticism about the use of a very rigid conflict resolution structure had been dispelled by their experience of the effectiveness of the process.

The block organization has continued to flourish. Conflicts were faced head-on, which if allowed to fester could have caused its demise. The personal conflict between Thomas and Mrs. Jones, who were absent from the conflict resolution meeting, has continued unresolved.

V
Bibliographies

WORKING IN GROUPS

Dynamics of Groups at Work, by Herbert A. Thelen (University of Chicago Press, 1954). Readable book, includes sections on membership, leadership, roleplaying, different kinds of groups, and other basic issues.

Dynamics of Planned Change, by J. Watson Lippitt and B. Wesley (Harcourt, Brace and World, 1958). The application of group dynamics and an analysis and theory of community conflicts to the whole field of social change. Basic reading for anyone actively engaged in social change.

Group Processes, An Introduction to Group Dynamics, 2nd ed., by Joseph Luft (National Press Books, 850 Hanson Way, Palo Alto, CA 94304, 1970). Short, basic and readable. The best brief discussion of important issues in group dynamics.

"Guidelines for Reaching Consensus," by Jay Hall, *Psychology Today,* Nov. 1971.

A Handbook of Structured Experiences for Human Relations

Training, in 6 vol., edited by J. William Pfeiffer and John E. Jones (University Associates, Inc., 7596 Eads Ave., La Jolla, CA 92037; 1969-1977). An excellent collection of activities and games that can be used in a variety of group training settings. Activities are easy to reproduce and contain step-by-step instructions; they can easily be adapted to suit unique needs and designs. Not a text.

A Manual for Group Facilitators, by The Center for Conflict Resolution (CCR, 731 State St., Madison, WI 53706, 1977, $5.00). Includes exercises and reading lists for further study.

No Bosses Here: A Manual on Working Collectively, by Vocations for Social Change (VSC, 353 Broadway, Cambridge, MA 02139, $3.50). "A guide for people who are working in a collective or are thinking about starting one."

Roads to Agreement, by Stuart Chase (Harper Brothers, 1951). A readable book with a good chapter on Quaker consensus. Some anti-labor attitudes with which we do not agree, but a good chronicle of various ways conflicts are solved in the U.S. Also includes examples of a variety of decision-making processes.

The Silent Language, by Edward Hall (Fawcett Premier, 1959). A study of nonverbal forms of communication and cultural differences as expressed by nonverbal cues. Focuses on the cultural aspects of "body language."

CONFLICT RESOLUTION AND CRISIS INTERVENTION

The Art of Negotiating, by Gerald Nierenberg (Cornerstone Library, 1975). An introductory work on the techniques and strategies of negotiating.

Building Communities for Social Change, by the Training/ Action Affinity Group (MNS, 4722 Baltimore Ave., Phila., PA 19143, 1977, $3.00). One chapter on resolving conflict in social change communities.

Conflict Regulation, by Paul Wehr (American Association for the Advancement of Science, 1776 Massachusetts Ave., Washington, DC 20036). An excellent introduction to conflict theory and conflict regulation processes.

"The Ethics of Social Intervention: Community Crisis Intervention Programs," by James Laue and Gerald Cormack (Community Crisis Intervention Center, Washington University, St. Louis, MO 63130). Outlines assumptions and techniques involved in crisis intervention in the community. Has a major focus on how weaker parties can be strengthened so that negotiations can occur.

The Functions of Social Conflict, by Lewis Coser (The Free

Press, Glencoe, IL, 1956). A book which details the positive benefits of conflict.

International Conflict for Beginners, by Roger Fisher (Harper and Row, 1969). An excellent book on negotiation strategy both informal and formal. Focus is on the international level but many of the concepts can be applied on the community and personal levels.

Making Peace, by Adam Curle (London: Tavistock, 1971). Includes one of the best chapters on the theory of conflict and conflict resolution available as well as chapters on successful resolution of conflicts from the personal to the international level.

Parent Effectiveness Training, by Thomas Gordon (Wyden Press, 1970). Includes a description of the ''No-lose'' problem-solving process for resolving family conflicts.

NONVIOLENT (CIVILIAN) NATIONAL DEFENSE

Civilian Resistance as a National Defence, edited by Adam Roberts (1967; Pelican, 1969). A valuable anthology on problems of defense in general, case studies of nonviolent resistance, and the prospects and problems of a nonviolent national defense policy. Doesn't shun hard questions.

War Without Weapons: Non-violence in National Defense, by Anders Boserup and Andrew Mack (Schocken, 1974). A critical analysis of the literature on the subject.

Moving Toward a New Society (Chapter 10) and *Strategy for a Living Revolution* (Chapter 8) discuss civilian defense in the context of revolutionary change (see Bibliography of Part One for these books).

HERE'S TO THE PEOPLE

Words and music by P.J. Hoffman
© 1976 P.J. Hoffman

go But those who seek will some-day find, And that is why we are here. CHORUS: But what is in a cir-cle, And what is left with-out? Let's keep one mind to the cen-ter and one mind all a-bout.

We are but some of the many folks
Whose lives often feel like they're full of holes.
Making pains, losing gains,
Until there seems no place to go.
But those who seek, will someday find,
And that is why we are here.

CH: But what is in a circle,
      And what is left without?
      Let's keep one mind to the center,
      And one mind all about.

Now we have come around the common wine.
Let's make a toast to our gathered lives:
Lift your glass, look around,
And take in the friends you have found.
Thank the lord, thank yourself,
And feel the old fears yielding.   (CH)

Here's to the people who have no home.
Here's to the people who suffer alone.
We're secure, but hear the call,
To try to tear down the walls.
This our life, and this our mind,
To be at one with all.   (CH)

Part Three

Developing Communities of Support

When people work alone on difficult social, political or economic problems, they often become isolated, overwhelmed and discouraged. The problems encountered are usually too pervasive for one person to understand and correct alone. People need acceptance and support for the difficult work they do, but it is rarely found among people who disagree with or are threatened by unfamiliar activities.

A community of support can be a variety of things, but for use in this part of the manual the following definition is adequate:

> A *community of support* is an environment in which people's mutual needs are met and various aspects of their lives are shared. It need not include living in the same house, but it must include an intention to articulate shared needs and provide ways of meeting them.

For people engaged in sustained social change activities, support communities are important in several ways:

• They offer opportunities to explore working and living arrangements that are consistent with people's goals—a good place to face the inconsistencies between the way we live and what we are trying to build in the large society as a whole.

• Cooperative economic arrangements release time and material resources for a variety of uses. Individuals have more time to develop their resourcefulness and work on projects.

• Encouragement and support through difficult projects and personal crises is more possible.

• Flexibility, skills in interpersonal relations, and cooper-

101

ative work patterns are learned in the process of maintaining and enriching community life.

• They offer opportunities for people to deepen their understanding of problems and to explore cooperative ways of working for agreed upon changes.

• Collective evaluation of individual and group behavior and style of work offers opportunities for improvement on a variety of levels.

I
Maintaining Community

Several elements seem to need attention if a supportive community is to be developed and maintained. These aspects will vary in importance depending on the goals of the group and the larger political and economic context in which the group exists.

Many of the activities are described in structured terms which may put some people off. Some may seem so obvious as not to need mentioning. Our experience has been that awareness of the need for an activity can lag or even disappear. Our goal is not to create an artificial or super-structured environment, but to clarify and encourage what we have found to be important on a fairly regular basis. The self-consciousness of the structure will decrease with use and we can all proceed even more freely with the joyful business at hand.

The Training/Action Affinity Group (MNS) of Philadelphia has compiled a guide for people who want to live or work collectively. *Building Social Change Communities* has sections on getting started, conflict resolution, nuts and bolts of communal living and relationships in community. It is available from 4722 Baltimore Ave., Phila., PA 19143 for $3.00.

1. MULTI-DIMENSIONAL SHARING

Community grows as people increase the quantity and quality of experiences they share. Alienation—separation or estrangement—develops when people's lives become compartmentalized into rigid roles. Relating in a variety of ways to those with whom we work or live helps us to integrate our lives and to develop more satisfying relationships.

Kinds of sharing:
• Long-term group living. Ex: Teachers and students in a

102

small, cooperative living arrangement at a boarding school.

• Short-term group living. Ex: retreats, intensive live-in workshops.

• Cooperative work projects. Ex: as part of an ongoing campaign, regular or special repair or maintenance of shared spaces such as the group's meeting room or community living areas. Constructive work projects in the neighborhood.

• Worship or group meditation. Probably most successful if people's different styles and needs are accepted and a variety of approaches are used.

• Shared meals, including cooperative planning, preparation and clean-up.

• Fun. Ex: singing, improvisational or folk dancing, bike rides, canoe or camping trips, picnics, celebrations of accomplishments of the group. A good resource for encouraging group interaction around simple structures is *Games*, by Frank W. Harris (Eastern Cooperative Recreational School, c/o Jesse C. Kaufman, 2834 Holley Dr., Yorktown Heights, NY 10598).

• Hugs and massage. Can be shared in a variety of ways and places. Especially good during extended work activities and after long meetings. Use *The Massage Handbook*, by George Downing (Random House and Bookworks, Berkeley and NY, 1972).

• Social change activities. Ex: street speaking, street theatre, planning and carrying out a campaign, training workshops, conflict intervention, building an alternative institution.

• Research, discussion or personal sharing groups. Good topics are economics, sexism, alternatives, a special local crisis, a recurring problem in the support community.

• Relaxed, unstructured two person conversations. Can include physical activities such as a walk or massage, and can focus on any topic, joyful or scary.

2. AN ECONOMIC BASE

Economic independence is important both to the individual and to the group engaged in social change. For the individual, economic independence means having enough income to meet basic needs without holding a full-time job unrelated to one's focus of concern. Groups should not plan to depend on uninvolved contributors or institutions for income because financial support is likely to stop once the actions of the group become controversial or threaten their interests. The following are suggestions which make economic independence more possible.

For individuals:

• Live simply. Cutting down on consumption will greatly reduce money needs and help to free you from the irrational demands made by our wasteful culture.

• Work part-time at manual labor, semi-skilled work, free-lance jobs (tutoring, etc.) which will provide necessary income and give needed contact with people from a variety of social and economic realities.

• Work full-time for short periods, freeing yourself for more relevant non-paid work later.

• Share full-time work in cooperation with one or two others, when the type of work permits. A shared full-time paycheck can frequently support two or three.

For groups:

• Set up an alternative business. Ex: print shop, food co-op, waste recycling, bicycle repair, bread baking, house repair, restaurant. Such an alternative is most exciting when it embodies characteristics of a better society and relates to other social change work you are doing. See section on "Constructive Program."

• Offer social change related services. Ex: training sessions, speaking or discussion-leading, writing articles for publications sympathetic to the work you are doing.

• Exchange services to meet mutual needs without exchanging money. Ex: plumbing for child-care.

• Set up a skills collective which plugs willing people into available short-term jobs.

• Share use of appliances, vehicles, hand and power tools.

• Grow some of your own food.

• Work as a collective in an office or factory.

Resource:

999 Little-Known Businesses, by William Carruthers (Plymouth Publishing Co., Brooklyn, NY 1970). Lists and explains 999 businesses through which individuals can start to earn money full or part time. Gives concrete examples and helpful information for people interested in trying them.

3. TRANSFER OF SKILLS AND INFORMATION WITHIN THE COMMUNITY

Within any community people will vary in the amount and type of experience and skills they have. People with greater experience and skill will tend to fill more roles of responsibility and this can become a source of tension, especially for newer or less experienced members of the community. It is important that people with fewer skills be given opportunities to acquire these skills *while* they are performing respected community functions. It is equally important that people with more experience and skill be encouraged to share desirable responsibilities *without* being "attacked" for the valuable contributions they are making.

A support community should encourage its members to use the skills they have, without allowing them to take permanent or undue credit in those areas where their expertise is greatest. For a genuine transfer of skills to take place people need to use their talents willingly, teaching others as they do, and to leave time to learn new things from others.

Ways to share skills and information:
- Have people take on apprentice roles in areas where they want to gain skills or experience.
- Rotate responsibilities within a work or living group, so that people get experience with a variety of jobs and learn how they interrelate.
- Maintain open decision-making processes at all times, with general or rotated participation so that everyone's input is received, and everyone acquires experience. (See Decision Making and Decision-Making Tools in Part Two.)
- Develop "co-learning" relationships with others. Share problems and insights from your study and work on an ongoing basis.
- Define and discuss the functions of leadership. Examine ways people can learn to take leadership responsibilities.
- Have a series of workshops where anyone can organize a session around a skill s/he wants to learn or share with others.
- Encourage people with clear ability to assume responsibility in a particular area, to become thoroughly familiar with the job (with assistance), and then to pass it on to someone whom they have trained.

4. TEAMWORK

A more involved way to share skills is the team approach to working on a particular task. The team, collective, or affinity group forms out of a shared work focus and incorporates other dimensions. It should never become a clique closed to outside participation, but those who take major responsibility for sharing the work usually develop a close-knit and deeply satisfying relationship.

Advantages of a team experience:
- A complement of skills may be available from the various members, allowing for versatility and rapid learning as members

share skills with others.

• Individual members can use their talents more fully on a specific task when not required to carry responsibility for all areas of the work at once. The quality of work often improves when done in the context of the support and shared insights of others.

• A team can use its fuller resources to identify the specific problems of a new situation and make a more appropriate response.

• People learn to relate to each other as total persons rather than as holders of a single role. Interpersonal tensions can be worked through as they emerge. Members become more skilled in interpersonal relations and cooperative work. Times for relaxation and fun will need to be respected and can often be shared.

• Team work can be integrated with other life functions, e.g., shared meals or group naps when work periods are long. Living space can be shared, especially if work is done away from home, such as at a workshop or conference.

• Members of the team can support each other in times of emotional or financial need, or when casualties result from risks taken.

• Team members may find that extensive forms of shared economic responsibility make sense, e.g., income sharing or earning money by working in an alternative business together.

All these aspects of the team experience can be applied to a more general community. The team is simply more intensive and is an excellent example of multi-dimensional sharing at its best.

5. AFFIRMATION

Affirmation is communication of the positive nature of reality. It is a necessary tool for individuals and groups involved in social change. Oppressive social forces often rely on a false, negative interpretation of reality to wear down the resistance of progressive forces and to create discouragement or apathy. An effective activist will counter "authoritative pessimism" at every turn.

In times of difficulty, we need to find time for positive evaluation of our work. Long-range perspectives should be kept in sight and not obscured by short-term victories or defeats.

We need to consistently affirm ourselves and each other. All of us carry scars, mental and emotional, of innumerable past defeats, discouragements and put-downs. These tend to inhibit or discourage us from effective social action. Instead of flexibly and confidently developing and carrying out a program for change, we feel frustrated as we alternate between apathy and emotion-laden surges of reactive energy.

Affirmation is as critical to group growth as it is to an individual. A group which is unable to recognize the positive attributes of its members and of their accomplishments will be incapable of organizing effectively for change.

Individuals who are acting destructively toward people and are holding jobs that are not building a human society also need to be affirmed—especially as they begin to consider making major changes in their lives. Learning to affirm these people requires the ability to separate the person from the destructive role and to affirm the former while challenging and noncooperating with the latter. This is a critical skill for nonviolent organizers.

Affirmation can be practiced by appreciating, openly and persistently, positive aspects of oneself or of others. It should never be sarcastic or cynical. Be sincere, make full use of positive words, tone of voice, posture, and facial expression. The person affirmed may react with protests, resistance, even with laughter, tears, or anger, but these healthy expressions of feeling do not negate the truth of the statement. Affirmation, whether of oneself or another, is not a positive judgment designed to manipulate or control behavior. It is a real and accurate appreciation of the good which is apparent in each person just as s/he is, and it can be a powerful tool whether or not its immediate effect is satisfying.

The role of affirmation in building communities of support:

- Affirmation clarifies and reinforces our strengths and allows us to use them more consciously and effectively to create better alternatives.

- When undertaken as an ongoing, regular activity, affirmation expands the sense of trust and shared appreciation among group members.

- It helps us appreciate the growth occurring on the personal level even before its effects are seen on large-scale problems.

- Self-affirmation makes individuals less dependent on approval from others. This is especially important when working in hostile or indifferent environments.

- It helps protect us from continual negative messages that alienate, weaken, and distress us, e.g., TV commercials, billboards, and newspaper ads that bombard us with things we "need" to be prettier, sexier, smarter, or more popular.

- It increases the dimension of celebration in our lives.

• It helps us to project more clearly those positive qualities we perceive to be possible though not fully attained: e.g., community, cooperative work relationships, warmth and caring in our interactions with others.

• It develops and releases creative energy.

• It sometimes makes the collective accomplishments of a group far exceed those one could expect from its members taken as individuals.

Affirmation Exercises for groups:

Because our society negates people and groups in so many areas of their lives, we have found it valuable sometimes to structure time to share affirmations of each other. Affirmation exercises frequently occur at the beginning of group meetings and may be used during the meeting if tension or frustration arises.

These activities allow the caring and positive feelings which exist to be shared openly. They also offer time to practice so that affirmation becomes easier to share in unstructured situations. The suggestions below should not be used rigidly, but adapted, expanded, and added to.

1. Each person shares two things about him/herself that are good—one that is obvious to all, and one that few other people know.

2. Each person shares his/her most satisfying accomplishments of the past week.

3. Each person in the group tells the person on his/her right what s/he finds special about him/her.

4. For three or five minutes the group focuses on each person in turn, sharing specific or general things it appreciates about that person—such as times s/he has been helpful or creative things s/he has done.

5. People affirm each other nonverbally, with hugs or other affectionate gestures.

6. Sheets of paper can be posted where people can write things they appreciate about individuals. A separate sheet can be posted for each person. Hand tracings or self-portraits or symbols can be drawn on the sheet.

7. Members focus on the positive contributions of the household or work collective as a whole and list as many as they can within an agreed-upon period of time.

8. To counter a problem in group process (e.g., everyone is talking at once for fear no one is really listening) an idea can be chosen that *contradicts* the feelings causing the problem, and each person can express that idea to the next person, e.g., "I really want to hear what you have to say..."

6. COMMITMENT TO THE GROUP

In an ongoing, multi-dimensional community, several areas of group activity require a disciplined, intentional approach. Below are questions which many groups have found it necessary to ask themselves. The group will need to choose flexible processes to examine these areas.

• What is the focus of activity of individuals? This can be asked on a regular basis, when major decisions need to be made, or when conflicts surface. (See *Self-estimation* and *Warm Fuzzy* exercises and *Clearness Meetings*).

• Are we being sensitive to behavior which is destructive to the group or to specific members? Patience is required to discover the causes of such behavior and to find ways of non-cooperating with it while simultaneously appreciating the value and beauty of the person.

• Are we developing processes which allow sensitivity to personal needs *and* which expedite business?

• Do we approach work, expecially that related to social change, with a rhythm of research/action/evaluation/research/action/evaluation...or other disciplined approaches as needed?

• Do we set and periodically re-examine both long and short-term goals for the community?

• Are we pushing each other into roles rather than treating each other as full human beings?

• Do we deal creatively and responsibly with the needs of children in the community?

• Are we providing for the health needs of community members, by exploring alternatives to medical insurance, learning para-medical skills, sharing information on medical assistance, clinics, and other resources?

• Are we protecting the resources (emotional, financial, time) the community has by being clear which are personal, which are communal and which are available for public use?

• What are we doing about status and skill differences within the community that make it possible for some people to find desirable bread labor jobs and others no jobs or less desirable ones?

• Are we developing a balance between work and fun, high energy output and relaxed sharing, theoretical and practical aspects, group and individual needs, communal and private life?

II
Encouraging Interaction

The following are structures and exercises developed or used by various households and work collectives in the Movement for a New Society/Life Center community in West Philadelphia to improve the quality of interaction among members. What was useful for one group may be less so for another. These ideas are offered for imaginative borrowing.

COMMUNITY-BUILDING STRUCTURES

1. *Two kinds of meetings,* one for business, and one for sharing and discussion such as personal sharing, fun, pursuing a topic in depth, considering major questions or conflicts affecting the group.

2. *Work projects:* setting aside blocks of time for shared work on major projects. Ex: house repair or beautification, money-raising.

3. *Work teams* (usually of two) for routine chores. Ex: cooking, cleaning, mailings.

4. *Meeting for worship/sharing.*

5. *Special sharing session:* time for one or more person(s) to share what is important to them. Ex: reading out loud, music, a time of crisis in which s/he was involved.

6. *Gripe sessions.* 3-10-minute timed period where no positive comments or excuses are allowed. Accompany gripes with groaning, growling, etc. Follow it up with time for constructive suggestions, clarifications, positive feedback.

7. *Positive feedback session.* A few minutes for people to appreciate good things about the group or about each other and their interactions. This provides a good companion for the gripe session. Good to begin or end other kinds of sessions. For examples of exercises see *Affirmation*.

8. *"Kvetch" or gripe blackboard* for unloading negative feelings and gripes when one is unclear who is responsible. If a person feels responsible for the gripe s/he erases it and tries to eliminate the source of the gripe. If no one erases it, responsibility may be general, and discussion in a house meeting may be in order. Examples appearing frequently on "kvetch" lists are dirty dishes, mud tracked in, community supplies removed from community areas and not returned such as tape, scissors or chairs.

COMMUNITY-BUILDING EXERCISES

1. *Sharing Personal Growth Experiences* by Blair Forlaw

Purpose/Uses: To draw out common themes and problems in our lives. To share our personal growth experiences in a structured way. To help build a sense of community. Good for developing trust and closeness in a group; breaks down barriers by showing each person's vulnerabilities to life.

Description:

1. People take five minutes to think about their own lives. What provided the most stimulus to grow? What were "jolting experiences" in which you sensed growth? What have you done that seemed to help bring about change in your life?

2. Each person has a set amount of time (say 5 min) to relate these experiences to the group, while the others give him/her their full attention.

3. A recorder can list on a flip chart the variety of experiences and begin to pull out common themes from the group.

4. Group concludes with discussion on "how change occurs," focusing on list derived from group sharing.

Caution: A certain level of trust needs to exist in a group for this to work well. If enough trust exists, the level will deepen.

2. *Group Conversation* by Rachel Davis DuBois

Purpose/Uses: To share personal experiences in a non-threatening way. To increase people's understandings of each other as people. To help people from different cultures to appreciate each other. To show human commonalities across cultural lines.

Description:

1. The facilitator explains that each member of the group will speak in turn, sharing from his/her *own* experience about the same topic. No reactions, agreements or disagreements with other speakers' thoughts are allowed. (Useful topics are food, celebrations, family get-togethers, experiences with siblings, childhood houses or apartments, early memories of grandparents and parents.)

2. Use time limits so each will have a chance to speak without the session running too long. (One to five minutes each are recommended.) Time will vary depending on the particular question asked. It is helpful to give people a 30-second notice before their time is up.

3. The participants share first an early childhood memory around the topic, for example, "When I was five years old my

grandmother used to bake blueberry pie,'' etc. For the second round of sharing, people may recall a later experience, perhaps around early teens; and so forth. As members of the group are invited into the intimate scenes of the others' lives, the trust level rises.

4. If desired, a problem may be discussed—how families with different backgrounds can work together on a neighborhood issue, for example. The earlier sharing helps to show people their commonalities and provides a basis for understanding and solving their differences.

For additional information read *The Art of Group Conversation: A New Break Through in Social Communication* by Rachel DuBois (Association Press, 1963).

3. Other Exercises Useful In Building Community
Statements Exercise
Risk List
Life Line
Self-estimation or *Warm Fuzzy* sessions.

COMMUNITY BUILDING GAMES

Purpose/Uses: For fun, physical activity, and physical contact of a playful nature. Use when energy is low, group is bogged down, or people need to have fun together. Encourages creative thinking.

1. *Pretzel* (15 min for 15-20 people)
The group forms a circle and the game is explained. A few people who volunteer to untangle the group leave the room. One volunteer is needed for about every 12 people. The group joins hands and tangles into an impossible knot, *without breaking* any of the *hand connections* in the process. Volunteers return and try to untangle the group without disconnecting any hands.

2. *Build a Machine* (5 min)
One person starts a mechanical action. People attach themselves to the first mechanical action until a large machine has been built. More specifics can be given such as, Let's build a musical machine, a Christmas machine, or a giggle machine.

3. *Group Pantomime*
One person starts acting out a group activity. As soon as others figure out what is happening, they join the pantomime, until all have figured it out and have joined the activity. Example: tug of war, painting a room.

4. *Attention Expanders* can also be used.

112

WE CAN MAKE THE CHANGES

Words and music by P.J. Hoffman
© *1976 P.J. Hoffman*

We can make the changes if we want.
We can make the changes if we try.
Everything we want to see
We can make reality
We can make the changes, and we will.

CH: We will, we will, we will—
        Take heart, all those in the struggle.
        Our lives are where it begins.
        So celebrate through the hard times,
        'Cause we will win.

We can make the difference if we want.
We can make the difference if we try.
Our numbers may be very small,
We can grow and become all.
We can make the difference, and we will.   (CH)

We can make the new world if we want.
We can make the new world if we try.
All we do is make it show
And the old world's got to go.
We can make the new world, and we will.   (CH)

Part Four
Personal Growth

While social change takes place most effectively in the context of a community, there are many areas that the individual must take unique responsibility for. These include: developing disciplined work habits, nurturing emotional and spiritual growth, and maintaining oneself as a healthy, joyful, contributing member of the community. A successful program for change depends on the self-discipline of its members, including their courage, patience, persistence and skill level. The loving support of others provides the environment in which growth on the personal level takes place, but each of us is ultimately responsible for how and in what areas that growth proceeds.

I
Personal Disciplines

EVALUATING DISCIPLINES

The following questions help evaluate particular methods for their usefulness in promoting personal growth and societal change:

- Is there a way to evaluate this method and the effectiveness of its claims?
- Does this discipline claim to be the only valid one? The best? Can any method claim unique ability to promote personal growth?
- How much sense does this growth discipline make in terms of my personal experiences?
- Does this method help individuals relate more creatively to others?

• Is the organization which spreads this method using processes consistent with my goals in relationship to issues of shared leadership, racism, ecological soundness, etc.?

• Is this descipline available to people of all financial levels without humiliation? Do the financial demands made by the method prohibit participation by large segments of the society?

• Does it result in escape from social problems, or does it encourage societal change as well as personal growth?

• Does it help people change themselves to become more effective participants in a process of positive social change? Can this discipline be integrated into my continuing work for social change?

RE-EVALUATION COUNSELING

There are many disciplines people use as part of their growth process. Re-evaluation Counseling is one which fits many of the above criteria and has made a significant contribution to the on-going process of the Movement for a New Society/Life Center community in West Philadelphia. Because its theory and practice are integrated into meetings and are frequently used in the formation of exercises and tools, it is useful to include a brief description of it here.

Re-evaluation Counseling has no organizational connection to Movement for a New Society and maintains its own structure for spreading its skills. For this reason the specific process is not presented here. For information on classes in your area, workshops, and literature, write The Re-evaluation Counseling Communities, 719 2nd Ave., Seattle, WA 98109.

Re-evaluation Counseling is a process whereby people, regardless of age, education or experience, can learn how to exchange effective help with each other in order to free themselves from the effects of past distress experiences.

Re-evaluation Counseling theory provides a model of what a human being can be like in the area of his/her interaction with other human beings and the environment. The theory assumes that everyone is born with tremendous intellectual potential, natural zest and lovingness, but that these qualities become blocked and obscured in adults as the result of accumulated distress experiences (fear, hurt, loss, pain, anger, embarrassment, etc.) which begin in childhood.

A child can recover from distress spontaneously by virtue of the natural process of emotional discharge (crying, trembling, raging, laughing, etc.). However, this natural process is usually interfered with by well-meaning adults and older children ("Don't cry," "Don't be a sissy," etc.) who erroneously equate the emotional discharge (the healing of the hurt) with the hurt itself.

When adequate emotional discharge can take place, the person is freed from the rigid pattern of behavior and feeling left by the hurt. The basic, loving, cooperative, intelligent and zestful nature is then free to operate.

In recovering and using the natural discharge processes, two people take turns counseling and being counseled. The one acting as the counselor listens, draws the other out and permits, encourages, and assists emotional discharge. The one acting as client talks and discharges and re-evaluates. With experience and increased confidence and trust in each other, the process works better and better.

The person who learns to co-counsel well in a Fundamentals Class* will become part of an existing community of co-counselors locally which has close ties with other such communities in the United States and abroad. Co-counselors in these communities share many on-going co-counseling activities.

Relevance to social change:

1. This method operates on a peer-group basis. It is consequently inexpensive (the actual co-counseling is a free exchange of services) and can be extended to large numbers of people.

2. People concerned to change society need their loving, creative abilities freed for this work. Re-evaluation Counseling facilitates this.

3. Re-evaluation Counseling is taught in classes which often evolve into groups of shared support. These groups have no overt social change orientation but do tend to empower their members as responsible, rational, active participants in society.

4. In one existing social change community, Re-evaluation Counseling has been useful in solving community problems by (1) providing an effective means for individuals to explore distress within themselves which causes interpersonal tension; (2) helping individuals to gain insight into the distress of others, expecially those they are in tension with, and to find creative ways of approaching conflicts, (3) giving people resources for dealing effectively with the distress of other community members in crisis situations.

5. The process of Re-evaluation Counseling enables people to recover large unused (or rigidly misused) capacities for thinking about and acting on situations in their lives. Social

* A weekly experience organized by an authorized teacher of Re-evaluation Counseling.

change demands more than strong feelings—it demands consistently clear thinking unencumbered by emotional confusion.

6. Re-evaluation Communities are at present involved in what is called "permeation" (application of theory and resources of Re-evaluation Counseling to a wide variety of human activities). Examples are (1) providing the tools of Re-evaluation Counseling to members of minority groups, women, young people and others engaged in the struggle for human liberation, and (2) using these tools to transform and humanize existing oppressive institutions. The scope of Re-evaluation Counseling goes far beyond its usefulness as a tool for personal growth.

DIET, EXERCISE, CLEANLINESS AND ORDER

It may seem too obvious to mention, but we feel it important to note that attention to physical fitness, good diet, and cleanliness is essential to personal growth and effectiveness. Both the individual and the community can find ways to encourage awareness of these needs and to meet them creatively. People who do not value themselves highly enough to take loving care of themselves and their environment should question seriously their participation in the solution of other social problems.

Diet: See "Cooking for Large Groups" for books useful in preparing simple, inexpensive and nutritious meals.

Exercise: Try Yoga or similar exercise. Read *Yoga, Youth, and Reincarnation* by Jess Stearn (Bantam, 1971, $1.50). Include regular times for physical activities such as walking, jogging, swimming, biking, canoeing, carpentry and games.

Cleanliness and Order: Explore cooperative methods for maintaining group work and living spaces, especially work teams and group work projects. When individuals' different criteria and approaches lead to conflicts, try "Processes for Conflict Clarification and Resolution," in Part Two.

II
Making Personal Decisions

Every person is faced with important decisions connected with work, community living and interpersonal relationships. Parents, friends and society at large offer us choices which may include equally exciting possibilities, or in which it may be unclear what the choices are. Sometimes the options will appear to be equally undesirable alternatives, and a search for new alternatives may be necessary. People who are attempting to build a new society and participate in it will need to make decisions of this sort.

Included here are both individual and group processes that can assist people in making better decisions. A person faced with a decision s/he cannot make could begin by trying to set goals; the decision may become clear quickly. Time spent on individual or 2-person exercises will, at the least, improve clarity and prepare one to make better use of a group session if called later.

Some decisions are particularly difficult and may affect other people directly. Some have major implications for you and your friends, such as change of career, joining or leaving a community, or changes in a primary relationship. In these cases there is tremendous value in getting substantial feedback from people in whose thinking you have confidence, as well as from those affected by the decision.

Shifting Gears by Nena and George O'Neill may be helpful to people who are making major changes in their life-style, vocation or relationships. The greater the care we give to our decision-making process, the more options we find are available for us, improving the chances that a right decision can be made.

PREPARING YOURSELF TO THINK CLEARLY

Past problems and traumas (as well as fears and expectations others have of us) can cause anxiety, making it difficult to think clearly about decisions which must be made. Below are suggestions requiring the help of another person. The first is a procedure in which anyone can participate and is explained here. The second and third require training on the part of the other person. See references for further information.

Think and Listen

Purpose/Uses: To think creatively about a problem or issue. To provide a structure through which an individual can give positive

119

attention to another while s/he thinks through a problem, without interfering with that thinking process. To provide a basis for further discussion, goal-setting or decision making with others.

Description:

1. The two find a comfortable place where they can face each other.

2. Each person takes a specified time (usually 10-15 min) to reflect (usually, but not necessarily, out loud) about a particular question, issue, or decision. The other person does not interrupt or comment, but listens carefully with relaxed interest. If the Thinker desires, the Listener may take written notes of the Thinker's ideas, or of decisions made. The Thinker does not explain ideas for the benefit of the Listener, but focuses on sorting or defining them solely for the benefit of him/herself.

3. Frequently the Listener will also want time to think. After a short break, if wanted, the Thinker can become the Listener and the process in step 2 is repeated. The new Thinker focuses on his/her own topic and is not expected to react to the ideas of the first Thinker.

4. This technique can be used by groups before decisions are to be made. Participants can pair up or form into groups of 3 or 4. Follow with a brief sharing of insights within the larger group.

Re-evaluation Counseling can be used to unload emotional distress which is blocking clear thinking. If no one is available who can offer you a counseling session, a good cry or laugh will be a great help. Find a trusted friend and let go!

Active Listening can encourage people to acknowledge feelings around an item for decision and think more creatively about a solution.

SETTING GOALS

1. Use *Force Field Analysis*. State clearly the decision to be made, such as "Should I leave this community?" "Should I join the _____ Action Campaign?"

2. Read "The Necessity of Long Range Goals" by Harvey Jackins (see *The Human Situation*).

3. Read *How to Get Control of Your Time and Your Life* by Alan Lakein. Use exercises included to prioritize goals and read suggestions for implementing them.

4. Use the *Time Line* exercise for each major task or event in your life.

5. List things you want to accomplish within a given period of time. Assign times you think they will take. Be realistic. Check against amount of time available. If less time is available than is needed, prioritize.

6. Use ideas or exercises found in the following books to help sort out your priorities:

> *Values and Teaching*, by Louis Raths, et al. (Charles E. Merrill Publishing Co., Columbus, OH, 1966).
>
> *Values Clarification*, by Sidney B. Simon, et al. (Hart Publishing Co., NY, 1972).
>
> *Value Exploration Through Role-Playing*, by Robert C. Hawley (ERA Press Amherst, MA, 1974).

7. Draw two circles representing day, week or month.

My time as I would like to spend it.   *My time as I spend it.*

  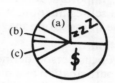

(a) with friends and family; (b) personal time; (c) social change activities.

Then ask yourself: How does my life have to change to allow me to spend my time as I would like to spend it?

RECORDING DECISIONS

A diary or a journal kept on a regular basis can be used to note goals and decisions when made and later serve as a resource to examine how effectively and in what ways you are carrying them out (especially helpful when kept for a project being undertaken). See Part Nine for more details on how to keep a journal.

Often date books, past and future, can provide useful answers to questions about priorities and actual use of time. Take a careful look at them before throwing them away.

REVIEW OF PRIORITIES AND FOLLOW-THROUGH

Choose a regular time to review priorities and set specific tasks. Intervals can be monthly, weekly, daily or all three. Before setting new tasks, check to see how well you followed through on your last list. If you are having difficulty following through, read *How to Get Control of Your Time and Your Life* by Alan Lakein. Find someone who could use support on follow-through and try a weekly calendar check and evaluation. Raise with each other questions around unreasonable scheduling and problems that prevent follow-through.

Self-estimation Session

A Self-estimation Session is designed to give individuals feedback from people with whom they are involved on a long-term basis, such as fellow workers, house mates or students of a class under their guidance. It is meant to help one evaluate how s/he is performing at a specific task, by sorting out those things done well and areas where improvement is possible or necessary. It is particularly helpful when people are trying to decide to leave or join a group or the most important place to put their efforts.

It is important for those in leadership positions to undergo frequent self-estimation. Where leadership functions are shared, everyone in the group may take a turn at self-estimation.

Description:

1. Focus person defines carefully what is being estimated. Ex: my participation as a member of the house last year; or how well I performed my job the last 6 months.

2. In twos or threes people take 5-10 minutes each to think aloud and unload feelings of distress about the person to be discussed. (Do this away from his/her presence.) Think about things that s/he did well and how you perceive s/he can improve.

3. People return to the large group.

4. The focus person estimates him/herself by taking an agreed-upon amount of time to talk about:

    a. strengths in relation to the topic

    b. weaknesses

    c. how s/he wants to change, and

    d. specific goals s/he may wish to set.

5. Each member of the group takes about 5 minutes to speak to points in number 4 above in regard to the focus person.

6. The focus person comments on anything that has been said and sets new goals where appropriate.

Variation: *Warm Fuzzy*. A less extensive, less structured period of self-estimation recommended for each group member in turn over a period of time. The "warm fuzzy" person prepares ahead of time to share about things that seem important—outside factors that affect his/her involvement in the group, pending decisions involving priorities and use of time, how this relates to the house (if it is a living unit) or work (if it is a collective) and the people in it, and areas where feedback from others would be helpful. This takes 10-15 minutes. An additional 10-15 minutes are allowed for specific feedback and/or general responses from the others. Feedback should include both positive and negative aspects. If feedback has been mostly negative, the session can end with **Affirmation** of the person and his/her participation in the group. Try to keep the tone one of listening and thinking, focusing on and responding to the person rather than going off on tangents or discussing related ideas.

USING THE CLEARNESS PROCESS*

A "Clearness Meeting" is a process through which an individual asks for support and feedback from people s/he trusts and respects. It is a process in which clarity is sought, not approval or permission. It is a mutual striving for a good decision and the surfacing of factors important to consider, rather than a judgment about the person or direction being sought.

The clearness process provides a way for the group to express care and love to an individual by giving him/her the benefit of the group's collective affirmation and sensitive critical feedback.

A clearness meeting can be called any time individuals (or groups) feel the need to make a decision or examine their lives in relation to basic directions such as change in community or collective, future plans, or facing a particularly difficult and perhaps recurring problem.

Preparation by an Individual for His/Her own Clearness Meeting

The "focus person" (as we will call the "person going through clearness") should prepare in advance for the meeting. This time can be fruitful in itself, but it is crucial for the success of the clearness meeting.

• Reflect and meditate, writing down thoughts and questions. Relax.

• Take time to talk, informally, with others who have information and experience which will help enlighten your decision-making process.

• Find someone with whom you can surface and release stress or upset associated with aspects of the decision to be made.

• Choose people for the clearness group who know you fairly well and represent a variety of perspectives and involve-

* Excerpted in large part from *Clearness: Processes for Supporting Individuals and Groups in Decision-Making*, by Peter Woodrow.

123

ment with you, such as living situation, work collective, and social change campaign. From three to seven people are recommended.

• Choose a facilitator from the clearness committee so that you can give your full attention to listening and responding. The facilitator should be someone who will *not* get over-involved in the emotional aspects of the situation. (See Role of the Facilitator below.)

• Meet with the facilitator before the meeting: (1) Clarify the question(s) to be brought to the meeting. (2) Clarify the task of the clearness group. (3) Draw up a tentative agenda that meets the needs of the focus person and the group. (4) Consider the general Questions for Individual Clearness, listed below.

Role of the Facilitator

Where decisions to be made have a strong emotional component for either the focus person or members of the clearness group, the facilitator has to be particularly capable of keeping the meeting moving and people's attention actively engaged on the topic. If people get sunk in heavy matters, silence, a break, a song or other *Attention Expander* is appropriate.

While keeping in mind the needs and process of the whole group, the facilitator should give particular attention to the needs of the focus person, checking periodically to make certain s/he is getting the kind of support as well as feedback s/he wants and needs from the group and protecting the focus person from unfair or hostile dumping of feelings or distress by another member of the clearness group.

See Part Two for information on how to facilitate a meeting.

Role of the Clearness Group

• To be supportive and affirmative while also raising forthright questions. To offer a balance between recognition of good thinking and clear but gentle challenges of fuzzyheadedness or false assumptions.

• To raise questions pertaining to the implications of decisions.

• To suggest additional options.

• To point out assumptions or motivations involved which may be preventing or forcing particular decisions or actions.

• To evaluate the practicality and merit of ideas, decisions, and solutions being explored.

• To remain sensitive to the needs of participants, especially the focus person, to express feelings as well as ideas.

- To point out areas where more information is needed and suggest how such information can be obtained.
- To participate in formulating a solution to a problem when desired. This is particularly important when others are directly affected by the decision being made.
- To offer follow-up help as individuals, as decided in the clearness meeting, or to reconvene as a group at a later date if needed.

Questions for Individual Clearness

Below are suggested questions, not all of which will be appropriate for every clearness meeting. Posting answers to questions in abbreviated form may help people later when posing questions for the focus person. If answers are reproduced and distributed before the meeting, only a quick review will be needed. If the clearness is for a person joining or leaving a collective or community, that group will want to generate questions to meet its own needs.

1. What are the events that have particular relevance to the decisions being made? Be personal and brief. (max. 10 min)

2. What are your goals, both long and short-range, for personal growth and social change work?

3. What are your sources of learning, support, and affirmation?

4. What are your basic necessities in order to function creatively?

5. What are your present commitments? (A pie chart of how time is spent may be useful.)

6. What are the implications of your proposed action/ change for your community, both those closest to you and the wider community of support?

7. What are your dreams and what do you perceive are those things holding you back from reaching them?

8. What are the positive and negative factors in each of the options being considered? (The group might help the focus person do a *Force-field Analysis* of these factors.)

Sample Agenda   (3 hrs recommended)

The agenda should be specific enough to help the focus person get feedback or make decisions as needed, but flexible enough to allow the participants to generate new options and ideas for making the best decision. The focus person should participate in tailoring the agenda to his/her needs.

Present the agenda at the beginning of the meeting and ask for the group's approval before proceeding. If changes are suggested it is important that the focus person agree that these changes will help meet his/her needs for the meeting.

• *A Meal* or other informal experience can be shared—*optional*. (Allow enough additional time.)

• *Gathering*, with singing, excitement-sharing, something that awakens a sense of community.   (10 min)

• *Agenda Review.*   (5 min)

• *Choosing Recorder.* We recommend a process of shared recording so that all members can participate. Notes can be read later by focus person and questions and suggestions pondered further when more time is available.

• *Sharing Good Time with Focus Person.* Each person can describe at least one good time s/he shared with focus person.   (10 min)

• *Statement of the Question for Clearness and Review of Expected Role of the Clearness Group.*   (5 min)

• *Checking for Personal Biases.* People who have clear prejudices or strong feelings before the clearness process begins should state them so focus person and other members of the group can be more objective in understanding questions asked and suggestions given.   (5 min)

• *Sharing from Focus Person* on questions for clearness, explanation of proposed directions or options, etc.   (30 min maximum)

• *Questions of Clarification.* Not a time for discussion or feedback.   (10 min)

• *Break.* Be imaginative.   (10 min)

• *Brainstorming Strengths of Focus Person.* Have someone record on chart.   (5 min)

• *Silence*, reflection or worship.   (10 min)

• *Brainstorming Questions/Concerns from Clearness Group.* It is good to get out initial questions to see scope of discussion possible. Selection of questions may need to be made, based on time factors.   (5 min)

• *Feedback.* Raising of questions, open discussion, generation of more options. Usually good to leave time fairly unstructured.   (60 min)

• *Next Steps and Follow-up.* It is often good to ask focus person what are the next steps as s/he perceives them. Also, ask each member of the group how s/he intends to follow up, if appropriate.   (10 min)

• *Evaluation.* May start by asking focus person whether s/he has reached greater clarity and, if so, how. Note both positive and negative aspects of the meeting so the next clearness meeting can be even better.   (5 min)

• *Closing.* A joyful celebrative occasion. Don't get back into the business of the meeting.

III
Bibliography

Clearness: Processes for Supporting Individuals and Groups in Decision-Making, by Peter Woodrow (Movement for a New Society, 4722 Baltimore Ave., Phila., PA 19143, 1976, $1.25 plus 35¢ postage). A thirty-page manual including suggested agendas for different kinds of decision-making meetings, developed by people in the Philadelphia Movement for a New Society/Life Center community.

The Human Situation, by Harvey Jackins (Rational Island Publishers, P.O. Box 2081, Main Office Station, Seattle, WA 98111. $5.00 paper). A collection of articles on various concepts of **Re-evaluation Counseling.** Three articles expecially recommended are "The Necessity of Long Range Goals," "The Logic of Being Completely Logical" and "The Flexible Human in the Rigid Society." Each article is available separately for 50¢.

How to Get Control of Your Time and Your Life, by Alan Lakein (Signet, 1974, $1.50). Can be ordered from NAL, 1301 Avenue of the Americas, New York, NY 10019.) Written for business executives, this book offers an extremely optimistic outlook and procedure for self-empowerment through efficient management of time. Exercises are offered for prioritizing goals and suggestions are given for undertaking achievement of these goals in the most appropriate times of one's day/week/month/year.

Shifting Gears, by Nena and George O''Neill. (Avon Books, 959 8th Ave., New York, NY 10019.) Talks about steps people have to go through to make changes in their lifestyle, vocation and relationships.

Organize for POOR POWER
G.R.I.P.E.
Grass Rooters
Interested In
Poverty Elimination!

Part Five
Consciousness Raising

Consciousness raising is a process of helping people recognize their hurts and see how these have social causes. This process can include:

- understanding what it feels like to live the life of someone different from yourself;
- finding out what you think about world issues;
- understanding your relationship to larger social-economic-political issues;
- understanding the ways in which you are oppressed;
- understanding the ways in which you may be oppressing others;
- finding out that you are not powerless;
- regaining control over your own life.

People often define consciousness raising as a process in which you encounter information, usually consisting of someone else's *personal* experience, which you find personally convincing, and which alters your belief and future behavior. Hearing several black acquaintances describe what it felt like to attend a high school with racist practices, for example, may move you to participate in supportive action with blacks for changes.

Consciousness raising includes this personal dimension in which individuals encounter real experiences in the world and change personal behavior. But consciousness raising, for us, also includes understanding the broader implications of hurts people experience in such a way as to enable them to act on societal problems to prevent unnecessary hurts from recurring. This process is accelerated when reflection and dialogue occur in a smal group where individuals feel safe to share feelings and problems. Exercises and structures can be used within these

129

groups to help people reflect on the social causes of personal problems.

We have found an understanding of consciousness raising to be essential among people working for broad-based social-political-economic changes. An important stage in the change process occurs when large numbers of people perceive their own hurts, understand how existing institutions oppress them, and develop motivation and confidence in pushing for change. In *Strategy for a Living Revolution*, George Lakey calls this the stage of "cultural preparation," in which "private problems become political issues as the people develop a collective will and an understanding of struggle." To understand the fuller implications of consciousness raising for the on-going process of change, see "Stages in a Program for Change" under Part Seven.

In this section we include resources we have found helpful in our own consciousness-raising process individually and within small groups.

EXPLORING YOUR WORLD

Consciousness raising does not happen in isolation. It requires exposure to a variety of human experiences. Some possible activities are:

• driving through a poor section of a large city, followed by driving through the richest section;

• visiting people in elegant suburban homes and in ghetto homes;

• participating in a neighborhood safety patrol in an urban residential area;

• court watching, especially in local magistrate's or Justice of the Peace courts;

• comparing prices and quality in ghetto and suburban stores within 20 miles of each other;

• visiting, writing to, or working with prisoners in a local prison;

• visiting migrant labor camps and talking to migrants about their life there;

• listening to conversations at cocktail parties;

• working with children that run away from middle class and upper class homes;

• reading books like:

    Bury My Heart at Wounded Knee, by Dee Brown (Bantam, 1972)

    The Closing Circle, by Barry Commoner (Bantam, 1972)

    Lessons from the Damned: Class Struggle in the Black

Community, by the damned (Times Change Press, c/o Monthly Review Press, 116 W. 14th, New York, NY 10011, $2.75 plus .35 postage)

Manchild in the Promised Land, by Claude Brown (Macmillan, 1965)

Voices from the Plain of Jars, by Fred Branfman (Harper, 1972)

- living on a welfare budget for 1 year;
- participating in a social change project;
- watching documentary reports on major social problems.

THE CONSCIOUSNESS-RAISING GROUP

Mere exposure to "harsh realities" doesn't necessarily lead to a change of consciousness and a resolve to action. Reflection on these experiences and dialogue about them within a group is important for better assimilation of information.

A commonly used form is the consciousness-raising group; several people with common problems who share their experiences and reflect on them together. A consciousness-raising group can provide the emotional safety and support necessary for members to feel hurts and articulate them. Hearing others share similar problems helps people realize that their problems are not just their own fault. The support of the group can help individuals overcome feelings of self-blame and self-doubt. Drawing connections between personal hurts and the structures of society motivates people to confront actively problems rooted in oppressive attitudes and institutions. In the safety of a consciousness-raising group, where the quality of reflection and dialogue is good, people tend to make these connections more easily.

There are a variety of ways to structure interaction within a consciousness-raising group. People can:

- share a common experience like those listed above and follow it with group reflection and/or evaluation;
- explore personal feelings and fears around difficult topics such as spending money, sexuality, use of drugs, exploitation of _____ by _____, lack of adequate employment;
- share with several close friends things such as living space, income, child care, food preparation;
- participate in a consciousness-raising workshop (see Part Six for information on how to put one together).

CONSCIOUSNESS-RAISING EXERCISES

Exercises explained below can help groups explore the relationship between personal problems and societal causes.

131

These exercises can be used by any consciousness-raising group but were designed for groups that want to apply their efforts to their work for social-political-economic change.

Exercises and tools listed elsewhere in the manual that can be used by consciousness-raising groups are:

Evaluation of almost any activity
Group Conversation
Sharing Personal Growth Experiences
Web Chart including both variations

1. *Statements Exercise*   (1½-2 hrs for 5-10 people)

Purpose/Uses: To help share ideas in an atmosphere of equal participation. To intensify discussion about a particular topic. To develop group awareness about a topic of their choice. To develop an appreciation of the diversity and strength of people's own resources. Expecially useful in groups that have not established a high trust level of have a problem with unequal participation.

Materials: 3x5 cards, pencils for each participant, chalkboard or flip chart.

Description:

1. Trainer and participants decide what topic they want to focus on. The topic or theme is stated in question form and writen on chalkboard or flipchart. The theme should be specific, such as "What is the first step we should take to effect change in _____ institution?" rather than "Changes in this institution."

2. Participants are given 3x5 cards and pencils and asked to write down their response to the topic. Their response can be in the form of suggestions or questions. Encourage brief responses. (5 min)

3. Cards (unsigned) are collected and shuffled. The trainer explains that the cards will now be passed around the circle, each person reading one card on the top. For one minute only the reader of the card is allowed to comment. The trainer should enforce the timing and not permit others to interject their opinions before one minute is up. At the end of one minute, the trainer says "one minute" and others in the group are allowed to comment on the card or the initial response to it. The time keeper should stop the discussion after two minutes even though discussion may be lively. (Strict enforcement of time limits is usually alienating but very important to keep discussions from going off on tangents, to allow for continual interjection of new ideas, to help people capsulize their thinking, and to insure equal participation. Explaining this at the beginning may help.) The

top card is then put on the bottom and the whole pack is passed to the next person. A person can respond to his/her own card, if s/he happens to draw it, or put it back into the pack. The cards are kept in a pack rather than passed separately so people will focus attention on the discussion at hand instead of concerning themselves with a response to their own card.

4. Be certain to get full agreement to use the discipline in #3 above.

5. When everyone has taken part and the cards have gone around, follow with full group discussion, for a period depending on the time left and the quality of the discussion.

Variation #1: Using pictures rather than written statements.

Description:

1. Provide magazines, such as *Ebony, Better Homes and Gardens,* or *Sports Illustrated*, which portray our society colorfully. Give each person 5 minutes to select a picture that says a lot about society, and ask participants to think about what they would like to say about the picture. Pictures can be provided ahead of time in a pile from which participants can choose.

2. Have each person in turn show a picture to the group, saying what s/he likes or dislikes, how it makes him/her feel.

3. Record these positive and negative reactions on a chart as each person presents his/hers.

4. Ask group to turn negative reactions into positive "wishes" for a new society, thus beginning to "picture" the new society in outline form.

Variation #2: As used in conjunction with questions brainstormed in *Macro-Analysis* seminars.

Purpose/Uses: To use material generated by people themselves.

Description:

First week: Brainstorm questions on given topic and list on a chart. Number questions.

Second Week: Shuffle numbers and pass out. Each person responds to question corresponding to number s/he picked.

2. *Risk List* *   (1 hr)

Purpose/Uses: To get people talking. To help them discover and investigate fears preventing them from getting involved in social change activities. To help people get to know each other.

---

* Original idea developed by Mary Fancher.

Can be used early in a weekend session to start people thinking about their own level or type of involvement.

Description:

1. Choose a question relevant to the group; e.g., "What would you be willing to do to end militarism?" The trainer may list 10-20 actions with varying degrees of risk involved, or actions may be brainstormed by the group. Let each person rank those actions according to his/her ability or willingness to do them, marking a cut-off point beyond which s/he would no longer act.

2. Divide participants into groups of not more than six members each. Ask members of each group to list factors they feel are most important to consider before taking a risk. Small groups may wish to consolidate lists of important factors.

3. *Option #1:* Ask individuals to rank actions following the discussion. Were there any changes in attitudes? If so, why? *Option #2:* Ask each small group to rank actions according to its willingness to participate as a group.

Caution: Trainers must take care that the risk list of actions and the questions for discussion are relevant to the group. Facilitators of small groups need to point out when discussion becomes judgmental. The exercise is not intended to divide the group or stigmatize individuals as less courageous than others.

Sample Risk List: *What would you do to end militarism?*

1. Write a letter to your congressperson. 2. Write a letter to the editor of the newspaper. 3. Work for the election to public office of a peace candidate. 4. Join a peace group. 5. Invite a draft resister to speak to your church group or club. 6. Participate in a vigil or demonstration. 7. Spend some time distributing leaflets downtown or at a shopping center. 8. Circulate a petition downtown or door to door. 9. Organize a campaign to get a local company to convert from producing war materials to producing civilian goods. 10. Refuse to pay Federal telephone tax (which is used for war). 11. Visit your local draft board or IRS office and confront employees about their jobs. 12. Give shelter and assistance to a GI who is AWOL and on his way to Canada. 13. Refuse to pay the military portion of your income tax and urge others to do likewise. 14. Publicly urge 18 year olds to consider not registering for the draft. 15. Join in mass nonviolent civil disobedience to convert the Pentagon into a life center, free clinic, etc. 16. Quit your job for one year to work full time in the peace movement. 17. Participate in blocking the operations of your regional IRS office or local draft board. 18. Participate in the destruction of

draft or IRS files. 19. Perform a citizen's arrest on a high government official.

3. *Life Line*   (45-60 min)

Purpose/Uses: To apply the techniques of planning and analysis to people's personal lives. Gives individuals a sense of past, present and future in their lives. Personal nature can build trust among participants.

Materials: Paper and crayons or pencils.

Description:

1. Each person takes a large piece of paper and a pencil or crayons and spends 15-20 minutes drawing a life line (or several) depicting past, present, and future events in his/her own life. The group should focus on a particular category such as work experiences, relationships with others, awareness of sex role oppressiveness or sense of community.

2. If there seems to be a good feeling of trust, have participants come back together and give a brief explanation of their life line charts to others. They could be posted in a gallery or kept as personal references.

Example:

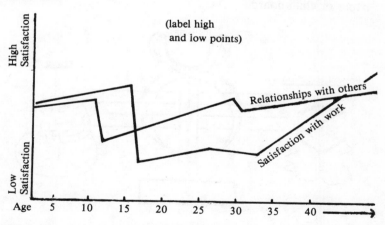

Variation: For examining relationships between personal life and work as seen by men and by women.

1. Have participants draw 3 or 4 life lines to show (1) highs and lows or "generally the way I felt"; (2) work; (3) personal relations/growth; or (4) other categories.

2. Examine what effect life lines (2), (3) or (4) had on life line (1).

135

3. Participants share insights with group. Facilitator can call attention to differences between men and women informally or list on a chart.

4. *Ice House Exercise*   (2 hrs)

Purpose/Uses: To help individuals develop a vision of how they want their lives to look in the future. To identify positive forces which help individuals to change and negative forces which hold them back. To identify the people who would be affected by a change in the individual's life. To identify a person's support community. To identify areas of one's life that one can control. To help identify the steps needed to change one's own life. To share visions, solve common problems, and build community. To help people understand what's involved in making decisions, and take more control over that process. This tool can be used to examine a total life change such as "living a simplified life," to examine just one part of life, such as "my vision for meaningful work," or to figure out what needs to happen next in a social change campaign.

Description:

1. Trainers place the following chart on a large piece of paper or chalkboard.

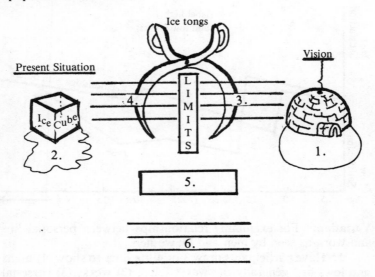

1. Description of Future	4. Forces Holding Me Back
2. Description of Present Situation	5. People Affected by Change
3. Forces Which Help Me Change	6. Steps I Must Take to Change

2. Individuals copy the chart and fill it out as numbered. Facilitators may want to assist individuals who have trouble with any of the 6 sections. If #6 is the problem, it may result from inadequate information in steps 1-5.   (45 min)

3. Participants form into groups of four, each using 10 minutes to share the information on his/her chart. Other group members may ask questions.

4. After all group members have shared, take 15 minutes for open discussion of insights gained through the exercise.

5. *Whole Person Exercise*   (In two parts: 1½ hrs each)

Purpose: To help people think about the forces that have acted on their lives. To think concretely about the next steps in their lives as part of a revolutionary process. To help people answer the following questions: (1) What are the forces, personal and social, that are encouraging me to work for change? (2) What are those things that prevent me from accomplishing my goals? (3) Are my long-range goals for myself consistent with my vision of the revolution? (4) What place do my decisions about my immediate future have in my long-range goals? (5) If I become involved in the revolutionary process, to whom am I responsible? (6) What part does my next step or decision play in freeing others to become part of the revolutionary process?

Description:

This exercise is usually done in two separate sessions. Either part can be done without the other, but they were designed to be used together. Preparation of the circles may be done by individuals before each session and brought to the group to be shared.

Since this exercise produces some very personal information, facilitators should explain at the beginning that group sharing will follow preparation of personal charts. Persons can choose not to show their charts and simply share verbally instead.

PART ONE: *"Life Forces" circle*

1. If both parts are to be used, the trainer describes briefly the whole exercise. Referring to a sample "Life Forces" chart, the trainer gives instructions for Part One.

2. By themselves participants list the major forces that have acted in their own lives to form who they are and their attitudes toward social change. These forces should include both positive and negative experiences in areas such as: personal history, family, economics, education, social status in community, and strong personal experiences. These forces are written around the

outside of a large circle. Arrows can be used to show that the forces acted on the person from outside. Inside the circle, corresponding to each of the forces, should be an area which states the resulting dilemma, feeling, positive direction, or question which is a result of that force. If this is done during group meeting time, allow 45-60 minutes.

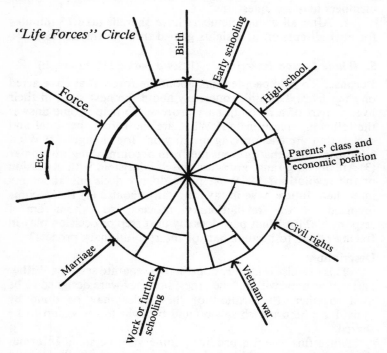

"Life Forces" Circle

3. The circle, when finished, is shared in small groups of 3-4 persons. Each person has from 5-10 minutes to share his/her circle and insights. It is helpful to allow 2 to 3 minutes for feedback from others after each person has shared his/her circle.

4. Following small-group sharing, the large group can discuss insights. Some points that may be considered are: (1) We are never free from the forces that have acted upon us until we come to terms with them. Nothing in our past ever just disappears. (2) Looking at forces is a way of understanding the nature of our connection to the society that we live in. (3) We cannot deny what our own history says that we are. We do not become new persons overnight, but change and grow, rooted in our own history. (4) A large part of working for social change is dealing with one's own experience of oppression. (5) Under-

standing our own history and coming to terms with it is the way we organize on the basis of self-interest—that is, to identify our oppressions and join others with similar oppressions. (6) Understanding the forces that have acted on us enables us to choose where to work intelligently and not reactively on the basis of what we are running away from.

PART TWO: *"What Next" and "Long Range Goals" Circles*

1. Referring to the sample circles, the trainer gives instructions for Part Two.

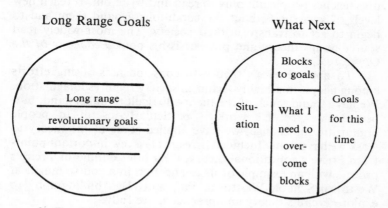

Long Range Goals

Long range
revolutionary goals

What Next

Blocks to goals

Situ-ation

What I need to over-come blocks

Goals for this time

2. Participants fill in the circle for long-range revolutionary goals, keeping in mind the questions: What do I want to happen in my life with regard to my ideas and values about social change? Where do I see my life headed?

3. Next, they fill in the circle of "what next," looking ahead 6 months to a year. This circle has three sections: (1) the present situation, (2) my goals for the next 6-12 months, and (3) the blocks to my goals, including things needed to overcome these blocks.

Under the section on "present situation," people should consider: With whom will I be working? Where will I be living? From where will my support come? and What will the focus of my work be?

Under the section on "blocks to my goals" and "things needed to overcome those blocks" people should consider: What other resources can I draw on? People? Community? Other groups? If the blocks cannot be overcome, am I locked into the situation or do I have other options? Are the goals for this period consistent with my long term goals?

If steps 2 and 3 are done during group meeting time allow 45-60 minutes.

4. Each person shares his/her circle (5-10 min), reflecting on the experience. More general insights are then shared in the full group.

THE EDUCATIONAL THEORY OF PAULO FREIRE AND ITS IMPORTANCE FOR RAISING CONSCIOUSNESS

Paulo Freire's work with illiterate adults in northeast Brazil and Chile has become a source of great interest among educators and organizers for social change. The process of education he uses teaches people not only to read and write but to reach new levels of awareness about the conditions around them and to begin to act to transform their society. The most widely read source on his theory and practice is his book *Pedagogy of the Oppressed*.

To apply Freire's theory to consciousness-raising efforts among people in a highly technical society requires imagination. We have found much of the theory difficult to understand; but, because we feel his work is particularly useful to people organizing for change, we have applied some of his theory to work we have done. Included here are (1) a few important points from Freire's educational theory, (2) a brief outline of Freire's process with an example of its application in a course taught at Westtown School, Westtown, Pa., and (3) a bibliography to explore Freire's theory and practice more fully.

1. Some Important Points from Freire's Educational Theory

The major task of human beings is humanization, the process of becoming more human. This process of growth includes being in touch with our needs and aspirations, emancipating labor, overcoming alienation, affirming people as persons and not objects, developing new visions of what it means to be human, and awakening our consciousness to the necessity of developing strategies and tactics that will help us attain our vision. The goals of all people should be to liberate themselves and those that oppress them. Education is one process for liberation; unfortunately, educational processes and programs frequently turn into instruments of domestication rather than liberation.

Two processes of education known to us are the Banking form and the Problem Posing form.

Banking/Anti-dialogic Form of Education:

The banking, or narrative, form of education turns the student into an object or receptacle into which the teacher makes deposits of material to be learned or retained. The teacher's job is to "fill" the students with information. The material to be retained is frequently alien to the student's existing situation. Rarely is the object of the student's study the reality around him/her. Teachers are judged or evaluated by how well, using a narrative method, they fill students with information.

In contrast to the banking method is the dialogic approach. Freire believes that knowledge develops from people's relationship with and inquiry into the world around them. It is the result of dialogue which allows people to invent new ideas and re-invent solutions to human problems. There are basic contradictions between the theory and practice of the banking form of education, which excludes dialogue, and Freire's theory of how students gain knowledge of their world. The banking form creates a dehumanized situation for both the teacher and the learner and perpetuates the oppression of the latter. This oppression is found in the following attitudes and practices that are commonly encountered in the banking form of education:

- "the teacher teaches and the students are taught";
- "the teacher knows everything and the students know nothing";
- "the teacher thinks and the students are thought about";
- "the teacher acts and the students have the illusion of acting through the action of the teacher";
- "the teacher chooses the program content and the students adapt to it";
- "the teacher is the subject (in the grammatical sense) of the learning process, while the students are mere objects." *

The banking form of education does not foster creative ability; in fact, it is a tool of domestication and control used by oppressors to "change the consciousness of the oppressed, not the situation that oppresses them."**

The banking form, with its abstract focus, frequently mythologizes reality and attempts to conceal certain facts about how people exist in the world. The process and content create attitudes in the learner that prevent him/her from acting to change unjust social conditions, allowing authorities and institutions of oppression to control his/her life. People who are concerned with real liberation and are opposed to oppression cannot subscribe to a form of education where learners are viewed as blank slates to be written upon by an all-knowing teacher.

* Paulo Freire, *Pedagogy of the Oppressed*, p. 58.
** Ibid., p. 60.

Problem Posing/Dialogic Education:

People need to explore a dialogic approach and enter into a process which poses problems about the participants' world which can be discussed by the group.

The first step in moving from the banking/narrative process to the problem posing/dialogic process involves resolving the student/teacher contradiction which exists between the two approaches. To resolve the contradiction, the teacher and the student must undergo attitudinal changes which affect how they behave in their roles. The change for the teacher involves becoming a co-learner and co-investigator of the world *with* the student rather than *for* the student. The students must also change, in that they must break their patterns of inactivity, relying on the teacher to think and act for them, and take a position of co-learner/co-actor with the teacher. Students and teachers are responsible for a process of reflection upon the world and then action upon *their* perceptions to attain mutual growth and liberation.

The subject of study in the problem-posing process is the world around the co-learners, both student and teacher. This process attempts to de-mythologize reality so as to empower people to act and transform the world. The process of de-mythologizing social attitudes, practices, and institutions requires critical dialogue and thinking not included in the banking/anti-dialogic form of education. If education is to be truly liberating, it must focus upon the existing situation of people, allow them to reflect upon their condition, and empower them to change it.

Discovering People's Themes:

The beginning of the educational/learning process involves a critical examination of the world around the co-learners, students and teachers. The goal of the examination is to uncover the *themes* which dominate the lives of the people.

Themes include: the basic needs of the people, their aspirations for a different life, their oppressions, and the thoughts and actions that they might use to liberate themselves from their oppressions. Themes vary in size from large societal themes, such as political oppression in Latin America or alienation from meaningful work in the United States, to smaller sub-themes which are more specific and peculiar to a particular region or institution.

It is important to remember that all themes are linked. A major goal of the problem-posing approach is to reveal the connections between social oppressions so that people can develop an over-all approach to change.

Each theme contains several different components. One of

these parts is a *contradiction*. Contradictions are the opposing forces within a given social problem which are the motivators for change. For example, women are treated differently from men on the job market. Women are frequently denied employment in particular types of jobs for cultural, traditional, or sexist reasons. This theme, which is common to many women in the U.S. today, reveals two forces: first, a societal behavioral pattern which defines women's roles and limits their work possibilities, and second, the ideal that women and men should be treated equally. The struggle between the forces which encourage static roles for women and the forces which encourage human liberation and equality is embodied within the theme of women's condition in the job market. *Revolutionary education should expose contraditions so that people can reflect and act upon them.*

Themes also contain or imply *limit situations,* the particular forces which prevent people from becoming more human, and *limit acts*, the actions that people can take to break through the limit situation.

The problem-posing process seeks to expose the contradictions through critical analysis, discover the limit situations, look for limit acts, and empower the people to act upon their perceptions and conclusions.

2. The Process Step-By-Step

An outline of the process used by Freire follows. The left-hand column describes the theoretical development of the learning process while the right-hand column describes the concrete experiences used in an adaptation of the Freire process to life in a contemporary high school. For more information on the course itself, see The Problem Posing/Dialogic Approach under Part Six: Training and Education.

EXAMPLE OF THE APPLICATION

FREIRE THEORY

I. Preliminary Investigation

- Facilitators investigate the existing situation of the group with which the curriculum is to be developed.
- Secondary sources are used.

II. Investigation.

Meeting with the group

1. Explanation of the investigation process—finding the group's themes and then turning them into problems (codifications) to be examined (decoded) by the group.

1. Explanation of the investigation process—finding the group's themes and then turning them into problems (codifications) to be examined (decoded) by the group.

2. Discussion on the theory/process of education.

3. Gaining group approval for participation in the learning process.

4. Asking for volunteers from the group who will be co-investigators for themes with the facilitators. (Co-investigation is part of the learning process; it develops proficiency in critical analysis.)

Investigation

1. Facilitators and participants* make concrete observations of the conditions of the group (work, play, social customs, authority, religion, etc.).

—Observations by the facilitators should be as value-free as possible.

—These observations take apart (de-codify) the people's life in order to examine it in more detail.

2. Evaluation

—Draw up brief reports of findings

—Look for nuclei of contradictions (small contradictions in everyday life which might have societal causes), and look for possible limit situations.

—Investigate with the group the level of its awareness of the

---

* Facilitators and participants *both* play an active role in this learning process. The term "facilitator" refers to a person who also performs a specialized role of thinking about and helping the group through the learning process.

OF FREIRE'S THEORY

APPLICATION IN WESTTOWN HIGH SCHOOL

I. Preliminary Investigation

• Facilitators held discussions with initial contact person about type of training desired.

• They learned about the school, students' environment, courses, extra-curricular activities, gripes, etc.

II. Investigation

Meeting with the class

1. Explanation was made of the development of the training process and its different parts: training for nonviolent action, group dynamics, and Macro-analysis.

2. Explanation was made of the Freire theory of education, with discussion and questions.

3. The class's approval was sought and gained to begin to find themes and develop curriculum.

4. Explanation was made of how the Statements Exercise and Brainstorming allow the whole class to participate as co-investigators of themes.

Investigation

1. Facilitators and participants used the Statements Exercise and Brainstorming to explore themes:

—*Statements Exercise*—Each participant, facilitators included, brings a picture, poem, object, etc. to the first class which expresses how s/he sees and feels about our society. All the things that people bring are placed in the middle of a small group (six). Each person takes an object, which is not his/her own, and explains to the group (1 minute) how the object does or does not reflect his/her view of society. There is a second minute for other members of the group to respond. The facilitator records information shared. These statements indicate the group's themes.

—*Brainstorm* and select goals—In small groups (six) people brainstorm their goals and expectations. Each small group selects its five major goals and presents them to the group. Goals are recorded on large sheets of newsprint. The whole group combines and modifies goals until satisfied.

2. *Evaluation*—The group organized themes and looked for contradictions and forces that prevent people from becoming more human. It approved the themes it felt were most important

145

THEORY (Cont.)

limit situations. (The same limit situations for different groups in different geographical locations may imply different themes and limit acts.)

—Group must begin to recognize different limit situations which have not been tested by action.

III. Codification: Making the Theme into a Problem

Codification

Team of investigators selects several themes and the contradictions contained within the themes to develop into a problem.

Guidelines for Codification

1. The problem must represent a familar and easily recognized situation of the group being investigated.

2. The nucleus of the problem, the contradiction, must not be overly clear nor overly perplexing. The problem should allow for a variety of solutions.

3. The problems (codifications) should be organized into a thematic fan; themes should connect in that the analysis of one should open up in the direction of other themes. The themes should make up a total picture of the lives of the group.

4. Contradictions within one problem should include contradictions which are part of a system of contradictions under study.

5. The problem must relate to the felt needs of the group.

Codification (Problem) Types

The first codification is a very simple one; it serves to introduce the group to the theme and to the process of dialogic examination (decodification). This is known as an "essential" codification. The "essential" codification is followed by other "auxiliary" codifications which broaden the theme and are more difficult. The combination of "essential" and "auxiliary" codifications (problems) gives the group a chance to examine the totality of the theme. "Individuals who were *submerged* (dominated) in reality, merely *feeling* their needs, *emerge* from reality and perceive the *causes* of their needs."

Codification (Problem) Possibilities

    Simple

        Visual—pictures, movies, film strips, etc.

        Tactile—encounter/group dynamics, etc.

APPLICATION (Cont.)

to explore. (See the list of goals from the Westtown class listed in Part Six under Course Design A.)

III. Codification: Planning for the Problem-Solving Process

Facilitators selected themes—Facilitators brainstormed all the possible ways to present the themes that the group had selected. They selected the ones that most clearly presented the themes.

Facilitators selected problems to be decoded

1. Facilitators selected the questions (a) "What are violence and nonviolence?" (b) "What are violent action and nonviolent action?"

2. Questions were turned into problems which the group would examine (decode); through dialogue they would clarify their concepts of violence and nonviolence.

Facilitators translated themes into exercises for problem solving

1. **Brainstorming** the characteristics of violence and nonviolence, comparing the results, and arriving at a group definition of each term.

2. **Violence/Nonviolence Social Good Chart**—to clarify the differences between violent and nonviolent action and to explore some of the personal and societal values which qualify their perceptions.

3. **Hassle Line**—an essential codification situation (one that introduces the group to the process and to a new theme): A teacher finds a student smoking a cigarette in the woods. Smoking is forbidden by school policy. One participant plays the teacher and another the student.

4. Group **Roleplays**—auxiliary codifications (those that develop the theme and help introduce new themes and problems). Group will be invited to break into small groups and construct a roleplay which involves personal violence/nonviolence. The roleplay will then be presented to the group as a whole for evaluation. The facilitator, who will lead the evaluation, will help the group: (a) clarify the problem, (b) explore feelings, (c) explore causes, (d) invent possible solutions, and (e) test those solutions (limit-acts) by repeating the roleplay.

THEORY (Cont.)

Auditory—newspaper clippings, brief reports, records, songs of the group, poems, etc.
Compound
Combinations of simple ones above.
Activities such as *Street Speaking, Radical Street Theater, Roleplaying, Strategy Games, Quick Decision* exercises, *Situation Analysis*, etc.

Hinged Themes—themes which connect one thematic problem to another—may be introduced by the facilitators to ease the transition from one problem to another.

IV. Decodification—Problem Solving

• Group selects a theme that has been turned into a problem (codified), examines it, discusses it, explores causes and limit situations and possible limit acts.
• Facilitator acts as coordinator of decodification by listening, challenging individuals, and posing problems, using the codified problem and its answers.

V. Interdisciplinary Study and Final Codification

• Themes are categorized into different social science disciplines and a detailed study is made. Each social scientist then presents a proposed breakdown or elaboration of his/her theme, noting the contradictions and possible problems that could be created from them. Different themes are discussed and modified and the rest of the team makes suggestions. The group explores hinged themes, those themes which facilitate the transition from one major theme to another. A bibliography is prepared.
• Final Codification

VI. Represent to the People Their Own Themes in the Form of Codifications

VII. Decodification—Problem Solving (Problems—Causes—Solutions—Actions)

APPLICATION (Cont.)

IV. Problem Solving

• Facilitation team presented exercises developed in step III as the proposed agenda for the session and gained the group's approval to proceed. (If a group does not agree that the proposed material will meet some of its goals and expectations, alternative themes and codifications must be presented.)

• Group participated in *Brainstorming, Violence/Nonviolence Social Good Chart* discussion, and *Roleplaying*.

• Facilitators led *Evaluation*. Group looked for high points, low points, statements on what individuals learned, how the goals and expectations could have been more successfully explored, and what would have improved the session.

V, VI, VII

• Because of limited time or resources, the last several steps were dropped. The team then continued to elaborate and develop on the themes already discovered by this group.

3. Bibliography of Freire and Freire-related Resources

"The Adult Literacy Process as Cultural Action for Freedom," in *World Development: An Introductory Reader*, Helene Castel, ed. (Macmillan Co., 1971). Examination of consciousness raising, using practical examples from Freire's experiences in Latin America.

"Cultural Action for Freedom," *Harvard Educational Review,* May and Sept. 1970. (Also available from Center for the Study of Development and Social Change, 1430 Mass. Ave., Cambridge, MA 01250.)

"Education for Awareness: A talk with Paulo Freire," in *Risk,* vol. 6, no. 4, 1970. (Available from the World Council of Churches, Publications Service, 475 Riverside Drive, Room 439, New York, NY 10027, 75¢.) A lively and less formal slice of theory and thought from Freire.

Paulo Freire: A Revolutionary Dilemma for the Adult Educator, Occasional Paper #32, Stanley Grobowski, ed., (Syracuse University, 1972). (Available from Clearinghouse on Adult Education, 107 Roney La., Syracuse, NY 13210, $4.00.) A collection of writings and bibliographies about experiments using the Freire process.

Pedagogy of the Oppressed, by Paulo Freire (Herder and Herder, 1970). The basic statement of theory by the Brazilian educator whose work in increasing literacy led to insights into the way people's consciousness is changed when they enter into a critical dialogic relationship with their world. Written from a third world perspective, the book's primary thesis is that education is not neutral but is either for the domestication or freedom of the people being educated. Freire's theories have many applications for "first world" situations.

Towards the Societal Transformation of America's Imperialist Environment: The Applicability of the Pedagogy of Paulo Freire, and other Latin American Action and Reflection upon the Social Change Process in the United States, by Philip E. Wheaton (EPICA, 1500 Farragut, NW, Washington, DC 20011, 1975, $1.00). Appendix includes a list of groups using Paulo Freire's methods whose insights contributed to the document.

EASY DOES IT

Words and music by Ellen Deacon
© *1975 Ellen Deacon*

Easy does it, easy does it.
I always knew there was more for me
Than fighting hard to set myself free.
So I quit fighting and let myself be—it's in me.

Easy does it, easy does it.
I always figure there's something wrong
When I must struggle too hard to be strong.
So then I let go and think of this song—it's in me.

Easy does it, easy does it.
Sometimes your feelings make things look tough,
But you can think even when it gets rough.
Just trust yourself and it's easy enough—it's in you.

Easy does it, easy does it.
The beauty in you just grows like a seed,
With love to nurture and water and feed.
The strength you have is all that you need—it's in you.

Easy does it, easy does it.
Like a leaf that falls to the ground,
Spins and whirls and dances around,
You'll settle on the truth to be found—it's in you, it's in me.

151

Part Six
Training
and Education

Training as we use it is a structured learning experience that is experimental, cooperative, and egalitarian. Co-learners share responsibility for facilitating their own education, through which they learn individual and group skills necessary to resist oppressive forces and to act to improve their living situations.

The content of our training is developed from the interests and concerns of group members. Through the use of a variety of tools, people are empowered to examine their world and their own feelings and needs, to identify personal or common problems, to develop structures which help them to understand problems, and to make changes in their lives and the world around them.

This training process has frequently been referred to as "nonviolence training" or "training for nonviolent action," because many people first used it while participating in nonviolent action. Whenever actions require a particular style or approach because of a commitment to nonviolence, it is appropriate to refer to this as training for nonviolent action. This manual, however, reflects expanded uses of training, and for that reason "training for social change" is a more accurate description of the process. People whose basic commitments are humanistic or religious in nature, whether or not they have a commitment to nonviolence, have also used our training process with success.

I
Why is Training Important?

People want to act wisely and positively to improve their living situations but usually feel powerless to resist undesirable trends or make needed changes. As a result of the type of education most of us received, we often are unclear about our own needs, are confused about the nature and causes of problems, lack concrete organizing skills, and fear conflicts which surface when we try to make changes. New training processes are important because they help people retrain themselves out of customary ways of reacting into creative, spontaneous ways of responding to problems and initiating alternatives.

More specifically, this type of training:

• develops skills in a variety of areas such as conflict resolution, democratic decision making, organizing a campaign or alternative institution;

• promotes a common analysis and helps people choose effective strategy and tactics for change;

• introduces cooperative ways that people can learn about and change their world;

• promotes the development of local communities of support and a network of communication among them necessary for sustained work for change;

• helps people share and evaluate mutual experiences, learn together and build mutual support;

• prepares people for long and short-term struggle for change;

• allows ideas, skills and organizing methods to be developed and tested first in practice situations where risks are easier to take and mistakes are less costly;

• develops skills for clear thinking in crisis situations which require quick and creative responses;

• identifies specific organizing problems;

• helps the group evaluate experiences and develop principles by which problems can be solved in future organizing efforts;

• teaches methods of creating trust and solidarity that can be effectively applied to withstand discouragement and repression.

II
Training
Its Basis, Its Uses

BASIS OF OUR TRAINING PROCESS

Included in any training process are components which influence the way people learn and use their skills. When fully incorporated into the training process, these components become the basis for people's personal activities and the institutions they will build. The training process explained in this manual consciously includes components which reflect the kind of society in which participant/trainers wish to live. Some of the basic components are listed briefly below. Most are covered in more depth in other sections of the manual.

Making Decisions Which Affect Your Life—Large institutions, social pressures, and family expectations influence the way individuals live. Economic and emotional rewards and punishments are offered for various behaviors. Often decisions are mandated or are made unconsciously. People who learn how to identify their own needs are in a better position to take more control over their lives. The training process encourages people to make conscious decisions and develop small groups of support for creative follow-through.

Consensus—The use of consensus decision making permeates the training process. Though consensus takes practice and is sometimes more time-consuming, people feel more included and decisions made are usually wiser and more enthusiastically implemented.

Voluntary participation—When people attend a training session or workshop against their will, they not only learn less but also usually disrupt the learning process for others. When working in schools or other institutions where attendance is compulsory, it is necessary to explain carefully the importance of voluntarism to the process and encourage only interested people to stay. If in the middle of a training experience an individual begins to doubt the willingness of his/her own participation, trainers/facilitators should make clear that withdrawing from the training session is an acceptable course of action.

Identifying Needs and Acting On Them—Many people are trapped by the myth that governments, corporations, teachers, and other professionals have better information than they do and are in the best position to analyze people's needs. The training process assumes that individuals and groups are able to identify their own needs and act on them. The emphasis is upon helping people to develop skills needed to identify and meet real needs.

Affirmation—Our society frequently gives critical, negative evaluations of people which in time contribute to feelings of inadequacy. This negative societal behavior can be countered by creating an atmosphere of acceptance and appreciation which allows people to realize their potential more quickly. Genuine affirmation of people's positive qualities and accomplishments is a crucial step in empowering them to take charge of their learning and decision-making processes. For more information see *Affirmation* in Part Three.

Cooperative Group Learning and Community Support—For basic institutional and personal changes to occur, people must work creatively with others and receive mutual support. The training process encourages cooperative learning, through which co-learners can share information and insights and build on each other's ideas. Community-building activities help develop a level of trust which nurtures individual learning and provide opportunity to work together on common goals. Given the difficulty of most social and personal problems, cooperative involvement provides an important opportunity for people to support each other, practice making group decisions, and share skills and resources to implement decisions.

The Useability of Skills—Skills learned through training for social change, whether theoretical or practical, are usable in a variety of situations. Since participants are in charge of the training process, they can choose to learn those skills that are most quickly transferable to their immediate situation.

Human Values—The training process recognizes people as more important than the roles they fill or the institutions in which they function. The focus is on the growth and development of people as a basis for structural change. When structures threaten people's welfare, they must be changed to reflect the needs of people. As a result an emphasis is placed on positive human qualities such as openness, truthfulness, and refusal to inflict hurt on others. An awareness of people's potential for good and their ability to take responsibility for their lives in creative ways is essential for training to succeed.

Change and Conflict—Change and conflict are here to stay. The problem facing us is how to participate in the decisions that change our lives and how to respond to conflicts in positive and creative ways. Training offers processes and skills which can be used to mediate and resolve conflicts with greater success.

Sharing Feelings—People need outlets for strong feelings, which if criticized or blocked can stifle clear thinking, prevent learning and growth, and cause frustrations. Sharing feelings with others can release tensions, free energy, and unfold new perspectives on problems. Our training accepts feelings as an important part of the social change process and offers structures through which people can release and share feelings at appropriate times without hurting each other.

CONTENT AREAS AROUND WHICH TRAINING HAS BEEN USED

Because the main purpose of training is to prepare people to solve their problems, the training process has been used in a variety of content areas. Some of these are briefly described here. Sample workshops in most of these areas are included later.

Community Building—The foundations for successful resistance and on-going struggle are groups of people who have a sense of community and support in their relationships with each other. Training tools such as *Affirmation Exercises, Listening Exercises*, and structures for sharing experiences and feelings have aided groups in developing good interactions which make change more possible and life more fulfilling.

Consciousness Raising—Within small groups, people explore personal hurts and discover their social causes. Tools such as the *Statements Exercise* develop awareness about personal and societal problems, while the *Web Chart* and the *Whole Person Exercise* can be used to connect personal problems with their institutional causes.

Democratic Decision Making—For social change groups to act efficiently, they need to have an effective decision-making process. Training for democratic decision making provides groups and institutions with skills that allow them to examine their group dynamics, solve group and individual problems, learn better facilitation, develop a process of shared leadership, and use consensus. Decision-making skills help people discover their own needs, determine priorities for work, establish creative and humanizing work relationships, and develop processes for evaluation.

Conflict Resolution—People who are living or working together eventually come into conflict with each other. Conflict resolution training helps individuals and groups to manage or resolve conflict situations within or between groups. Some of the skills include: negotiation/mediation structures, dialogue skills, third party presence techniques, and nonviolent intervention.

Conflict resolution ranges from the resolution of personal differences to intervention for defusing violent intra-community conflicts.

Crisis Intervention—Crisis intervention training teaches skills needed by groups managing large group situations with a potential for rioting. Dealing with immediate post-crisis situations is also important. Skills in this area include marshaling, negotiation, observation, and third party intervention.

Nonviolent Action—A characteristic defining nonviolent action is that participants learn to respond even to violent attacks with disciplined nonviolent behavior. Training for nonviolent action usually includes (1) preparation for the action through roleplaying, strategy games, analysis of the event and on-going evaluation, (2) learning action skills such as making decisions under stress, leafleting and street speaking, and (3) learning practical skills such as basic first aid and cooking for large groups. The focus of training is often on preparation for one event and the clarification of what is to be done by specific people. An expanded form of nonviolent action training is the campaign-building workshop. In addition to teaching preparation, action, and practical skills, campaign-building offers skills in developing an analysis, theory, vision, and strategy and in choosing tactics which help participants reach long and short-range goals.

Nonviolent Civilian Defense—Nonviolent civilian defense refers to the defense of a culture or a way of life, as opposed to defense of territory, by a civilian population using nonviolent means. There are numerous historical examples of nonviolent civilian resistance (see *The Politics of Nonviolent Action*, by Sharp, and *War Without Weapons*, by Boserup and Mack), although little training was involved in preparing the population for the action. Training for future nonviolent civilian defense can take the form of simulations, strategy games, and extended roleplays which allow prospective defenders to experiment with organizational forms, strategies and tactics.

THE RESPONSIBILITIES OF TRAINERS AND PARTICIPANTS

A *trainer* is a person who is given primary responsibility for planning or leading a session or workshop. S/he usually has more information or experience than other participants and may get permission to direct a group for hours at a time. It is the trainers' responsibility to see that preliminary planning is done, options are discussed with participants, and the format is acceptable to trainers and participants.

Participants agree to undergo the training experience together and make clear contracts among themselves and with trainers as to the length, content and process involved. Participants should make decisions about their training to the fullest extent possible and feasible. If participants are inexperienced, trainers may at first be given more decision-making responsibility or a large degree of freedom to suggest options. Participants, however, always have final responsibility for their own learning process and need to agree from the beginning as to the basic purposes and content of the workshop.

Good *facilitation* is necessary throughout a session or workshop. This responsibility may be assigned either to trainers or to participants, or shared between them. A facilitator is aware of the process of training and oversees sessions when group decisions need to be made. The more experience participants have with facilitation, the more able they are to share this function.

Sharing the role of the trainer: Many of the tools suggested in this manual are simple to use and can be quickly explained by any participant. Sometimes trainers are needed due to the complexity or special requirements of a tool. Inexperienced trainers can guide a group through most of the activities by carefully reading them in advance. When using training for the first time, a group may need or want a person experienced in the process. It is important to note that where a trainer is required, the roles of participants and trainers are mutually exclusive and need to be well defined. Using this manual as a resource, groups will be able to share the role of "trainer" among their members from session to session.

USING TRAINING RESOURCES

While training ourselves and others for effective social change work, we have used special tools. Many of the tools described in the manual did not originate with us, but we have used and refined them, and when they have not met our needs we have developed others.

A *tool*, to us, is something that is useful in work for social change, just as a hammer, a saw, or a construction crew is useful in building houses. Tools include group exercises and games used in training sessions, but larger processes like macro-analysis, peer counseling or nonviolent action campaigns can be regarded as tools for social change.

We have tried to distinguish between a *game*, a tool with

rules which dictate both structure and content, and an *exercise*, a tool where participants provide the content and where the structure can be changed to meet the needs of the group. We have also tried to distinguish between a *game or exercise*, a tool which assists in the learning process, and an actual *skill*, an ability learned.

Suggestions for Use of Training Resources

1. Be flexible. Training should be tailored to fit the needs of participants—the right tool at the right time.

2. Carefully explain exercises and games the first time they are used—including the simpler ones. Terms such as "brainstorm" and "evaluation" may have a general meaning for many people, but don't expect familiarity with the specific structure used.

3. Most skills and tools can be learned well through intensive 1-day to 2-week workshops. See descriptions of workshops below for planning suggestions and examples.

4. Evaluation is a skill that should be used repeatedly in learning and using all other skills and tools.

5. Practice in real situations is essential for developing a high degree of competence in action, facilitation, and practical skills.

6. When skills and tools learned in the past are needed again, especially just before difficult events, it is often wise to plan a refresher workshop.

Steps for Choosing Tools or Designing New Ones

1. Define the problem. Aspects to consider are: (a) What are people's needs as they experience them? (b) What are the group's needs as it stated them in its list of goals and expectations? (c) What are the trainers' perceptions of what people need? (d) Which exercises have people responded to positively and which negatively? (e) What emotional tensions or other problems in the group need to be countered?

2. Brainstorm visions about the best experiences that could happen in the group. Include possible exercises that might be learned and effects on the development of community.

3. Brainstorm "old" tools that might meet the needs of participants.

4. Combine old and new ideas or develop a totally new exercise. Affirm each other's efforts. Negating people's ideas causes defensiveness and stifles creativity. Assume that an idea might work and try to build on it before discarding it.

5. Polish new tool. Clarify how it works. List steps in presenting it to the group. Correct any flaws.

160

6. Evaluate the tool. (a) Does it help to meet people's needs? (b) Does it help participants develop new insights into the problem or situation? (c) Does it raise new questions? (d) Is the exercise too risky for participants? (e) Is it clear enough for others to use the tool later?

7. Try it with the group.

8. Ask participants to evaluate the effectiveness of the tool and project how the tool could be improved or better used.

III
Workshops

Short and intensive periods of training, lasting from three hours to two weeks in length, have been found to be effective for learning social change theory and skills. This section includes guidelines for construction of a workshop, components to consider when designing sessions, and sample workshops in a variety of areas.

CONSTRUCTING A TRAINING WORKSHOP

When planning a training workshop, it is essential to consider the goals and expectations of participants from the very beginning. When people are exploring a general area of interest, such as group dynamics or conflict resolution, it is often useful to develop a general idea of what might be included, have a variety of resources on hand, and include participants in the process of deciding goals for the workshop.

Sometimes content and process of a workshop can be determined in advance. This is particularly true when participants are being prepared for a limited event, such as marshaling at a demonstration or organizing a specific action campaign. When workshops planned in advance lose excitement or relevance, the process should be stopped while goals and expectations of participants can be discussed and, if necessary, renegotiated.

When participants are to be included in the planning of the workshop, the following guidelines may be useful.

Planning the First Session

1. Compile all information known about the group or individuals participating, including (a) history, (b) stated goals and expectations, (c) past successes and failures, (d) personalities, and (e) strengths and weaknesses. If the group has functioned as a group prior to this workshop, gather any news clippings about

161

or literature by the group. Talk with group members individually or collectively.

2. Given what is known about the group, consider what we as trainers would like to see happen to the individuals and the group as a result of the training experience. What do we perceive they need? What can we provide? What are our goals?

3. Check on situations which may modify the process and content of the workshop.

    (a) Are people's goals for the workshop feasible? Do individuals have conflicting goals?

    (b) What are the needs of the immediate community?

    (c) How can this training experience connect the participants to a network of people working in social change?

    (d) If training is being done inside an institution, what are the expectations of the institution?

    (e) If training is for an action project, what logistical information is needed?

4. Given information gathered in steps 1-3, brainstorm tools that could be used to reach goals.

5. Identify what is to be covered during the first session.

6. Identify the tools or exercises that will be used during the first session, allotting time blocks for each item.

7. Review proposed agenda for the session so that all planners are clear about what will be done.

8. Divide facilitation responsibility among the trainers.

Possible Agenda for the First Session   (2¾ hours)

- Introduction of trainers.   (5 min)
- Explanation of *Affirmation* and how participants will use it to introduce each other.   (5 min)
- *Affirmation Exercises to Introduce Each Other.*   (20 min)
- Explanation of (a) trainer's role, (b) the process for the workshop, and (c) how following sessions will be constructed to meet the participants' goals and expectations.   (8 min)
- Agenda review and getting group agreement to proceed. (3 min)
- *Determine Goals and Expectations* for the workshop. (15 min)
- Exercise(s) to build community, develop trust, increase understanding as to how the group functions and/or give opportunity to work on a common task. Include evaluation of exercise(s). A variety of exercises for these purposes is available in the manual under Group Dynamics, Community Building or Consciousness Raising.

• *Brief Evaluation of a Meeting.* (5 min)
• Closing. Share things which allow people to end a session feeling good, such as affirmations or a short, enjoyable game. (5-10 min)

Presenting Proposals to the Group

1. Review proposed agenda. Explain the purpose of each exercise and how it relates to goals and expectations agreed upon by the group.

2. Get verbal agreement from the group for trainers to facilitate for the group *and* get approval of the proposed agenda.

3. If the group fails to approve the proposed agenda, (1) request information on how the agenda could be modified to better meet the group's needs, (2) take a break if necessary so that trainers can develop a new agenda, and (3) involve participants in the planning wherever possible.

Planning Later Sessions

1. Check out how trainers felt about the previous session and how they worked together. Trainers need a chance to unload accumulated tensions and feelings, blow off steam, and relax.

2. Review goals and expectations of the group, focusing on priority goals.

3. Share insights gained by trainers as to what the group needs.

4. Clarify what trainers can and cannot do. If participants are expecting trainers to function in roles not acceptable to trainers, e.g., trainers are expected to be therapists for one or more deeply distressed individuals, decide what needs to happen.

5. Select tools and exercises for the balance of the workshop, combining old ones or developing new ones where necessary.

6. Build an agenda and allocate time blocks. Divide responsibilities.

DESIGNING SESSIONS WITHIN A WORKSHOP
Contracting With the Group

Early in a workshop trainers need to get the approval of the group for them to train, facilitate, and make proposals for learning exercises. Participation is voluntary. Trainers working in institutions where participation in classes is not voluntary need to be especially careful to explain the voluntary nature of training sessions and to try to contract with the group. Trainers should make a verbal contract with the group at each session. If maximum learning and involvement are to be achieved, it is important for participants to agree to the content and the process.

Use of Facilitation Tools

Tools like *Introductions, Brainstorming* and *Time Limits* should be used regularly as needed. See "Tools Used Frequently at Meetings" under Part Two.

Pace

Sessions need to move rapidly enough so that participants do not get bored but not so fast that they get lost. Pace can be regulated by:
- trainers' energy and enthusiasm;
- a balance of physical activities with intellectual ones;
- a balance of highly emotional experiences with neutral ones;
- the time of day for which an exercise is planned (see energy levels);
- use of time limits.

Energy Levels

Groups have energy levels—the amount of emotional, intellectual, and physical energy or attention that can be focused upon an activity. Energy level will vary from session to session and can change even within a one-hour session. Trainers need to be aware of different group energy levels in order to plan experiences that maximize learning.

Variables which may affect energy levels include:
- amount of time individuals have worked/slept prior to the session;
- how emotionally or intellectually tiring the activity is;
- time of day or week;
- degree of emotional involvement with the topic;
- ability of trainers to design activities that are energizing and that have high participant involvement.

When energy levels are low:
Possible causes: People are tired, trust level is low, people are afraid, previous session has been mentally or emotionally exhausting.
What to use: *Affirmations, Attention Expanders,* Community-building Exercises, a break, games, a group nap.

When energy levels are high:
Possible causes: People have had enough rest, material is interesting, there is a good balance between intellectual and emotional activities, the pace is good, community has been built and people feel safe in the group.

What to use: heavier intellectual material, mini-lectures, *Macro-Analysis* sessions.

Energy Levels at a General Training Workshop

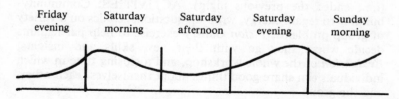

Friday evening	Saturday morning	Saturday afternoon	Saturday evening	Sunday morning

Friday Evening—Energy level is usually low because people have either worked all week or traveled to get to the workshop. Meeting new people is threatening to many, and energy level will be low until people feel safe in the group. Primary task for this session is to develop a feeling of safety for the participants, or the depth of sharing in later sessions will be impaired. Enough intellectual content should be included that participants feel time has been well spent. Groups that already know each other need time to re-connect and enjoy each other, but less time may be necessary for building community. ACTIVITIES: *Affirmation* of individuals, Community-building Exercises.

Saturday Morning—Energy level is high because of trust developed the previous night and, it is hoped, participants are rested. ACTIVITIES: Short *Affirmation* or Community-building Exercises which reaffirm the level of trust felt the previous evening. Heavier intellectual material, such as mini-lectures, *Macro-Analysis* sessions. Light, energy-producing exercise at the end of the session.

Saturday Afternoon—This is usually the lowest energy level during a weekend. The causes include time of day, the fact that people "worked" during the morning session, and the fact that people may have stayed up late the previous night and tiredness has caught up with them. ACTIVITIES: High energy exercises such as *Roleplays, Strategy Games*, with high participant involvement and physical activity. (Speeches and lectures put people to sleep.) Use *Attention Expanders* frequently. Leave a portion unscheduled so people can nap, exercise, and relax as needed.

Saturday Evening—The group may get a second burst of energy. Trust/comfort/security level is higher. Session needs to be shorter than the others so that the group can have unstructured time to spend together. ACTIVITIES: Light, active exercises to begin, heavier intellectual material in the middle, and a good community-builder at the end.

Sunday Morning—Energy level is at medium range because people are tired from late nights and concentrated learning periods. There is also a general feeling that the workshop is over (i.e., ended the previous night). ACTIVITIES: Community-building to regain energy, wrap-up questions, clinics on a variety of group problems, *Vision Gallery* exercise to help participants decide where they go with their new skills and insights, *Evaluation* of the whole workshop, and a closing time in which individuals can share good things about themselves, each other, and the group.

Trust Level

Trainers need to recognize the degree of openness to sharing feelings, thoughts, or new experiences exhibited by the group. Exercises can be structured to encourage people to share, but activities that are too threatening will cause participants to withdraw or resist. The threat level decreases as trust and community are built. Activities which help to build community include: *Affirmation Exercises*, shared work and play, and personal sharing (see Part Three: "Developing Communities of Support" for suggestions). Exercises such as the *Whole Person Exercise* should be used only after a high level of trust has been built within the group.

Transition between Sessions and Topics

Frequently the subject matter changes from session to session or within a session. Trainers need to facilitate a smooth transition from topic to topic and to help link new topics with information previously explored. This can be done by (a) transitional statements or (b) an agenda review with an explanation of how the new material meets the goals and expectations of the group. When a topic continues from one session to another, trainers can briefly sum up past work and state specific areas of activities for the new session.

Physical/Material Needs

Is the room large enough for the whole group? What comforts are available: chairs, rugs, light? Is there space for small groups to work? Is adequate food available? Are there food preparation facilities? Is the location of the workshop sufficiently removed from distractions, noise, or other happenings, so that participants can concentrate? Have provisions been made for child care?

End of Sessions and Workshop

Sessions and workshops need to end with the participants feeling good about themselves and each other. *Affirmation* or

166

Community-building Exercises are important to use at these times. Each session should end with a *Brief Evaluation*. Participants should have a sense of completion and feel good about stopping. A later time should be set to handle burning questions. Steps for further action should be defined.

SAMPLE WORKSHOPS

Note: All tools listed in bold italics are explained in other sections of the manual and can be found by using the index. *Explanations* included after these tools *are only supplementary.*

FACILITATION AND DEMOCRATIC DECISION-MAKING WORKSHOP   (3 sessions, 2½-3 hrs each)

SESSION #1:   (3 hrs)
- Introduction of trainers.   (5 min)
- Agenda review.   (10 min)
- An explanation of the process of facilitation and how the workshop will be developed around the interests of the group. (10 min)
- *Affirmation Exercise to Introduce Each Other.*   (30 min)
- *Determine Goals and Expectations* for the weekend. (20 min) Things participants may expect to learn: How to facilitate a business meeting. How to facilitate consensus. What consensus is and how it differs from voting; from parliamentary procedure. How to cope with hostility when facilitating a meeting. What to do about people who dominate meetings. What to do about people who block consensus. How to organize a meeting. How to plan an agenda. How to keep people's attention for long periods of time. How to keep people from feeling that the facilitators have all the control. What to do about people who never speak. What to do when you cannot reach consensus. How to know when a group is ready to make a decision.
- Community-building or group dynamics exercises. Use early in the workshop to help the group work together better later on. Example: *Elephant Game*.   (90 min)
- *Brief Evaluation of the Meeting*   (10 min)

SESSION #2:   (3 hrs)
- *Attention Expanders*   (10 min)
- Short talk on trainers' contracting with a group for approval of the agenda.   (5 min)
- Agenda review and contracting with the group for the proposed agenda.   (10 min)

- *Brainstorming* group maintenance and group task roles that are found in a good group. (1) Trainers explain that there are many roles that participants can play in a group. Some are positive and supportive and others block groups from acting. (2) Participants are asked to brainstorm things that people do in groups that are supportive and help the group reach its goals. (3) Participants are asked to brainstorm destructive actions that individuals play in a group. (4) The trainer explains that individual and group behavior is influenced by individual needs and past positive and negative experiences in groups. Facilitators need to be able to spot negative behavior patterns, identify needs of members, and keep things moving smoothly. (15 min)
- NASA Game—An exercise to explore consensus decision making and group decision making vs. individual decision making. (Found in the *Handbook of Structured Experiences for Human Relations Training,* Vol. I). (45 min)
- Short talk on consensus decision making, covering the following points: does not create in-group and out-group; requires flexibility and generation of better solutions; differences between consensus and voting. (10 min)
- Short talk on the role of the facilitator, agenda planning, etc. (10 min)
- *Roleplaying* problem situations found in groups, using those brainstormed by the group. (Optional: Trainers may act out problems in the roleplay format and give participants a chance to suggest ways of handling the problem. This is the same process used for *Quick Decisions* except that the problem is presented as a roleplay.) (60 min)
- *Brief Evaluation of the Meeting*. (10 min)

SESSION #3: (2½ hrs)
- *Attention Expander*. Three-person machine. (20 min)
- Agenda review and contracting with the group for the proposed agenda. (10 min)
- *Listening Exercises*. Explain each, practice and evaluate.
     Listening for feelings: Use *Active Listening* in pairs for five minutes apiece. Allow reflection time. Sample topic: problems I have when I facilitate a meeting. (20 min)
     Listening for content: Use *5-2-1 Exercise*. Reflection and discussion on the use of the tool can be done in pairs and then in the whole group. Sample topic: an important experience that has changed my life. (30 min)
- Short talk on problem-solving processes. *"No-Lose" Problem Solving* and *Small Group to Large Group Consensus*. (10 min)

• Simulated problem-solving exercise. (1) Participants form groups of 6-8 members. (2) Facilitators present groups with a task, such as designing a social change project for their community. (3) Group must choose a facilitator and complete the task. (4) Groups evaluate the facilitation, participation, and group processes for problem solving.   (45 min)

• *Evaluation* of the session and of the workshop.   (15 min)

CONFLICT RESOLUTION WORKSHOP   (5 sessions)

This workshop contains parts of several workshops facilitated for communities and schools that have had racial conflicts. It can be used before or after conflicts erupt. This workshop was designed for students and faculty.

Note: For reasons of space, in the later sessions of this workshop we do not always list *Attention Expanders*, "agenda review," "contracting with the group for the proposed agenda," etc., but it should be remembered that these are important and necessary parts of most sessions.

FRIDAY EVENING: (2½ hrs)

• Introduction of the trainers and explanation of why the workshop is being held.   (5 min)   The background of the conflicts can be given briefly.   (additional 5 min)

• Explanation of *Affirmation* and its role in conflict resolution and nonviolent social change.   (5 min)

• Use of *Affirmation Exercise To Introduce Each Other*. (20 min)

• Agenda review and explanation of how the content of the workshop will be developed.   (10 min)

• *Determine Goals and Expectations* for the workshop. (20 min)

What people may expect to learn: How better to handle hostile feelings. How to understand people of other races. How to handle conflicts that occur between students in the halls. How to develop a group of people in the school who can stop or prevent fights among students. How to prevent conflicts in the future. How to isolate potential conflicts and resolve them before they become destructive.

• Community-building and/or Group Dynamics Exercise (like the *Elephant Game*) to build community among the group members, to give them a chance to work together on a common task, and to explore how they function in a simulated conflict. Evaluate for 20 minutes minimum.   (1½ hrs)

• *Brief Evaluation of the Meeting*.   (5 min)

SATURDAY MORNING: (2 hrs)
  • *Attention Expander.*   (5 min)
  • Thinking and sharing about conflict.   (30 min)
Each person is a case study of experiences involving conflict and
its resolution. This exercise helps people to identify their own
strengths, weaknesses, and common experiences regarding
conflict.

The trainer explains that s/he will be asking the group
several questions. Everyone will have 30 seconds to think of a
response and 1½ minutes to share his/her thoughts within a
small group of three people.   (15 min on questions)   Follow with an open discussion of things learned through the
exercise.   (15 min)

Sample Questions: Think of a conflict that you had as a
child that has influenced the way you think about and handle
conflict today. Complete this sentence: "One of the most
difficult things for me in handling conflict is..." Complete this
sentence: "I function best in a conflict situation when..."
Complete this sentence: "A conflict situation in which I learned
a lot or did well was..."

  • Short talk on conflict which covers the following points:
(10 min)
  —Conflict is and will probably always be present.
  —Our goal should not be to eliminate conflict, but to learn
how to manage it creatively.
  —Conflict is bad only when it is handled destructively.
Conflict is a prime ingredient of change and growth.
  —Goals of conflict resolution should be: (1) to regulate the
conflict so as to minimize the physical or psychological damage
done to either party, and (2) to maximize the achievement of the
goals of the contending groups to the greatest extent possible.
  —Current conflicts are frequently exaggerated. The new
conflict may not be as drastic as it appears, and may be blown
out of proportion by participants because of similar past
conflicts with each other or other people. It is important to
separate current conflicts from past hurts.

  • *Quick Decisions*—Use situations drawn from the conflict
experiences of the group.   (15 min)
  • Learning to listen in a conflict—In order to resolve
conflicts, it is necessary to have at least one of the conflicting
parties or a third party listen carefully to what is being said by all
groups involved. The following steps can be used by facilitators
to help a group explore listening for content and for feelings.

Step #1: Identification of unhelpful behavior.   (7 min)
Trainer asks the group to brainstorm all unhelpful phrases or

actions that would-be listeners have used in the past. Examples are: "If I were you, I'd...", or "That reminds me of the time..."

Step #2: Listening for feelings and content.   (5 min)
The facilitator should explain the two roles of the listener. Listeners can help clarify issues and feelings in a conflict situation by restating what they hear being said or felt. Explain the chart.

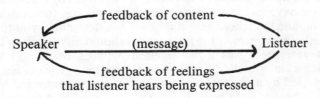

Step #3: Practice giving content feedback.   (20 min)
Use *5-2-1 Exercise*. Have speakers talk about "An important conflict with a friend or member of my family that I have resolved." Follow with a discussion on what participants learned about conflict resolution.

Step #4: Practice giving feeling feedback.   (20 min)
Remaining in pairs, each person takes seven minutes to talk about a problem or conflict that s/he is facing. The listener should use *Active Listening* to feed back the feelings s/he hears being voiced by the speaker. The listener should not dialogue with the speaker or make suggestions. *Note:* Because this exercise surfaces unpleasant feelings, participants may become upset. After step #4 is finished, trainers may need to allow a short time for people to release feelings, then use *Attention Expanders* to refocus on positive things.
   • *Brief Evaluation* of the morning session.   (5 min)

SATURDAY AFTERNOON: (2½ hrs)
   • *Attention Expander*—Magic Glob.   (15 min)
   • Short talk on *Roleplaying*—purposes for and description of.   (10 min)
   • *Hassle Lines*—Situations should be close enough to the group's experience so people can identify with them.   (15 min)
   • *Brainstorm*—Ask group to brainstorm conflict situations on which they would like to work.   (10 min)
   • *Roleplays*—Explain that behavior conflicts, those caused by an undesirable action, are easier to handle than conflicts over values. Trainer should select a conflict suggested by the group, ask for group approval, and develop a roleplay around it. Several situations can be used. Some situations may be tried

more than once, to experiment with different solutions. If more than one trainer/facilitator is available, roleplaying can be done in small groups.   (1½ hrs)

• *Brief Evaluation* of the afternoon session.   (5 min)

SATURDAY EVENING: *Simulation Game:* A Community Conflict   (2 hrs)

• *Sample situation:* (read to the group by the trainers) You are a group of students and faculty at Central High School. All of you have had some experience with training for nonviolent action, and the school administration has designated you to be a peacekeeping team in the high school should any conflicts arise. Last year there was a major clash between black and white students in which 80 people participated. The causes, as diagnosed by a special investigative committee sponsored by the school board, were lack of student power over their lives, an ineffective student government, a double standard for discipline of black and white students, and general tension between the races caused by family attitudes and economic segregation.

It is Friday. During the week there have been rumors of both black and white students carrying knives to school. There was a pushing incident around a drinking fountain yesterday that seemed to amount to nothing. At noon, a white student bumped a black student, causing the latter to drop his tray. A shouting match ensued, and the white student said that he would meet the black student after school with some of his friends to settle the conflict. At 2:45, when school let out, 15 students were involved in a fist fight in the parking lot. Several students and teachers and one policeman intervened. Three students were arrested, two black and one white. There were numerous fights on the way home from school, one of which resulted in a knifing and a trip to the hospital for a black student. His condition is unknown at this time. Rumors are flying that there will be a big fight on Monday when school opens. The administration is considering closing the school but has asked you to present a plan for lowering the tensions in the school and for handling conflicts which might occur Monday.

• *Part One:* It is assumed that all members of the group are interested in nonviolent methods of conflict resolution. Participants, working in groups of 6 to 8, create and outline strategies of conflict regulation and resolution. It may be useful to use a *Time Line* to clarify the steps to action. During the first 20 minutes, people consider what needs to be done between now and Monday, what groups need to be contacted, what additional information is needed, where sympathetic support can be found, etc. During the second 20 minutes, outline strategy for Monday morning. During the third 20 minutes, consider how basic changes in the school or community might reduce conflict in the school.   (60 min)

• *Part Two:* Begin a simulation game in which small groups will play black students, white students, police, and nonviolent peacekeepers. The situation should not be too close to the real conflict of the group, and people should not play a role that they play in reality. The scene begins when school opens Monday morning, 15 minutes before the first class. About ½ of the students have arrived.   (30 min)

• *Evaluation* of the exercise.

SUNDAY MORNING: Conflict and Institutional Change: A Campaign-building *Simulation Game*   (4 hrs)

• Introduction of the morning agenda.

Frequently community conflicts are caused by institutional injustices. People who are interested in conflict resolution must be as concerned about basic change in institutions which cause violence and conflict as they are about minimizing violence in an immediate "hot" situation. The task of the small group is to select a problem within the school or community and briefly use the following steps to develop an analysis, vision, and strategy to solve the problem.

A real campaign requires many more hours of thinking and planning than this; therefore, in order to complete this exercise within the time limits, trainers will have to keep tight *Time Limits.* For some of the small groups, depending on the issue they have selected, time limits may have to be modified. For example, some groups may need less time for analysis and more time to work out a vision.

Because this session requires a lot of difficult thinking and includes little physical activity, small groups may need several short breaks or *Attention Expanders.*

Frequently, when people participate in a campaign-building simulation, they have trouble distinguishing between reality and the simulation. Because of their excitement, they feel they are planning for a real campaign. Trainers need to stress before the exercise that this is a simulation and not a real campaign. In order to do a real campaign, group members must contract to work with each other on a definite project. During the morning they will have contracted only to learn about campaigns together. If at the end of the session participants decide to develop a real campaign, the group must form a new contract. Group members who do not want to become involved in their group's issue should be allowed to use the exercise as a learning

173

experience and not feel compelled to participate in an on-going action.

• Steps that Groups Can Use to Develop a Social Change Campaign.

Step #1: Facilitators ask the whole group to brainstorm problem areas in the school *or* community, but not both.   (10 min)

Step #2: The group is divided into small groups of 6-8 members who are interested in the same issue.   (15 min)

Step #3: Small groups examine the issue and focus on a manageable problem. For example, not "racism in the school," but different treatment for blacks and whites in the discipline office.   (10 min)

Step #4: The history of the problem or conflict is clarified so that everyone has common information.   (10 min)

Step #5: The parties involved in the conflict are identified: central, peripheral, potential allies, opponents, and neutrals in the change process.   (15 min)

Step #6: The structural environment of the conflict is identified: (1) the authority structures of the groups involved, (2) the communications channels that are available, (3) the channels that social change agents would have to go through to achieve "legal" change, (4) the larger political institutions or issues that affect the change such as school board or community institutions.   (20 min)

Break   (10 min)

Step #7: A vision of an alternative is developed that includes solutions to this problem. ***Brainstorm*** and try to reach consensus on a common vision.   (20 min)

Step #8: Small groups use ***Time Lines*** to outline the steps they need to take to achieve the change. Two time lines may be used, one for immediate steps to be taken within the next few weeks and the second for long range strategy.   (5 min)

Break—A stretch in place.   (5 min)

Step #9: Small groups share their analysis and campaigns for 5 minutes per group.   (15 min)

Step #10: Campaigns can be discussed over lunch.

• ***Evaluation*** of the morning and the weekend.   (15 min)

• Closing circle—Each person tells the person on the right something that s/he has appreciated about him/her during the weekend. The person receiving the affirmation goes next, and so on.   (15 min)

MARSHAL TRAINING WORKSHOP   (3 hrs)

This workshop was designed to train marshals in nonviolent peacekeeping skills for the January 25-27, 1975, Assembly to Save the Peace Agreement, Washington, DC.

- Introduction of the trainers.   (3 min)
- *Introduction* of the participants to each other. Each person gives his/her name and where s/he is from.   (5 min)
- *Affirmation*—Explain purpose of affirmation. Group divides into pairs and each person uses two minutes to share about a conflict situation in which s/he did well.   (8 min)
- Short talk on theory of nonviolent peacekeeping, using case studies.   (5 min)
- Background of the action—History, purpose, and groups involved.   (5 min)
- *Hassle Lines*—Explain. Use several situations in which a conflict occurs and/or violence erupts or is a potential. Use *Evaluation* to bring out important points.   (20 min)
  Sample situations:

    1. Person A, a well-known person in the movement, wants to go on stage and make a speech. Person B is a marshal who has been instructed *not* to let anyone on the stage who does not have Assembly approval. Person A does not have approval and verbally abuses the marshal.

    2. Person B is an irate participant at the Peace Assembly who wants to enter an already overcrowded room to listen to a speaker and has indicated s/he will push others out if necessary to get in. Person A is a marshal and wants to keep him/her out.

    3. Person A is a demonstrator who starts throwing stones over the White House fence at police in the yard. Person B is a marshal who tries to stop him/her.

- *Roleplay* of a fist fight between a demonstrator and a bystander who is heckling the crowd.   (15 min)
- *Roleplay* of a large group conflict situation.   (20 min)
- Break   (10 min)
- Briefing on medical emergencies.   (25 min)
- *Situation Analysis*—Present (1) route of march, (2) marshal placement along march route and strategy for facilitating marchers, and (3) strategy for marshaling the stage.   (15 min)
- *Quick Decisions*   (15 min)
  Sample situations:

    1. Demonstrator falls down in line of march.

    2. Demonstrator has a banner that is unacceptable to the coalition.

175

    3. Counterdemonstrators move toward march and harass participants.
- Question and answer period   (15 min)
- *Evaluation* of workshop   (10 min)

NONVIOLENT DIRECT ACTION AND CAMPAIGN BUILDING WORKSHOP   (5 sessions)

This workshop was designed to prepare trainer/organizers to develop and carry out a nonviolent action campaign opposing the construction of nuclear power plants.

FRIDAY EVENING: Community Building (3 hrs)
- Introduction of trainers.   (5 min)
- Use of *Affirmation Exercise To Introduce Each Other*. (25 min)
- Explanation of the training and facilitation processes. (5 min)
- *Brainstorming* the goals and expectations of the group. (10 min)
- Prioritizing goals.   (7 min)
- *Elephant Game* or other community building exercise. (2 hrs)
- *Brief Evaluation* of evening session.   (5 min)

SATURDAY MORNING: Macro-Analysis   (2¼ hrs)
- *Excitement Sharing*—People tell of something that is happening in their lives (to be done in pairs or in the whole group).   (10-15 min)
- Introduction of *Macro-Analysis*.   (5 min)
- Macro-Analysis session on nuclear power.   (1½ hrs)
    1. Reports on readings which were mailed to participants or distributed the evening before. Readings should be completed before the session.   (1 hr)
    2. Introduction of the *Web Chart* tool.   (15 min)
    3. Introduction of *Force Field Analysis*.   (10 min)

SATURDAY AFTERNOON: Introduction to Direct Action (2½ hrs)
- Sharing in pairs for 2 minutes each on "a time when I was afraid but was able to act."   (5 min)
- Sharing in fours for 2 minutes each on "a time when I was in a confrontation situation and did well."   (10 min)
- *Hassle Line* with several situations.   (25 min)
    Sample situation: Person A is policeman who pushes demonstrator and demands that the sidewalk be cleared where a vigil line has formed. Person B is demonstrator who feels s/he should be able to vigil on the sidewalk.

- Short talk on nonviolent campaign building with a direct action component. For content material see "The Direct Action Campaign" under Part Seven: Organizing for Change. (20 min)
  - *Quick Decisions*—Using several situations.   (15 min)
  Sample situations:
      1. Police throw tear gas canister into a crowd and begin to push people with night sticks. You are in front and the first to be pushed.
      2. A fellow demonstrator uses abusive language on police. You are 10 feet away from the demonstrator.
- Break   (5 min)
- Medical Briefing—Where information can be found on common injuries, tear gas, setting up medical teams, and victim counseling.   (15 min)
  - *Mass Roleplay* including evaluation.   (20 min)
  Sample situation: A group of demonstrators who oppose the construction of a nuclear power plant is blocking the road to the construction site by sitting in it. The police order demonstrators to leave and proceed to gas and chase them away.
  - *Brief Evaluation* of the afternoon.   (5 min)
  - Closing Activity.   (5 min)

SATURDAY EVENING: (3 hrs)
- Community-building activity.   (5 min)
- Explanation of nonviolent tactics found in *The Politics of Nonviolent Action* by Gene Sharp, and short talk on building campaigns, using a sample *Time Line*.   (10 min)
  - *Strategy Game* including 20 minutes for evaluation. (2½ hrs)
  - *Brief Evaluation* of the evening.   (5 min)

SUNDAY MORNING: (2-3 hrs)
- Community-building exercise—Building a three-person machine.   (15 min)
  - *Decision-making Structure—Sample Problems*
      1. Design a display of alternative power sources. (10 min)
      2. The night before an anti-nuclear power plant demonstration, the construction firm spreads manure on the field where the demo is to be held. What do you do? (3 min)
      3. What do you say to construction workers who will be out of a job if the power plant, which is in a depressed area, is not built?   (15-40 min)
- Open discussion on problem areas or particular interests. (30 min)

177

- Small discussion groups on the topic: "Where do we go from here?" Encourage groups to outline steps and be specific. (20 min)
   - *Evaluation* of the morning and workshop.   (20 min)
   - *Closing Circle*—Participants (1) share what they have appreciated about each other during the weekend, (2) identify the various skills and insights gained, or (3) project how these skills will be useful to them when they return home.   (15 min)

GROUP DYNAMICS WORKSHOP

Workshops in group dynamics should increase the participants' awareness of how groups function, improve the efficiency of the group, and raise the level of personal satisfaction among the group members. By using information in the section on Group Dynamics you can put together your own workshop based on the needs of your group. An excellent resource for group dynamics workshops is Lynne Shivers, 1006 S 46th, Phila., PA 19143. Two basic approaches for the structure of group dynamics workshops are suggested here. Use them as they seem helpful and develop your own.

Concepts Approach:
We recommend including exercises in each of the following areas:
1. Task and maintenance roles.
2. Decision making—We often use the NASA game. If you decide to use a different exercise, we recommend using one that allows the group to explore the use of consensus as a process for decision making.
3. Leadership.

Add exercises on additional topic areas according to the needs of the group and limitations of time.

Encourage people to remember their own experiences as participants in groups. Use these experiences as the basis for exercises whenever possible. After several exercises, ask people to recall past group experiences and to evaluate them in light of the information just learned. You may want to generate a list of new ideas on how your group(s) can function better and solve common problems.

Problem Solving Approach:
Brainstorm and list problems that participants are having in their group. Select several that occur frequently or are especially difficult to resolve.

Take each problem separately, construct situations, and roleplay each. Use other exercises that apply. Have printed materials available on group task and maintenance roles, leadership, and decision making; use pages of the manual when they apply. Repeat roleplays and test possible solutions.

Note: One advantage of this approach is that participants are quickly able to link theory and experience. However, this approach requires trainers that are skilled in designing exercises on the spot, and a group with self-learning discipline among the members.

CONSCIOUSNESS-RAISING WORKSHOP

By using exercises and tools in this manual, your group can create its own consciousness-raising workshop. The following elements seem essential:

1. Vision Building: Looking at real possibilities, not unattainable fantasies. Tools which can be used:

> *Vision Gallery*
> *Scenario Writing*
> *Brainstorming*
> Evaluation and improvement of your vision
> Case studies in Part One

2. Understanding methods of change: How do we get from where we are now to where we want to be? Tools which can be used:

> *Violent and Nonviolent Revolution*
> *Roleplaying*—with an emphasis on methods, their desirability and their end results.
> *Combining a Case Study with Strategy Game.*
> Discussing how change is occurring within yourselves and your own group by using the *Statements Exercise, Structured Speaking*, and exercises found under Group Dynamics.

3. Getting started: Your group should by now have developed a sense of mutual support and goals necessary to hold it together. The key insight in consciousness raising is that of understanding that people together can change reality—for reality is us and the way we live together. A process that will help you move into action is:

a. Choose an area in which you want to bring about change. Use *Brainstorming* and Priority Setting Tools.

b. Look at your resources, strengths, and weaknesses. How do you nourish strengths and overcome weaknesses?

c. Brainstorm criteria for a good project, always with an eye to how it applies to *you*.

d. Choose a specific action.

Additional Resources:
1. Consciousness-Raising Section in this manual.
2. Awareness/Action Workshops. Write Philip Wheaton, 1500 Farragut, NW, Washington, DC 20011. Available on request is "Philosophy and Praxis of Liberation Workshops," 8 pages including a description of and theory behind workshops. Include contribution for postage and printing.
3. MNS/LC in West Philadelphia. Trainers available to do consciousness-raising workshops similar to those in this manual. Write Consciousness-Raising Workshops, Attn: Ellen Deacon, Charles Esser, Christopher Moore, 4501 Spruce, Phila., PA 19139, (215) 662-5261.
4. Blair Forlaw, 1007 Lakewood Ave. N, Durham, NC 27701. (919) 489-1981.
5. Plowshare Community/Twin Cities MNS, 3628 Park Ave., S, Minneapolis, MN 55407. (612) 825-8644.

IV
Training in the Schools

During the past four years members of the Movement for a New Society/Life Center community in West Philadelphia have developed and facilitated courses and workshops in several high schools and universities, public and private. These have been on a variety of topics related to social change. Cooperation from students, teachers, and administrators has been high.

These experimental courses were designed to develop student and faculty awareness of the nonviolent social change process and skills and to encourage the participants to apply them to areas that affect their lives.

MNS/LC members have also worked in the Nonviolence and Children Program of the Friends Peace Committee, offering workshops to young people, their teachers and parents. Brief information on this area is included below under Working with Young People.

WHY OFFER COURSES AND WORKSHOPS ON NONVIOLENT SOCIAL CHANGE?

There is immediate need for grass roots groups to analyze, discuss, and act to solve a whole range of serious crises facing our society. People are needed who are aware of social problems and are skilled enough to bring positive changes. This requires that people have a practical and effective concept of change which empowers them to take charge of their own learning process.

Training for nonviolent social change:

- exposes students to macro-analysis: a society-wide view of social issues and their inter-relationships (the relationship between seemingly isolated social problems is examined, leading to a deeper and more complete understanding of the changes needed in society);
- helps students develop a vision of what they would like their society to be;
- provides skills to help students resolve personal and group conflicts;
- offers skills in a whole variety of areas related to social change;
- offers students the opportunity to participate in and understand the dynamics of consensus democracy (this experience is critical to the functioning of a democratic society and must be practiced to be learned);
- creates an experience of community and affirmation that is important for human growth;
- allows students and faculty to build a learning experience based upon their own interests rather than on a pre-determined curriculum (learning how to use this process of course development is one way that students and faculty may develop a continuing learning experience);
- offers a co-learner process which can dissolve the student/teacher, leader/follower barriers.

HOW TRAINING FOR NONVIOLENT SOCIAL CHANGE DIFFERS FROM MOST PEACE AND CONFLICT STUDIES COURSES

Since the late 1960s many courses in peace and conflict studies have been developed for high school and university students. For the most part these courses resemble traditional political science courses, except for a greater emphasis on world issues, world law, and "future" studies. The majority of the courses assume institutional change from the top down as the process of change for world peace. Students rarely focus on how individuals and groups can be directly involved in changing social, political, and economic policies which cause war. These courses focus on consciousness change through acquisition of information, rather than teaching skills which help students act in making changes.

181

Courses in nonviolent social change which use the training approach explained in the two designs below are different from many courses on peace and conflict. Some of the major differences are:

• *Training for nonviolent social change links consciousness raising and action.* Participants are able to explore their personal oppressions, community problems, and societal needs while they learn skills that will help them change these situations.

• *Training for nonviolent social change involves experiential learning on topics which concern the participants directly.* People usually become involved in peace and social change issues because of a personal experience which motivates them to act. Courses taught from this perspective try to recall this gut level experience which, combined with an intellectual interest in the issue, will motivate the participants to further reflection and action.

• *The content of the course is developed from the group's perceived needs.* From the beginning participants are involved in selecting the content of the course. As the course develops, the group learns to take control of the learning process through which information is studied and acted upon.

• *The course helps to create a lifestyle consistent with changes needed on institutional levels.* Participants are encouraged to look at nonviolent social change from a personal as well as a societal perspective.

• *Training for nonviolent social change focuses on learning skills.* Social change does not come about by consciousness changes alone. People need concrete skills that they can apply to their social problems. A course of this type allows people to look at skills and processes that have been effective in the past, to experiment with those that fit their situations, and to develop new skills and approaches when needed.

COURSE DESIGN A:
THE PROBLEM POSING/DIALOGIC APPROACH
(Methods of Nonviolent Social Change: 12 week course, 3 hours per week, used with 11th and 12th grade students at Westtown School, Westtown, Pa.)

The Problem Posing/Dialogic Approach has been used in high schools, colleges, and ad hoc groups of people interested in social change. The emphasis is on community building, consciousness raising and skill sharing before becoming involved in action and societal change. The process itself can be used to teach a variety of contents.

Goals: (Developed by trainers in pre-course planning)
- To affirm students' ability to make change.
- To transfer social change skills to students for use in a variety of everyday situations.
- To help students build and maintain community in the group.
- To broaden students' perspective on the full social change process from lifestyle to campaign development.
- To help students investigate what nonviolence means in our own lives and how it connects with the society at large (dynamics, philosophy, history, and practice).

Goals: (Brainstormed by students and agreed upon by consensus)
- To learn about the definition of nonviolence.
- To learn how nonviolence relates to me and others.
- To understand institutions, or things, that block change.
- To learn to cooperate in putting into practice things we learn.
- To experience community by visiting the MNS/LC community in West Philadelphia.
- To compare differences between militant nonviolent action and violent action.
- To learn action skills which can be used to wake up apathetic people.
- To explore the concept of internal violence and ecological exploitation in U.S. and Third World relationships.
- To learn what nonviolent social change requires of a person.
- To apply skills of analysis to social change situations.
- To learn history of the nonviolent movement.
- To examine differences between mental and physical force and pain.
- To build community in the group.
- To understand sexism and racism in institutions.
- To learn how to relate to people in authority.

Process:

The Problem Posing/Dialogic Approach involved mutual discovery by the students and facilitators of the group's *themes*, major questions about nonviolence and social change, and how these themes can be turned into problems or experiences that can help group members learn and clarify their feelings and ideas. The basic theory behind this approach, as well as a step-by-step description of how learning experiences are developed, may be found in the educational theory of Paulo Freire explained briefly in Part Five: Consciousness Raising.

Brainstorming and the *Statements Exercise* were used to discover the group's themes. This information was clarified and compiled by the trainers into a list of student goals. The list was presented to the students so they could check its accuracy and rank goals according to their priorities.

The trainers developed learning experiences and proposed them to the group. Frequently several options were suggested. The class could select one of the options, combine parts of the proposals, or reject them outright. If a proposed activity was rejected, the facilitators would ask for a short break and develop a new one. In this course students were not directly involved in planning each session.

Because the trainers had to commute a long distance to the school and often needed to plan before they arrived, the students' role was frequently that of a sounding board. Trainers made proposals to a small group of students to verify that content and process would meet the group's needs and expectations.

Decision-making skills were learned through group dynamics exercises, *Simulation Games*, and very short meetings during class sessions to clarify future agenda and handle group business. This process did not give students direct control over the content and process of the class, but it gave them power to direct the course in a general way and prevented them from getting bogged down in long meetings due to poor facilitation and lack of information.

Social change skills were learned through simulated experiences, like *Roleplaying*. The simulations allowed students to develop skills and confidence in a laboratory situation, make and correct mistakes, and strategize before dealing with real conflicts and issues. Community-building exercises, especially *Affirmation*, helped to develop team spirit and support among the participants.

Content: Course Outline

Length of Sessions: 45 minute class in the afternoon and 2 hour class in the evening once a week for 12 weeks.

SESSION #1:

Afternoon
* ***Affirmation Exercise to Introduce Each Other***.
* Explanations of the training and facilitation processes, how the course would be developed, and a history of training for nonviolent social change.

Evening
* ***Attention Expander***.

- **Determine Goals and Expectations** of the group.
- **Statements Exercise** with following variation: Students were asked to bring to class a picture, object, poem, song, etc., which reflected their view of society and something that they would like to see changed or enhanced. The object was put into the middle of the circle of a small group of five. Each person could select an object and reflect for three minutes on what the object meant to him/her. During a second two minutes, other members of the group could respond. The owner could respond or remain silent. Facilitators collected the student responses and examined them for common themes.
- **Brief Evaluation** of the session.

After Session Planning
- Facilitators compiled all information from Brainstormed priorities and the comments from the Statements Exercise. Common themes and interests were grouped and organized and topic for first content session of class was selected. (Students should be involved in this process if possible.)
- Facilitators developed a proposal for the content and process of the next session.

SESSION #2:
Afternoon
- **Attention Expander**—Touch Blue
- Facilitators presented themes and proposal for session in combined and organized form. Students verified themes and selected priorities. The group elected to look, for the first three weeks, at the definition of nonviolence, personal nonviolence, and questions of strategy, theory, and history.
- Explanation of the uses of **Roleplays** was followed by several **Hassle Lines**.

Evening
- **Brainstorming** the characteristics of violence and nonviolence.
- Discussion and introduction of definition of violence. A definition we used is: any act of omission or commission which does physical or psychological harm to an individual is violent.
- **Hassle Line**.
- Group broke into three groups to develop situations which they presented to the whole group. Topic: personal conflicts.
- Suggested readings for next session: selections which focus on nonviolent theory and case studies from **Stride Toward Freedom: The Montgomery Story**, by Martin Luther King, Jr., (Ballantine, 1958), *The Power of Nonviolence*, by Richard Gregg (Schocken, 1966), and *Conquest of Violence,* by Joan

Bondurant (Univ. of California, 1965). Three volunteers were recruited to give reports, using the *Macro-Analysis* format.

SESSION #3:
Afternoon
    • *Anger Tool*, using the syllable "Grr." The group broke into pairs and each person took a minute to talk about how s/he felt during the exercise. Then the whole group discussed the relationship of anger to violence.
Evening
    • The three volunteers reported on readings, using the *Macro-Analysis* format: a five-minute report followed by a ten-minute discussion, putting the emphasis on what most excited the reader and what questions were raised by the reading.
    • Continuation of the personal conflict *Roleplays* from last session.
    • Volunteers were recruited to read for the next session's Macro-Analysis report.
    • *Brief Evaluation* of the session.
    • The decision was made to see movies next session.

SESSION #4:
Afternoon
    • Film. 20th Century Production on Gandhi. (Good historical document but weak on analysis of nonviolent action. To obtain, call your local library or inquire of CBS-TV.)
Evening
    • Reports on readings, using a *Macro-Analysis* format. Case study on Salt March in *Conquest of Violence*, by Joan Bondurant (Univ. of California Press, 1965); "Norwegian Resistance" in *The Quiet Battle,* Mulford Sibley, ed. (Beacon Press, 1963); and scenarios on nonviolent change in *Moving Toward a New Society*, chapter 11, by Gowan et al. (MNS, 4722 Baltimore Ave., Phila., PA 19143).
    • Movie. "The Voyage of the Phoenix," available from MNS, Phila.

SESSION #5:
Afternoon
    • *Attention Expander*   (10 min)
    • Listening exercise. The *5-2-1 Exercise*. Topic: How I deal with interpersonal conflict.   (20 min)
Evening
    • *Attention Expander*
    • Discussion with whole group on "the kind of participant I am in a group."   (30 min)
    • NASA Game or other exercise in consensus decision making.

- *Brief Evaluation* of the session.
- Discussion of possible topics to cover in next part of the course. The group selected sexism.

SESSION #6:
Afternoon
- Look through magazines to see how sex is used to sell products and create myths about the "ideal" woman and man.
Evening
- *Attention Expander*
- Reports on readings.
- Discussion on readings in small groups.
- *Brief Evaluation* of the session.
- Decision to continue exploring sexism.

SESSION #7:
Afternoon and Evening
- Roleplays in small groups on "sexist situations I have known." Situations were first suggested by the trainers and later by participants.
- Sharing in small groups of women and men. Men discussed times they have seen women treated unfairly. Women discussed personal oppressions which they experience because they are women.
- *Brief Evaluation* of the session.

SESSION #8:
Afternoon and Evening. Focus on racism and nonviolence
- *Attention Expander*
- Case studies of personal experiences with racism were presented by trainers. Participants shared other personal experiences.
- *Statements Exercise*—Topic: "When I first recognized that people were different racially and were treated differently."
- *Brief Evaluation* of the session.
- Discussion of what to do during the last four weeks of the course. The group decided to focus on alienation next.

SESSION #9:
Afternoon and Evening. Alienation
- *Attention Expander*
- Sharing in groups of five. Each person talked for 5 minutes on the topic: "Experiences that have raised my consciousness about social problems and that have helped me grow."
- Discussion of how alienation prevents growth.
- Reports. Chapter 1 of *Pedagogy of the Oppressed*, by

Paulo Freire (Herder and Herder, 1970). *The Pursuit of Loneliness*, by Philip Slater (Beacon Press, 1970); focuses on the middle class as an oppressed group.

• Group discussion using the following questions: What do oppressed people have in common (women, blacks, students)? How does oppression relate to violence? Is it possible to feel as if you are both the oppressed and the oppressor? Do you have any insights on how to deal with oppression nonviolently? Discuss noncooperation.

• Group planned weekend trip to the MNS/LC community in West Phila.

• *Brief Evaluation* of the session.

• Deciding what to do next. The group decided to spend the last several sessions on nonviolent campaigns for social change.

SESSION #10:

• Weekend at the MNS/LC community. Activities included a workshop on political puppetry and guerrilla theater. The group performed its theater action on the street.

SESSION #11:

Afternoon and Evening—Focus: Social change campaigns

• *Attention Expander.*

• *Web Chart* on how oppressions are linked.

• Short talk on the steps in a social change campaign.

• Group *Brainstormed* social problems participants wanted to work on and broke into small groups. Each small group selected an issue, developed on paper a model campaign, and returned to the large group to share it.

• *Roleplays*. Topics: Confrontation and negotiation.

• *Brief Evaluation* of the session.

SESSION #12:

Afternoon and Evening

• *Life Line Exercise*, focusing on how working for social change fits into each participant's life.

• Individuals shared their life lines.

• *Evaluation* of the course, written and oral.

• Discussion of how class can be an on-going group. Participants set up future meeting times and selected facilitators.

Evaluation:

The Problem Posing/Dialogic Approach requires sensitivity, flexibility, and creativity on the part of the trainers in helping the group identify its themes (goals and expectations) and then in planning experiences which will help the group learn. By learning to build and use new training tools, a group can clarify what it wants to learn.

Students need to be involved in planning the course. Time should be arranged when the facilitators and students can plan together. In some sessions students may play the role of a sounding board, but in others they may participate fully. It is important for students to learn how to plan learning experiences for themselves after the course is finished.

An important consideration in building a cohesive and active group is the development of group dynamics and facilitation skills. Students need to practice these skills. If a class is well prepared in them, it will be able to continue as a social change group after trainers/facilitators have left.

Frequently, when the course is over, a group will just have arrived at the point where it could engage in a social change campaign. Trainers should be willing to spend additional time with the group until it is able to facilitate its own meetings and develop its skills as needed.

If students get interested in an on-going project, they should be encouraged to continue as a group. Contact with other nonviolent social change groups will be necessary to maintain momentum.

Teachers as well as students should be encouraged to enroll in the social change course. This is important because (1) teachers will come into contact with students and staff with a social change perspective and skills, (2) the school will have persons skilled in group process to give continuity, (3) teacher involvement means that someone in the power structure can learn social change skills and become a student advocate, and (4) the Problem Posing/Dialogic Approach will introduce new teaching methods to teachers.

COURSE DESIGN B: THE ISSUE/PROJECT APPROACH
(Methods of Nonviolent Social Change: 8 week course, 5 hours per week, used with 11th and 12th grade students and several teachers at George School, Newtown, Pa.)

The Issue/Project Approach requires a high degree of skill on the part of the trainers and a large amount of self-discipline among participants. The trainers have used it only once in a course for schools. This approach is recommended for groups that have a general background in social change or that are already focused on an issue.

In spite of problems, students and teachers were able to use the skills they learned to make significant changes in their personal lives as well as in the process and content of future courses at the school. The results included a course in Methods of Nonviolent Social Change coordinated by a student and a teacher, major revisions in the teaching of history at the school, and individual involvement in numerous social change projects outside of the school.

Goals: (of trainers)
- Teach students the skills and methods of nonviolent social change.
- Help students transfer the skills to their everyday lives.
- Build a sense of community in the group.

Process:

Several months in advance, three trainers began meeting with the head of the history department, gradually adding a few other teachers and students. After much negotiation and planning, agreement was reached to offer a course in Methods of Nonviolent Social Change. A meeting was held with interested students and teachers at which the trainers shared their vision of a course to be jointly developed by trainers, students, and teachers. A process of co-learning was developed by scheduling pre-course planning meetings when most of the interested students and teachers could attend. The school schedule was modified to extend the length of sessions. Trainers met and talked with other teachers and administrators on numerous occasions to introduce them to the process and content of the course.

Trainers structured a three-week introduction to nonviolent social change theory and process. Activities such as *Affirmation* were designed to promote sharing and community. Case studies of past nonviolent actions, particularly those involving students, were presented to raise consciousness about theory, strategy, and tactics. Possible issues were discussed, and alternative visions were explored, using basic exercises and tools. A great deal of time was spent on the development of a decision-making process so that the group could direct itself during the last part of the course. A weekend retreat at a social change community was planned by the group to develop better community spirit and to provide opportunities to learn about social change from people involved in it.

During the last five weeks of the course, participants selected an issue and worked on it, using stages in a social change campaign as their basis. Throughout this process students were to learn skills of community building, consciousness raising, evaluation, group dynamics, personal growth, and direct action as they were needed. Decisions were to be made by the group in meetings facilitated by students.

Stages in a Social Change Campaign

Gathering Stage:

Focusing—Focus on issues in which students are interested. Work in small groups.

Analysis—Research problems. Understand their context.

Define Goals—Explore a variety of possible alternatives. Define long and short term goals.

Preparation for Engagement—Develop a strategy for change and prepare for social change activities.

Engagement Stage:

Cultural Preparation—Talk about the problem/issue with people affected by it (what needs to be changed? why?) and share ideas about alternatives.

Negotiation—Discuss problem with people who appear to be blocking changes.

Confrontation—Act directly to change the situation.

Content: Sequence of Activities for First Four Sessions

SESSION#1:

Introductions of participants, using *Affirmation Exercise.* Each person introduced self and shared two good things about self, one that the group might know and one that was known only by the individual.

• *Introduction of the course.* Facilitators explained the basic goals; presented proposed agenda for the first four sessions and sought approval; distributed reading material which would be discussed periodically; and explained about keeping a personal and group journal to record what happened during the course.

• *Planning.* Facilitators proposed that the participants visit the MNS/LC in West Philadelphia for an intensive encounter with people working on various social change projects. Participants listed tasks that needed to be done in order to make the trip, divided into work groups to carry out the tasks, and planned to report back to the whole group.

SESSION #2:

• *Affirmation Exercise.*

• *Scenario Writing.* Individuals were asked to write scenarios describing the steps they would need to take to reach their vision. Scenarios would be shared at next class meeting.

• *Discussion* of readings about high school students who have been involved in social change.

• *Planning* for the weekend.

SESSION #3:

• *Affirmation Exercise.*

- *Check-in* and general discussion about how the course has gone so far.
- *Scenario Sharing.* Individuals shared their scenarios in groups of five. Each small group wrote a joint scenario including a strategy that the group could take to reach its vision.
- *Group Planning.* Setting up book shelves, rearranging the furniture, developing a dictionary of social change terms using file cards.

SESSION #4:
- *Affirmation Exercise.*
- *Reaction/feedback* on how course is going.
- *Presentation of social change theory by trainers*—principles of nonviolence, theory of *Affirmation*.
- *Group journal.* Discussion and organization.
- *Brainstorming* issues around which the group might like to develop a social change campaign.

Evaluation of Course Process:

The original plan for the course was to develop a class meeting structure in which all decisions would be made by consensus and facilitated by a student. Instead, we found it useful for the experienced trainers to facilitate the first several class meetings, demonstrating the necessary skills. A workshop on facilitation and practice in small groups would probably help the students learn the skills more quickly than would throwing them directly into a class meeting. We have found this to be true in the other seminars we have facilitated.

Full planning in a group of 18 proved impossible. We rapidly moved to a small group of two students and two facilitators. This process was more efficient, but the students were frustrated by the fact that facilitators knew more and that students were frequently in the position of approving or disapproving facilitators' proposals. To better share the planning process, students needed to know more about available resources. A manual like this that includes a variety of resources would have been helpful.

Because most trainers are products of teacher-dominated classrooms and reject that model, and in an attempt to encourage student initiative, trainers frequently withheld information needed by students to take responsibility. This is a common problem among progressive and free-school teachers. Trainers must take great care not to dominate the decision-making process, but they should offer information and encourage students to acquire skills which empower them to control their own learning situation. Many training tools, such as *Simulation*

Games, can be set up by trainers. These games allow the students to explore particular areas and still use the expertise of the facilitators. The difficult balance of helping, yet allowing students to take responsibility, is one of the hardest tasks of a trainer.

Evaluation of Course Content:

The first two weeks in which a structured introduction was presented were clearly important for student consciousness raising. The traditional structure, with trainers deciding what information was to be covered, was much more comfortable to students than the unstructured second half of the course where they had to direct themselves.

Community-building activities built trust and openness in the group. Community feeling developed, reaching a high point during the weekend spent together visiting a social change community. When the group returned to the boarding school environment, the sense of community dropped rapidly and, in spite of efforts to regain it, never reached the levels experienced earlier. The students' own evaluation was that the fragmented and busy schedule and lack of community spirit at the school made it difficult to maintain community spirit among class participants.

Trainers need to consult the students very early in the course to find out what issues or social problems they are concerned about. Exercises in this course could have been better developed around students' concerns.

Affirmation Exercises in front of the full group are threatening. Breaking into pairs has a lower threat level and serves a similar community-building purpose. When the trust level has been built up, group Affirmations work well. At the end of a session, affirmations or a short, fun game leave people feeling good. A "closing circle," in which people hold hands or put their arms around each other, is especially effective.

The students had difficulty in selecting a social problem to work on. This was due in part to the lack of interest among the juniors and seniors in changing their immediate school environment. They were more interested in focusing on what they would do when they left. Also, focusing itself is a difficult process. Most students were unable to select an issue and move into the Engagement Stage by the end of the course.

Trainers can help students focus their concerns as a group by (1) presenting group dynamics exercises which allow groups to see how they function and how they can improve, (2) teaching specific decision-making and priority-setting tools, (3) presenting concrete decision-making structures, (4) structuring simu-

193

lated decision-making experiences, (5) offering decision-making opportunities on simple issues to build skill and confidence for more complex decisions, and (6) pointing out to the group when it is making successful decisions and when its process is good.

Trainers who work with groups that select issues with high emotional involvement or distressful past experience need to be prepared to counter depressed feelings with lots of affirmation and community building. If the group does not develop a positive base from which to work, it will either sink into greater apathy and feelings of powerlessness or will move toward more violent responses.

Institutional social change is too big a step for many students. When this is true, trainers need to focus on the personal problems of the individuals, being careful to help the students see the links between their personal oppressions and societal phenomena.

Students who exhibit severe emotional distress should be encouraged to seek help outside of class. Trainers can use their own skills to listen and encourage release of tension and hurt. Trainers should not be embarrassed to ask a student to leave the course if his/her needs for personal attention conflict with the agreed-upon goals of the course.

Participants can be encouraged to select an issue which has a lower emotional investment and a higher possibility of accomplishing a change. Success breeds confidence, and larger issues can be tackled later.

WORKING WITH YOUNG PEOPLE: PRESCHOOLS, GRADE SCHOOLS, TEACHERS AND PARENTS

Young people frequently suffer indignities because of their age. Often their choices are severely limited in basic areas such as what they eat and wear, with whom they associate, where they live, and how much money they have to spend.

Patterns of submission and oppression are learned at a very young age. Although adults can often remember in detail unpleasant and unfair ways they were treated as young people, they frequently use a variation of this hurtful behavior when they associate with younger people.

There is evidence that in each generation more people are becoming aware of how the day to day treatment of younger people by adults shapes behavior. Thus they can encourage change for the better.

Ending injustice to and oppression of younger people means to encourage them:

- to take responsibility for decisions about the structure and events of their own time;
- to develop their natural abilities to handle difficult situations;
- to appreciate themselves and others;
- to contribute directly to society as creators, producers and discriminating consumers.

The authors feel that working with young people on creative responses to their own problems is important. Many of the resources appearing in this manual have been used with younger people and others can be adapted to meet the needs of the particular situation.

Resources Available For Working with Young People:

1. *A Manual on Nonviolence and Children*, by Stephanie Judson, et al. (Friends Peace Committee, Phila., approx. $5 plus postage). Theory and activities on affirmation, sharing, cooperative games and conflict resolution. List of books for children and adults. Accounts of work in schools, and approaches for teacher support and parent support work, developed by the Nonviolence and Children Program.

For information on where the Nonviolence and Children Program has worked and additional resources available, contact Friends Peace Committee, 1515 Cherry, Phila., PA 19102.

2. *Children's Creative Response to Conflict Handbook*, by Priscilla Prutzman, et al. (Quaker Project on Community Conflict, New York, 1975, $3.50). Practical and useful information. Includes sections on Introductory and Loosening-up Exercises, Personal Affirmation Exercises, Community and Cooperation Building Exercises, Communication Skills, Conflict Resolution, Teaching Nonviolence with Puppets, Finding Solutions and Collecting Information from a Group, and Themes. Also includes information on planning workshops, and 16 sample workshops.

For information on where the Children's Creative Response to Conflict Program has worked and other resources available, contact Quaker Project on Community Conflict, 133 W. 14th, New York, NY 10011.

3. *Parent Effectiveness Training: The Tested New Way to Raise Responsible Children*, by Dr. Thomas Gordon (New American Library/Plume Books, 1970, $4.95). Book and course give adults a workable language of acceptance through which many

conflicts between parent and child can be resolved, without the use of power, to meet the needs of *both*. Process equally useful in adult-child and adult-adult relationships.

For nearest 8-week course in Parent or Teacher Effectiveness Training, write: P.E.T. Information, Effectiveness Training Associates, 531 Stevens Ave., Solano Beach, CA 92075.

4. Pamphlets by Edward Myers Hayes (AFSC, 821 Euclid Ave., Syracuse, NY 13210).

Roleplaying in the Classroom (1974, 8 pp, 10¢). How to use roleplaying with young children.

Puppetry as a Teaching Tool (1974, 5 pp, 10¢). Puppetry as an affective development tool.

An Approach to Improving Classroom Communication (1974, 7 pp, 10¢). Listening and communication exercises for young children.

HOW TO GET A COURSE OR WORKSHOP INTO A SCHOOL (OR OTHER INSTITUTION)

Organizing From Outside

A frequently asked question is, "How did you get in?" Here are some suggestions which have helped in the past.

• *A written proposal*—Draw up and circulate a proposal among people you think might be interested. Talk to them about it and ask them who they think might be interested.

• *The administration*—The principal, headmaster, or director of a school or organization may be open to innovation and change. Facilitator/trainers can talk directly with an administrator or negotiate for training sessions.

• *A friendly teacher or student*—Frequently, trainers can find a sympathetic teacher or student who can increase interest among other staff members and students in developing a course and bringing in outside trainers. A demonstration class can be held to increase interest.

• *A parent support group*—A support group of parents and/or graduates can frequently provide the needed leverage to get a social change course into an institution.

• *A weekend workshop for teachers, students, and parents* —A weekend workshop on "Teaching Peace and Social Change" can be organized and sponsored by the school or by another local group. If trainers have good contacts, they can organize and run their own workshop, an effective method when school administrators refuse to let them in. Teachers and students who have been trained can share what they learn with other staff members and students in the school. In this type of workshop, it is important that at least two people from each school come to the sessions so they can support each other in their social change efforts when they return. Weekend workshops often lead to an invitation for trainers to hold workshops in schools and universities. They also allow students to meet people with a radical analysis which they might otherwise not encounter. In the long run, holding teacher training workshops is an effective strategy for change. Public schools provide good recruiting grounds for large numbers of people of all backgrounds. Training teachers to teach social change skills multiplies the number of people who can teach these skills. *Note:* Before attempting to train teachers or other trainers, it is wise to have a variety of social change experiences oneself, such as teaching courses, running a project or campaign, or resolving a conflict, as well as experience in group dynamics and democratic decision making.

• *An after-school workshop*—If you can't get in during the day, try an after-school activity period. If necessary, you could register yourself as a club. An after work activity can be a successful organizing strategy in other institutions too.

• *A crisis situation*—Frequently a crisis in a community, school, or organization will open doors to training in creative and innovative responses. When people's normal approaches fail to solve critical problems, groups become open to alternatives. Trainers need to be aware of potential crisis situations and prepare training and organizing sessions to meet people's special needs.

• *The union*—An area which we have not explored, but one which seems to make a lot of sense, is organizing people through their unions. Workshops could be set up on democratic decision making, teaching the use of a democratic process, conflict resolution, negotiation skills, and direct action skills. Sessions with union members on social change strategy for themselves and society could also be beneficial.

Organizing From Inside

For those already within the institution, the task may be easier or more difficult depending upon the school and community.

Some general guidelines for those working from within are:
• Be clear about what you are doing. Know your material and the format of the course you want to facilitate.
• Develop a community of support among students, staff, and parents. An isolated teacher or student is much less likely to

be successful than a group of concerned people.

• Ask for help if you need it from sympathetic groups, lawyers, and training resources.

• Spend some time with your support group developing an analysis, strategy, and tactics which apply to your particular community, school, or organization.

• Develop an over-all strategy and vision, but limit what you do so that you are not over-extended. One good course on nonviolent social change with 18 students and teachers is better than a poorly organized effort to raise overall consciousness in the school. Larger issues and groups can be tackled after a successful base/support group is established.

Schools that Have Sponsored Courses or Workshops in Nonviolent Social Change

High Schools:

Cinnaminson Alternative Public High School, Cinnaminson, NJ

George School, Newtown, PA

Oakwood Friends School, Poughkeepsie, NY

Putney School, Putney, VT

West Catholic High, Philadelphia, PA

Westtown School, Westtown, PA

Colleges and Universities:

Earlham College, Richmond, IN

Friends World College, Kyoto, Japan

Glassboro State College, Glassboro, NJ

Gustavus Adolphus College, St. Peter, MN

St. Joseph's College, Philadelphia, PA

Stockton College, Pomona, NJ

Syracuse University, Syracuse, NY

Temple University, Philadelphia, PA

University of Colorado, Boulder, CO

Villanova College, Villanova, PA

Williams College, Williamstown, MA

Graduate Schools:

Antioch/Putney, Putney, VT

Rutgers University, New Brunswick, NJ

School of Social Work, University of Delaware, DE

Other:

Pendle Hill, Wallingford, PA (Quaker Center for Religious and Social Study)

V
Resources

For resources on working with young people, see Working With Young People above.

BOOKS AND PAMPHLETS:

Marshals: What Do They Do? How Do You Train Them? by Robert Levering, et al. (MNS, 4722 Baltimore Ave., Phila., PA 19143, 1970, 14 pp. 60¢). Includes specific exercises and suggestions for organizing and training marshals for vigil, moving march, mass rally and indoor assembly.

Nonviolent Action Training In Japan: As a Project in East Asia of IAD, by Charles Esser and Christopher Moore (AFSC, International Affairs, Attn: Roberta Levenback, 1501 Cherry, Phila., PA 19102, 1972, 18 pp, $.90 plus postage). Explores use of nonviolence training in a foreign country.

Nonviolent Training: A Manual, by Carl Zeitlow and Brian Yaffe (Zeitlow, Troutville, PA 15866, 115 pp, $2.50 unbound, $4.00 bound looseleaf, $1.00 mailing). Good information on training, especially as it relates to developing strategy and carrying out a campaign. Originally compiled and used for the May Day actions of the People's Coalition for Peace and Justice in 1971; now includes much additional information.

A Study of Training Programs for Nonviolent Direct Action In The United States, by Lynne Shivers. (Write to the author, c/o MNS, 4722 Baltimore Ave., Phila., PA 19143, 1969, 66 pp. Price on inquiry.) Not a training document per se, but a review of training programs up to 1968 and a good theoretical discussion of training, with suggestions.

Towards Nonviolent Revolution, by Narayan Desai (1972; available from Gandhi Institute, Box 92, Cheyney, PA 19319, $3.00). Several chapters on training and the uses of training.

Training for Nonviolent Action for High School Students: A Handbook, by Bidge McKay (Friends Peace Committee, 1515 Cherry, Phila., PA 19102, 1971, 50 pp, $1.00). Training from a student context with examples and appendix.

Training for Nonviolent Action: Some History, Analysis, Reports of Surveys, Charles C. Walker, ed. (Walker, Box 92, Cheyney, PA 19319, 76 pp, $2.00). Focuses on training for demonstrations, including training of marshals and evaluation of training programs.

Cheyney, PA 19319, 76 pp, $2.00). Focuses on training for demonstrations, including training of marshals and evaluation of training programs.

FILM SOURCES:

American Documentary Films, Inc., 336 W. 84th, New York, NY 10024 (212) 799-7440 *or* 397 Bay, San Francisco, CA 94133 (415) 982-7475. Produces and distributes a variety of films especially documenting liberation struggles. Write for catalogue.

Newsreel, 332 7th Ave., New York, NY 10001. Nationwide organization of activist filmers. Will arrange screenings or mail films to interested groups. For information on films or other offices, inquire.

GROUPS TO CONTACT FOR ASSISTANCE IN TRAINING:

It is possible for people to use the resources in this manual to begin or continue their own training processes. If, however, you need help in initial efforts, you will find resource people under Part Ten: Groups to Contact, listed alphabetically by state.

Some of these groups will send teams of trainers to your area upon request. Reimbursement for travel and expenses is usually expected, and sometimes modest honoraria are necessary or recommended.

Both long and short-term training programs are held in the Philadelphia Movement for a New Society/Life Center for people who live outside of Philadelphia. Participants live in the MNS/LC community during the training period and share equitably in living expenses and community work with other community members. Note specifically 1-year training opportunities available through the Training Organizing Collective and 2-week General Training Programs offered several times a year by the Medium-Term Training Organizing Collective. Write for schedules. (See Part Ten for addresses.)

WOMAN POWER

Words and music by Rachel Rubin and Wine, Women and Song
© *1977 Rachel Rubin*

Everyone knows you can't keep a good woman down.
Now they're knowin' we are growin' stronger all around.

CH: Woman power, woman power, woman energy,
      No surprising, we are risin' far as the eye can see.

Building houses, making music, raising children too—
Woman power keeps us moving, strong in all we do.   (CH)

In the office, in the restaurants, in the factories too,
We are rising, organizing all that women do.   (CH)

We've got poets, we've got painters, we've got printers too.
We are singing, we are bringing women's words to you.   (CH)

Up in the hills and down in the cities, all the world around,
We're not sitting' and lookin' pretty—
    —we won't be held down.   (CH)

Repeat first verse and chorus.

Part Seven
Organizing for Change

It is a hopeful sign that so many people are organizing for change around basic issues. People are uniting to challenge large corporate interests, to democratize organizational structures, and to develop alternatives.

We believe that fundamental changes are needed in our political and economic system and in our human relationships. Centralized institutions where decisions are made by a few need to give way to decentralized and cooperative groups of community people, who make decisions that affect their own lives personally and communally.

It is not easy to make such changes. We need to reclaim power in all areas of our lives, putting our mental, emotional and physical resources to work in meeting human needs. Groups of people organized effectively *can* challenge and stop the destruction and misuse of community and environmental resources and can create new alternatives to replace rigid and inefficient institutions.

We personally know many people who are working together on basic problems and making necessary changes. We believe it possible for others to gather together their common sense of decency, their resources, their goals for a good society, and solve the problems that face them. As we search for solutions, we need to develop creative approaches consistent with our goals. When crises arise or we gain new information about a situation, we need to be open to designing new strategies and tactics and not be bound by old models of change.

In the other nine parts of this manual are resources we have used in our own training/organizing efforts. These resources have helped us to develop skills in numerous areas including analysis, strategy, group process, personal and group decision making, and conflict resolution. In Part Seven we offer suggestions on how these skills may be used in organizing for change. We hope they are helpful to you in your work.

I
Getting Started

CHOOSING A FOCUS

Choosing a focus requires that people have real goals for themselves, others and society. To establish these goals, people need to investigate what is happening in the world around them and what they and others are thinking. Taking enough time to share with others is important in making the friends and allies which will help us to act on goals. Individual problems that a group decides to focus on may be complex and confusing. Taking the time to research and share information before choosing a focus is often necessary.

When choosing a focus, the following suggestions are helpful:
• Meet with a group of people (3-10) regularly to talk about and try out ideas you are researching.
• Investigate past and present efforts for change in your area and the world.
• Develop a broad analysis of major problems in the society and their causes.
• Create a vision of how you would like the world to be.
• Develop a theory of how change occurs.
• Focus on the causes, not the manifestations, of problems.
• Investigate the relationship of the political/economic causes to common, personal problems which you and others feel.
• Think about your own goals.
• Select an issue which you find exciting and challenging.
• Select an issue which connects with other social problems.

Select as carefully as you can. There is a limit to what one group can do, so choose a manageable piece of an issue. While working on one aspect of a problem, you may discover deeper causes. Evaluate the new information, and choose a new focus if that makes sense. A variety of resources are available in Parts One, Five, Six, and Eight to help groups focus.

DEVELOPING GROUP DISCIPLINE AND SKILLS

For groups to accomplish difficult, long-range goals, careful attention needs to be given to the development of group discipline and skills. For this reason the relation between training and organizing is important. Training can create a process in which trust grows, problems are examined, skills are learned and shared, and solutions are tried and evaluated. A good ongoing training program can also build group discipline, which helps prevent actions or reactions which bring disorder to, or work against the objectives of, the project.

Part Six: "Training and Education" describes a training process currently used in several organizing efforts. As groups organize for change, their participants' own experiences and information can be incorporated into this ongoing training process to improve group discipline and skill. Resources described in the rest of the manual can help facilitate this process.

CRITERIA FOR SELECTING A PROGRAM FOR CHANGE

There are a number of factors, in addition to the determination of the organizers, which strongly influence the success of a program for change. If participants hope to effect basic changes in the society, attract the support of large numbers of people, and persist until their goals are accomplished, the following aspects of programs should be included wherever possible:

1. *A clear description of the problem* which:
   - points out the problem's basic causes;
   - describes the problem in terms of failure of existing institutions to meet current needs;
   - makes connections between issues and political and economic aspects of the problem;
   - makes connections between personal problems and institutional causes.

2. *Clearly-stated, achievable goals* which include:
   - clear short and long-term objectives;
   - the removal of the causes of the problem so that the problem doesn't manifest itself in other forms or recur later on;
   - a shift in resources of people and money from maintaining unimportant or unjust institutions to providing needed services and supporting constructive change;
   - a shift in power to a more democratic direction (a change in policy alone is not adequate);
   - a vision of what the future can be like economically, politically and socially.

205

3. An alternative for people which includes:

• a replacement for what one is opposing; a solution to the problem;

• an opportunity to try out alternatives which are proposed for a broader scale;

• an opportunity to achieve desirable ends by creating organizations which encourage self-help and group initiative;

• opportunities for people to learn basic skills and information needed (1) to carry out independent self-help programs and (2) to cooperate with other groups in developing networks of support;

• community-building and outreach structures and experiences which connect people with others involved in similar efforts.

4. Actions vividly conveying the message in socio-drama form which:

• cut through liberal dialogue and academic discussions;

• reduce the problem and solution to a picture which tells the story without the need for verbal explanations;

• show a clear violation of widely held values like justice, democracy, personal safety;

• include attention-holding drama (e.g., involve elements of personal risk, civil disobedience, etc.);

• are a new form of communication, a clear and effective message which encourages people to become involved.

5. A way to fuse constructive programs with direct action to achieve a permanent change. The combination of 3 and 4 above.

6. Opportunities for involvement and shared responsibility.

• Decentralization and democratic decision-making, reflected in the way the program is organized. (See "Building Organizational Strength.")

• Involvement occurring on many levels. Allows for increased participation of people through direct action; support of those in direct action; constructive program; work in activities of low visibility such as education and research; giving of money or gifts in kind.

7. Programs/actions fairly easy to duplicate.

• They should focus on issues where people feel oppressed. Issues should be timely and affect large numbers of people.

• Program and actions should have potential for bringing about national or transnational changes, especially important if the issue is a transnational one.

• If public consciousness does not already exist on the issue, it should be perceived by organizers to be easily aroused by consciousness-raising activities.

- Good sub-issues should be available as handles for the larger problem.

8. An element of dilemma for the guardians of unjust institutions and practices.

- If activists are allowed to continue, they make the changes they want. If guardians try to stop the activities, public attention is drawn to the issue and reveals the undesirable truth about the guardians and the unjust institutions over which they preside. (See Dilemma Demonstration.) It reveals a violation of democratic values, or contradiction in values.

9. The ability to sustain and build until needed change is achieved.

- Issue should be clear and present over a long period, increasing in importance with time.
- It's important to have a generating theme* making possible further change and release of additional people into struggle.
- There should be potential for eventual success.
- It should be possible to organize the issue into a number of steps or smaller issues, so that small successes can be achieved along the way to the basic change.

CHOOSING TACTICS

Tactics are actions selected to accomplish specific objectives. They include the way people and materials are organized for the action. Careful selection of tactics is important because they are the most visible part of your program. People are attracted or frightened away by the choice of tactics and the way you implement them. If people are impressed by your tactics, they are likely to want to know more about your analysis and strategy for change.

Tactics should:

- be consistent with the general, overall plan of action (see Planning a Strategy);

---

* A generating theme, as used here, is an issue which can encourage and involve a variety of additional people on related issues or connected problems. For example: the B-1 bomber/peace conversion campaign raises issues of disarmament, ecology, U.S.-Third World relations and government expenditures for weapons rather than for social needs. Peace activists, ecology groups, and social service groups have been drawn into the campaign.

• clearly state the issue to people even if they disagree with the tactics or would choose other methods;

• be tested out before using them in real action situations. Tools for testing the usefulness of a tactic are *Roleplays, Force Field Analysis, Flow Chart, Quick Decision,* and *Situation Analysis.*

Example of tactics chosen to accomplish stated goals and strategy.

Goal: Develop safe, non-polluting and decentralized sources of electrical and mechanical energy in the U.S.

Strategy: To build ecologically sound energy supply sources on a decentralized basis while preventing highly centralized power companies from constructing nuclear power plants, wasting non-renewable resources, and polluting the environment.

Tactics used to succeed: Street speak and leaflet on a variety of related issues, design and build alternative power supply systems, create resource and education centers to teach people the skills they need to develop their own energy supply systems, creatively confront police attempting to close down safe, local energy sources.

When the goals is complex and the problem affects many people, as in the example above, many groups will need to work on different aspects of the problem. Tactics will need to be as flexible and varied as the situations in which they are used.

A variety of tactics is available depending on the goals and strategy chosen. For a description of 198 tactics used in nonviolent resistance and action, see *The Politics of Nonviolent Action, Part Two: The Methods of Nonviolent Action,* by Gene Sharp.

II
Building Organizational Strength

No direct action campaign can sustain itself for long without strong constructive programs which meet people's basic needs and which illustrate through practical work the goals of

---

* For a fuller discussion of this topic read pp 66-101 in *Strategy for a Living Revolution,* by George Lakey.

the campaign. Likewise, a group which demonstrates an alternative program to meet people's needs will find it necessary at times to launch action campaigns to challenge conflicting government and corporate interests. For example, people who develop a regionalized food production and distribution program which produces high quality foods, provides more satisfying jobs for workers, and causes less environmental damage will need to resist attempts by food conglomerates to maintain a monopoly on food markets, and to challenge the right of speculators to maintain control of land resources. Whether your immediate focus is an alternative program or a direct action campaign, an organizational base is essential, and on many issues organizational strength will need to be transnational and include thousands of organizing groups.

When working for systemic changes, organizing needs to occur on three levels: (1) the organizational framework, (2) the constructive program and (3) the direct action campaign. A program for change may begin by organizing on any one of these levels, but if lasting, widespread change is to occur, organizing on all three levels will eventually be necessary.

A. THE ORGANIZATIONAL FRAMEWORK

An organization is an arrangement of people and their relationships into a structure for the purpose of accomplishing common tasks.

Bureaucratic organizations with a board of directors or an executive committee, a paid staff, and a clearly designated hierarchical structure are often effective in achieving goals, such as lobbying for legislation, training people for a specific job, or redistributing land. To maintain their budget, these organizations usually appeal to a broad constituency which may or may not be involved.

Political parties, also hierarchical in their organizational form, are usually oriented towards selling a candidate to the masses of people rather than engaging in dialogue with them on real issues.

There are elements of bureaucratic structure which are important to any organizing effort, such as standardized routines for handling problems or agreed upon rights and responsibilities of individuals to the group, but there are also some negative aspects. Hierarchical structure which removes policy making from people who will be affected and impersonality which produces alienation are aspects which need to be corrected.

As we build a better society it is necessary to develop

209

organizational structures which reflect and support the values for which we work, both because these structures are visual examples by their style of activity, and because they will in many cases replace poorly functioning institutions.

New organizational forms are needed which can help people deal with their own most pressing issues, and can renew and encourage cooperative activities, infusing cultural richness back into people's political and social lives.

This manual encourages experimentation with forms of people-centered organizations which (1) can stop institutions from acting out destructive policies on people or the environment, (2) can challenge undemocratic institutions and profit-centered industries, and (3) can restore or gain grass-roots control over decision making.

There are several aspects we would like to see incorporated in the organizations we are developing:

• Liberation of individuals and groups to act on their own best insights.

• Rapid, open dissemination of information. An end to privileged information.

• People freed from social patterns or roles. Everyone given equal opportunities to learn skills and share in all aspects of the work, increasing the resourcefulness of all participants.

• Widespread sharing of training/organizing skills among individuals and organizations.

• Broad sharing of leadership skills and responsibilities so that creative programs can be developed and carried out simultaneously in many locations. When repression strikes, the movement cannot be stopped by hitting a concentrated center or removing the charismatic leader.

• Decisions made by the people affected by them.

• Economic control of organizations by the people who operate them. No dependency on contributors outside the organization by whom the program could be controlled.

• Decentralized structure based on concepts of self-sufficiency of local groups.

• Meaningful and satisfying work for all participants.

• Community support to allow people to resist oppression, personal and institutional. People who feel connected with each other.

• Institutions which are responsible to wider economic, ecological and social needs of the community.

• People enabled to work on short, middle, and long-range goals.

- Problems solved in ways that allow people in other parts of the world also to meet their basic need for a meaningful life.
- Incorporation of policy into internal structure to combat racism, sexism, elitism, ageism, nationalism, classism, etc.
- Connection with a transnational network committed to equality, local autonomy, universal peoplehood, and equitable distribution of wealth and power. Rejection of use of military power to maintain privilege.
- Participative democracy/discussion encouraged among peers on the great issues of the day.
- Activities rooted in common purpose and community.
- Connections between concrete issues/problems and fundamental causes reflected in the programs chosen.

The organizational framework we have found to be most supportive of our goals as stated above is small groups linked together in a voluntary "life center" and/or network (see below). Through this structure small groups maintain autonomy while being able to join with other groups to work on difficult projects of common interest. Once agreements are reached, everyone is encouraged to participate in carrying them out. As the basic institutions in our society continue to malfunction or break down completely, new organizational models will be welcomed and sought after by the casualties of the old order.

The Small Group (4-12 people):

Advantages of the small group as the basic organizing structure:
- The internal structure of the group can be informal. Time on bureaucratic problems can be saved, leaving more time for work on the chosen task or developing skills among members.
- Skill-sharing can occur easily. Leadership functions can be shared or rotated so everyone learns them, and other skills, such as fund raising, typing, and song leading, can be exchanged.
- Each member can participate in decision making. It is possible to learn to make decisions by consensus, a more inclusive basis for working together. (See Consensus Decision Making.)
- The group can be more experimental. It can take positions or undertake projects that might upset a larger constituency if it depended on one for funding or permission.
- Everyone can have a chance to wrestle with problems and issues of injustice and think critically about analytical and strategic questions.
- Members can develop enough trust and commitment to support each other through personal or group crises.

211

• Members can support their own activities. Funds can be sought for specific projects, or members may all work together in an economic alternative or have jobs outside of the group. Incomes can be shared if desired.

• Members can focus and concentrate on a task and/or issues in such a way as to see results and build confidence. Meetings of the membership for shared work, decision making and fun can be held frequently.

• Frequent and multi-dimensional sharing among members can make it difficult for undercover agents or provocateurs to infiltrate and disrupt activities.

• Groups can grow and divide as cells. New groups can begin and different aspects of the same problem can be cooperatively worked on without sacrificing any one group's goals or style for another's.

For small groups to function well, it is important to have all of the following:

• A clear process for joining and leaving the group.

• Clear procedure and structure for decision making with clear lines of authority and responsibility. The more difficult the task to be done, the clearer these need to be. Everyone in the group can be involved (if s/he wants to be) and should know who will be doing what.

• A self selection process for deciding who does what, infused into many aspects of the program. Participants could give preliminary thought to selected questions before coming to a meeting where decisions are to be made together. Things considered by the Tool Box* training collective were:

> My reasons for wanting to participate.
> Perceived task(s) to be done and needs to be met.
> Skills and resources I have which would make a strong and effective contribution toward fulfilling those tasks and meeting those needs.
> Disadvantages I see in my participating.
> Projected length of involvement.

Responses were shared briefly and freely with all other participants and a consensus sought for the right people for this aspect of the program.

• A process to deal with personal distress, interpersonal and intra-group conflicts.

• An ongoing process of skill sharing and personal support.

---

* The Tool Box was a Philadelphia based MNS training collective that trained only outside of Philadelphia 1972-73.

- Ongoing evaluation sessions:
  to help individuals function better (see *Self Estimation Session* and *Making Personal Decisions*);
  to help groups evaluate ongoing activities of the group (see *Evaluation*).

Several types of small groups have so far been found useful. They are described briefly below with functions special to their particular types.

1. Action Collective (sometimes called the Nonviolent Revolutionary Group or NRG)—has a limited time commitment, sometimes as short as three months. An action collective:

- focuses on a specific issue like a nuclear energy moratorium, U.S. military intervention abroad, or a change in the food distribution system;
- researches and develops an analysis of a particular problem as the basis for long-term involvement;
- develops an action campaign to accomplish specific goals;
- may be the core organizing group for a campaign involving hundreds or thousands of people; or may engage in coalition actions as they seem appropriate;
- provides support for members as they engage in direct action projects.

Example: Citizens' Right To Know All About Nuclear Power organized to focus public attention on the biased nature of literature, films, and speakers presented by the Philadelphia Electric Company (PECO), especially at its Atomic Information Center, Limerick, Pa. Its demands specified ways that PECO should spend money to inform its customers about disadvantages of nuclear power, alternative energy sources, and conservation of energy. The collective was active 4 months and had about 10 members at any time, though there was considerable turnover in membership. Demonstrations usually included 30-50 people. Three broad goals were implemented during the existence of the group: 1) to increase public opposition to the use of nuclear energy in the Philadelphia area; 2) to develop training methodologies for nonviolent campaigns; and 3) to train people for nonviolent campaigns. People interested in organizing or training for action campaigns around atomic energy issues can contact Bill Moyer, 4713 Windsor Ave., Phila., PA 19143.

2. Working Collective—may have a duration of many years. A working collective:

- focuses on a task related to building a movement for

change; e.g., training, outreach, internal communications among the network; development of special tools or resources, providing money-earning opportunities for individuals, or building an alternative institution;

- develops an analysis, vision, and strategy as a basis for its ongoing work;
- provides satisfactory working conditions for the members of the group;
- may initiate action projects related to its area of work;
- may include special structures to develop emotional support and share incomes.

Example: The Philadelphia Macro-Analysis Collective, now five years old, has eight members, two of them original. They designed and periodically revise the macro-analysis seminar to help people study the root causes of social problems and use what they learn to develop campaigns for social change. Through a network of contact people, a seminar manual and a quarterly newsletter, over 250 macro-analysis seminars have formed in the U.S. and Canada. Members meet weekly, run an office, and support themselves through part-time work outside the collective. Grants are occasionally found for specific projects.

3. Organizers' Support Collective—may have a duration of several years but usually does not meet as frequently as a working or action collective. An organizers' support collective:

- provides emotional support for members engaged in organizing activities outside of the group, e.g., in factories, community schools, unions, etc. (members might be involved in similar organizing activities or in different ones);
- develops common analysis, vision, and strategy for members' own activities and the broader movement;
- helps members solve problems each may have in his/her own organizing situation.

The Life Center

A Life Center is a cluster of social change people organized in working collectives and communal households. If it is to continue as a dynamic center, some attention must be given to outreach, training, community support, personal growth of members, and action for change.

In life centers, members may:

- live in communes or extended families within walking distance of each other;
- consolidate efforts and finances in areas such as housing,

cooking, child care, medical care, transportation, recreation, and basic education;
* pool resources to release each other for greater involvement in projects for change;
* pool skills and energy to provide resource centers for others in the broader movement for change. Such centers focus on one or several areas such as research, training, building alternatives, or developing area-wide action projects.

Example: See a description of the Movement for a New Society/Life Center community in Philadelphia, PA, under Part Ten.

The Network

A network is our model for the interrelationship among small groups. Each group remains autonomous but cooperates with other groups toward the achievement of certain goals. Coalitions can be formed within the network by several groups and membership in coalitions can change depending on the type and complexity of the problem.

Functions of the network:
* Communicate information and ideas.
* Develop a network-wide analysis, vision, and strategy.
* Be a channel for groups to challenge and discuss the merits of other member groups' actions.
* Provide aid (financial or physical) for local groups in crisis situations.
* Do outreach to new people on a national level.
* Make decisions on wider policy. Decisions are then taken back to local collectives for approval.

Structures can be used within the network to fill the above functions. Some of these are:
Outreach Collective—Raises funds for network functions and special projects of member groups; encourages formation of new groups. May publish a general newsletter of activities of the network. Promotes the network's ideas. Membership may rotate among collectives or include individuals from a variety of collectives.
* Internal Communications Collective—Facilitates communications within the network, helps in coordinating resources and compiles directories of resources, human and material.
* Internal Newsletter—Shares information, resources or debates of important issues within the network. Responsibility for publishing it may be rotated among collectives in different regions.

- Transnational Collective—Relates to groups and individuals in other countries. May coordinate an exchange program. Encourages other collectives to think transnationally.
- Network Meetings—at all levels—monthly in some areas, 2-4 times a year in regional areas and yearly at the national level. One or more representatives from each collective attend. The network meetings can make recommendations to local collectives, such as criteria for membership in the network and network communication. Groups may report on work being done, share resources, and discuss cooperation on compatible efforts.
- Celebrations—Gatherings of group members, their friends, and interested people. They are times for singing, games, workshops, and discussion groups.
- Forums on important issues and campaigns to be launched.
- Visits and exchanges—Groups or individuals from different locations may work and/or live together for a period of time, learning from each other. With careful planning this may happen on a transnational basis.
- Workshops—Any person or collective can organize or facilitate a workshop on any topic and make it available to people on as broad a geographical basis as they choose.

B. THE CONSTRUCTIVE PROGRAM: BUILDING ALTERNATIVES

The Constructive Program

The constructive program is the broad institutional and educational activity which gives tangible expression to the goals and values of a positive plan for change. It provides essential needs and services in a way that points out injustice or inadequacies in the existing society. It demonstrates the courage, intention, resourcefulness, and sincerity of the advocates of change. A constructive program can be organized to include social, political, or economic aspects, and is often so basic that it transcends immediate issues, political loyalties, and factions.

More specifically, the constructive program can:
- communicate, through example, goals of the larger organizing efforts;
- test, through practice, elements of the vision being projected;
- provide a concrete experience upon which theory can be developed and tested;

216

- demonstrate solidarity of organizers with the community;
- build popular support in the community for the broader program for change;
- support people facing injustice or natural disaster;
- back up and offer resources to those victimized by society;
- bring neighbors into contact with each other through work together on basic needs;
- help people integrate their working lives with their values;
- develop self-discipline, persistence, patience, endurance under hard physical work, initiative, cooperative working relationships, community spirit;
- develop self-confidence and skills needed for self-reliance;
- release tension and nervous energy;
- meet social, political, or economic needs inadequately met by existing institutions;
- build the independence of neighborhoods, regions, and the movement for change by involving people in the process of creating alternatives for themselves;
- develop independence from institutions that provide essential goods and services, thus the ability to withstand repressive measures from government and other institutions;
- remove support from existing oppressive institutions.

Examples of constructive programs. Constructive programs will vary depending on the issue, the context, and the length of the ongoing program for change.

1. The United Farm Workers organizing struggle in California established alternative food distribution facilities, medical care, child care and an auto repair shop that developed into a self-help community. The success of the long-term struggle for rights among farm workers depends on this constructive support system, which continues between the direct action efforts of particular campaigns.

2. The Columbia (NYC) Tenants Union combined constructive program with their direct action campaign when they encouraged poor people to move into houses about to be bulldozed by Columbia University for expansion purposes. The program offered poor people badly-needed housing the city had failed to provide, as well as valuable training in house repair skills. Strong community feeling developed among Tenants Union members and the newly housed poor.

3. The most notable example of the contribution of constructive program to a successful campaign was the village self-sufficiency movement developed by Gandhi and his

followers during the struggle for Indian independence. The program included the spinning and weaving of cotton as a village industry. Hundreds of thousands of peasants spun cotton at home and exchanged it for woven goods at village exchange centers. Other village industries and sanitation facilities were built. An active education program was offered in health, reading, writing, the national language, and technical skills. The need for the uplift of women and removal of untouchability was stressed. The program had the double purpose of increasing economic independence from Britain and developing a strong decentralized India. The program was essential in the success of the independence movement.

The Alternative Institution

Constructive programs which meet people's real needs can quickly gain support from the larger society, and may will grow into viable institutions. For these institutions to be real alternatives they must provide a clear choice between themselves and existing institutions. Alternative institutions can supply goods and services, provide jobs, maintain social order, or encourage political, religious, or social activities. To the degree to which these new institutions succeed in providing efficient alternatives, oppressive or inadequate institutions may weaken or dissolve. Several types of alternative institutions are listed below.

The Community Land Trust is a means to land reform. It releases land from the profit motive and short-sighted exploitation and provides it as a resource for all people. The trust takes land off the speculative market and frees it for people's uses regardless of ability to buy. A trust both buys and receives gifts of land and surveys the land to determine uses that would best meet human needs and sound ecological principles. The land can be leased to individuals or groups, often on life term leases, for uses consistent with the conditions of the trust.

For additional information read *The Community Land Trust: A Guide to a New Model for Land Tenure in America*. Two existing land trusts are New Communities, Inc., Lee County, Georgia, and Sam Ely Land Trust, P.O. Box 116, Brunswick, ME 04011.

Business and Repair Services provide needed income to workers and goods and services to consumers under experimental and satisfying conditions. Some of the services offered through such groups are house, auto or appliance repair, typesetting, and printing. Some of the products available through alternative businesses are bread, games, toys, furniture, kitchen utensils, and clothing. Experimental guidelines for such groups are:

• Have *workers* make decisions affecting workers, including type of work, services offered or products made, quality and safety of materials, work schedules, salaries, work benefits, withholding tax policies, and decision-making process.

• Share skills among workers based on interest. Show no discrimination based on sex, age, race, etc. Make efforts to teach each other practical, theoretical, and managerial skills as desired.

• Provide high quality work and/or safe products.

• Offer services on a sliding scale based on ability of the customer to pay (especially relevant for repair groups in multi-income areas).

• Give adequate information to customers to make possible intelligent decisions about the purchase of goods or services. Insist on the customers' right to know.

• Be willing to share skills and information with customers, especially about maintenance of products or repairs.

• Use surplus income, above expenses and fair wages, to benefit the wider community through reduced costs to customers, a seed fund for new non-profit businesses, or free basic services needed by the larger community.

• Encourage other groups to form rather than enlarging the group beyond a size which allows good conditions for working and decision making.

For assistance in developing such a business, contact the Federation for Economic Democracy, Washington, D.C. See Part Ten: Groups to Contact for information on resources the Federation offers.

Training and Education alternatives provide people with the theoretical and practical skills needed to take charge of their own lives and to be supportive of positive efforts for change in the larger society. Many of the skills essential to good organizing for change are *not* available through most established public and private schools. Areas around which training is badly needed are:

• making personal decisions;

• basic elementary skills for repair of house, car, and simple appliances;

• growing food, nutrition, and basic meal preparation;

• communication skills, written and verbal;

• managerial and organizational skills;

• taking initiative; taking charge of your own learning process;

219

- constructive release of tension, anger, and grief;
- understanding of and care for your own body;
- conflict clarification and resolution between two people or within small groups;
- developing family and community support systems;
- group decision making and facilitation;
- setting goals, choosing priorities, and evaluating performance individually and in groups;
- researching the causes of problems and developing an analysis;
- developing a theory, vision, and strategy for change;
- focusing on an issue and organizing to make changes, immediate and long-term;
- resistance to exploitation by persons or institutions;
- noncooperation and civilian defense;
- crisis intervention.

See "Groups to Contact" for groups which offer resources and/or training in these areas. Note particularly manuals available through the Organizers Book Center, Washington, D.C., or through local "How-To-Do-It" bookstores.

Care of Emotional and Physical Health—Numerous groups are becoming known for their insistence that individuals can and should exercise more responsibility for maintaining good health. These range from groups that make information or services available at a low fee to groups that teach disciplines which are used regularly. Such efforts are useful to organizing for change if they give people:
- information and services they need;
- skills which they can learn and use on an individual and peer group basis;
- good preventive health care;
- more freedom from the need for costly professional services and harmful drugs.

Examples are:
- Local medical clinics focusing on preventive health care.
- Women's health centers, which offer services for abortions and rape victims and give information on birth control and the care and functioning of the female body.
- The Re-evaluation Counseling community, which offers classes to learn skills in peer counseling and a wider support system for practicing counselors. See Part Four, Personal Growth, for additional information.

Neighborhood Safety Programs involve people in their own protection and the maintenance of social order. A good program

includes:
- organizing sub-areas for mutual support;
- a distress alert system;
- patrol of the area (can be nonviolent and shared by many);
- a broad educational program;
- training and leadership development program;
- a counseling and support system for victims of crime;
- positive working relationships with government officials and police in the community.

For a description of this program, see section III below, example #2: Organizing a Neighborhood for Safety.

Maintaining The Constructive Program

Existing institutions which feel threatened may attempt to stop or change the nature of the constructive program. Success also tempts people to forget original purposes. To keep constructive programs consistent with long-term efforts for change, people can:
- keep the goals and methods of constructive work consistent with their overall analysis and strategy for change;
- develop in others an understanding of constructive work in the context of the larger goals for fundamental transformation of the society;
- form a network of mutual support with other groups which share a common analysis and commitment to change.

When community people have acquired the skills necessary to carry on a constructive program, it can be handed over to them and new programs can be organized.

C. THE DIRECT ACTION CAMPAIGN

The *Direct Action Campaign* (or social change campaign) is a series of planned actions sometimes stretching over years, to achieve a specific goal, generally changing the structure or activities of an existing oppressive institution. Actions are usually highly visible to the public, and the element of confrontation is strong. The purpose of confrontation may be:
- to make public the group's conflict(s) with a specific institution;
- to dramatize an unjust situation;
- to expose moral contradictions in a group's stated goals and practices;
- to communicate different values and try to influence change.

221

The direct action campaign may be one of resistance, such as refusal to allow a strip mining company to remove Native Americans from their land. The campaign may be part of a carefully planned ongoing program for change, such as action by a housing group to demand that government funds be used to create a local, cooperatively-run house construction company in place of a munitions plant scheduled to be built in their area.

A direct action campaign as outlined here is based on a commitment to *nonviolence*—a discipline of non-injury practiced by participants. For such a campaign to succeed it is essential that, as a minimum, nonviolence be accepted tactically by each participant for the full duration of his/her involvement.

Though a nonviolent action campaign can proceed in unique and often unexpected ways, there are a number of distinguishable stages which seem to be necessary if the effects of social change are to remain. For general theory and discussion of these stages, we recommend reading *Strategy for a Living Revolution* by George Lakey. We list the stages below in our own format and include under each stage the activities likely to occur there. During an action campaign this section can be used as a check list.

Try to remember in examining the following that:
- stages will sometimes overlap or occur simultaneously;
- some of the activities suggested in one stage will occur in several stages, but have been listed only under the stage in which they will first occur or are most likely to occur;
- stages will take a longer or shorter period of time depending on the particular situation, the nature of the change sought, and the level of skill and experience of the participants;
- It will be evident that certain items need to be tackled before others.

The Stages of a Nonviolent Action Campaign can be illustrated as:

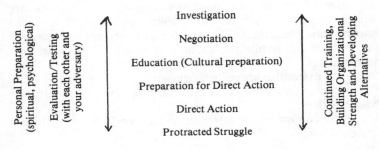

222

1. Investigation

Goals:
- Understand the nature and extent of the problem.
- Sort out participants' own relation to the problem and willingness to work on it.

Steps for Investigation:

a. Choose a manageable problem that interests all members of the group. The scope and complexity of the problem chosen is related to the length and type of commitment of group members. What are the real needs of group members in relation to the problem?

b. Define the problem in the context of its relation to social, political, and economic forces. Use *Macro-Analysis* format to focus on the particular issues involved.

c. Acquire information on the following:

> Community or national power structure. Who has the power? To do what?
>
> Role of press, police, and politicians.
>
> Sources of rumors.
>
> Attitudes of individuals and groups currently involved at all levels of the problem.

d. Meet informally with individuals, professional and non-professional, who are interested or involved in the problem. What do they know about the problem?

e. Investigate all possible solutions to the problem. Make every effort to resolve conflict through established channels. Document such efforts and make the results public. People will not want to join an action campaign unless they are convinced established channels have been tried and have failed.

f. Explore the sources of resistance to change by all people involved.

g. Explore the forces supportive of the changes you are proposing. Use the *Force Field Analysis* exercise.

h. Investigate alternatives:

> Define your own goals *long and short-term*. State goals in terms of a creative alternative or specific recommendations.
>
> Analyze alternatives available now and their inadequacies in solving the problem.
>
> Find next steps that community agencies and/or leaders are prepared to take.

i. Re-examine your definition of the problem and redefine it in light of additional information.

j. Give your information to the opposition and to the

223

public in a simple but thorough presentation, written as well as verbal. Include a statement of the problem, changes desired, and what you are asking whom to do by when? Knowledge is sometimes powerful enough to begin the process of change.

k. If changes are made, publicly acknowledge them and affirm the people making them.

l. Divide the problem into pieces and develop a strategy for action. If the group is large enough, it may divide and each subgroup begin working on a piece of the problem.

2. Negotiations

Goals:
- Help both parties understand each other and the reasons for their actions.
- Enable both sides to see each other as human beings.
- Clear up misunderstandings, rumors, inaccuracies throughout the campaign.
- Possibly achieve resolution of conflict.

General Guidelines:
- Establish ways to keep in contact with the opponent, and continue negotiation throughout the campaign.
- Approach people with whom you negotiate as potential allies.
- Cooperate with your opponent when you can do so on honorable terms. This will not weaken your position but can show your desire to serve the common good.
- Recognize the limitations of negotiation. It may serve as advance discussion or notification, but some issues will not be negotiable.
- Do not attempt to defame or smear the character of any of your opponents. Public acknowledgement of the cooperative and human aspects of your opponents will make future cooperation more possible and will encourage the opponent to maintain those positive qualities.

Steps to Negotiation:
a. Formulate the proposal for negotiation. Make it specific.

b. Choose a negotiation team and agree on the roles that its members will take. One person may act as facilitator, suggest breaks, caucuses, etc. One or more people may concentrate on making human contact. One or two may present the proposal and answer questions about it.

c. Roleplay the negotiation meeting until participants feel comfortable with their roles. Try out different strategies for the negotiation.

d. Prepare yourselves for negotiation. For example: meditate, worship, release distress, brainstorm good qualities of the opponent.

e. Negotiate with opponents. The first session may be mainly an opportunity to get to know the people on the other side, to find out their positions and options. Additional sessions may be necessary before clear agreements or disagreements can be reached.

- Sessions may be public or private, but make no secret agreements.
- Keep detailed records of all negotiations.
- If an agreement is reached, make it specific and in writing (signed if necessary). Ex: *Not* "We agree to take steps to end discrimination in hiring," *but* "We agree to appropriate X $ and free Y jobs by Z date."
- Keep a united front. Take time to caucus if necessary.
- Set a time for a second negotiation meeting or follow-up.

f. Keep your own constituency informed every step of the way. Make public any facts, decisions, or new information discovered during a negotiation session.

3. Education: (Cultural Preparation)

Goals:

- Make information available and bring about a full discussion of the issues at stake.
- Get support for the campaign.
- Put pressure on the opponent to change.
- Prepare the public for periods of confrontation to follow.
- Provide an analysis that enables the public to evaluate accurately official explanations of the problem and to see the social causes of private problems.
- Demonstrate that those with greater power are more responsible for the problems we face.
- Excite people's vision of future possibilities.
- Create indignation that such foolishness and exploitation is still allowed to exist.
- Help people discover their own abilities and power and develop a collective will to resist injustice.

General Guidelines:

- Focus the attack. Concentrate on the weakest points in the opponents' cause, policy, system.

225

• Make connections between abstract political issues and immediate bread-and-butter goals of the constructive program.

• Work through established groups where possible.

• Enter into dialogue with groups and individuals most affected by the injustice. When groups prove to be uncooperative, seek neutrality rather than open criticism from them. Look for things you may have in common and may wish to cooperate on in the future.

• Find ways to communicate your respect for the public. In campaign literature, be clear without talking down to the public or stereotyping their activities or response.

Methods:

• Canvass door-to-door. Leaflet on street corners.

• Publish truth through bulletins, letters to the editor, TV, speeches, petitions.

• Bring the skeptical or uncommitted face to face with the injustice through structured experiences.

• Develop new symbols and culture of life. Write songs, create posters, dances, etc., celebrate anniversaries of accomplishments of heroic actions, celebrate lives of those imprisoned or victims of injustice.

• Carry out *Street Speaking* and *Radical Street Theater*.

• Conduct *Teach-Ins*.

• Conduct workshops on history and practice of nonviolent action using tools, case studies, and films.

• Undertake limited actions, e.g., vigils, demonstrations, symbolic actions.

• Organize study groups similar to *Macro-Analysis* seminars.

• Hold training workshops to teach skills, raise consciousness and build community.

• Build alternatives to educate people about future possibilities.

4. Preparation for Direct Action

a. Plan preliminary strategy and tactics.

• Develop strategy and tactics with realistic view of the strength of yourselves and your opponent.

• Consider the vast array of nonviolent tactics available. See "The Methods of Nonviolent Action" by Gene Sharp (Part Two of *The Politics of Nonviolent Action*).

• Pick an appropriate target for the action.

• Select a form of direct action which expresses the

deepest truths and feelings that those undertaking it wish to communicate.

b. Set a clear nonviolent discipline from the beginning in order to:

- lessen the attraction for violence-oriented sympathizers;
- deter use of *agents provocateurs*;
- keep attention focused on the injustice or violence of the establishment;
- help protect the lives of demonstrators and adversaries;
- encourage overt expression of life and humanity clearly contradictory to the injustice being protested.

c. Indicate clear sponsorship, to lessen public confusion and counteract name calling, like "communists," "outside agitators," etc.

d. List jobs to be done. Areas to be included are:

- community relations;
- office management, mailings, phones;
- transportation;
- literature production and/or distribution;
- housing, food, child care;
- finances: preparing a budget, fund raising, bookkeeping, payment of bills;
- coordination of volunteers;
- communications;
- publicity, press information;
- continued negotiation with opponents;
- liaison with police, courts, and arrestees;
- key organizational responsibilities (such as calling a special meeting, communication of emergencies, etc.);
- training;
- medical care and physical safety.

e. Inventory resources available—human and material. Divide and designate responsibilities clearly.

- If the group is large enough, each area can be handled by a small team.
- Be aware of isolation, fragmentation, and dissension that can arise within and between small groups. Regular meetings of the total group should continue, with reports from each subgroup. When the goals of a small group have been accomplished, the group can dissolve and the

227

members be freed to join other working groups.

- Some special resources may need to be mobilized if they are not already part of your group, such as trainers, lawyers, or medical personnel. For legal assistance, check local law schools, a National Lawyers Guild or American Civil Liberties Union branch. For medical personnel, contact medical colleges or the Medical Committee on Human Rights chapter in your area.

f. Develop a *Flow Chart* and *Time Line* for the completion of all major tasks preparatory to the action. Check periodically to see that plans are going as projected.

g. Set up centers for the coordination of information. One in the area of most support. This may be the home of a participant or the office of a sponsoring organization. One near the location of the action.

h. Acquire necessary supplies:
- A good typewriter for cutting stencils.
- Dependable mimeo machine and supplies.
- Postage and stationery.
- Poster materials.
- Cars available upon request.
- Cots, sleeping bags, food, sanitary and medical supplies, etc.

i. Research permits, rules and regulations for projected activities. Get official information from police or city hall. Don't rely on assumptions of local people. Gather information about local police and jails, whether or not illegal actions are planned. Learn the names of all police or officials with whom you may be involved.

j. If supporters will be coming from outside the area, find housing, parking, food, maps, etc.

k. Encourage training for all participants in direct action. Especially important are the uses of *Roleplaying, Quick Decision* and strategy exercises. Use situations similar to expected actions. Mistakes can be made in a safe environment with plenty of time to evaluate and learn from them. Training should help people:
- identify, learn, and practice skills that will be needed;
- understand the opponent better;
- build morale and relationships among participants which can carry a group through trying times;
- reduce fears and tensions and prepare for confrontation;

228

- democratize the process by spreading skills of leadership throughout the group;
- build self-awareness and understand their own motives and reactions;
- re-examine their analysis, strategy, and tactics, and change them where necessary;
- handle disruptive actions of counter-demonstrators, citizens, or police and deal with provocation and reprisals;
- think clearly under stress.

l. Agree before the action on processes for decision making and communications. These are essential. Set up a phone tree for immediate notification. Write down all important messages, including from whom and where, to whom, who took the message, date, and time.

m. Have briefing sessions for all participants, where information is pooled and final decisions are made.

n. Prepare individually and collectively for the emotional and spiritual demands of the action through meetings for worship, meditation, prayer; meetings for clearness; community-building activities.

Where civil disobedience is planned (openly illegal actions), the following steps are also important:

o. Discuss policies concerning paying fines vs. jail; bail vs. no bail; complying with fingerprinting, giving information, etc. Appoint someone to coordinate bail matters regardless of policy. Consider policy of bailing out poor people instead of members of your group, if money is available.

p. Prepare people for what to expect if arrested:
- Their legal rights.
- How to go to trial.
- How to relate to guards and prisoners.

q. Explore carefully the role of those not planning to be arrested. What types of support can they give those in jail, their families, and their friends? How can they carry on the campaign?

r. When the number of people likely to be arrested is larger than fifteen, consider forming affinity groups. Affinity group participants take special responsibility for each other, helping keep morale high.

s. Deliver final strong verbal appeal for changes to be made.
- List specific grievances, past attempts to negotiate, concessions offered, and reactions to them.

- Set date actions will begin if minimum demands are not met.
- Put this in writing to policy makers.
- Inform all who may be affected.

5. Direct Action

Goals:
- Test the strength and determination of opposition forces.
- Humanize all parties in a dehumanizing, oppressive situation.
- Change a part of the exploitative social/economic structure.
- Achieve a reform of the system as part of a long-term strategy for social transformation. (See "Reformist Reform vs. Revolutionary Reform.")
- Noncooperate with an exploitative aspect of the society.
- Raise public consciousness and communicate information about the problem.
- Encourage duplication of the action elsewhere.
- Influence all people involved in the situation to be more supportive of (or less opposed to) your goals.

Guidelines for Direct Action:
- Choose the tactics of direct action in the context of the overall strategy. When tactics no longer support your goals, use other tactics, or take a break. When tactics work, declare your accomplishment, state the additional injustice, give your further goals, and go home promptly and joyously.
- Individuals and groups can be ranked on a spectrum of how they relate to the campaign as follows:

> Active participation
> Moral and/or material support
> Neutral
> Hostile wait-and-see
> Actively hostile

Decide which of these groups you wish to influence the most. Try to raise people in each group up to the next group. *
- Don't depend for unity on the mistakes of the opponent. When mistakes are made by the opponent, use them to educate the public as to the reality of the situation. Never fail to acknowledge the capacity of the opponent to recognize his/her own role in the problem and to desire a change.

---

* *A Manual for Direct Action*, by Martin Oppenheimer and George Lakey (Quadrangle Books, 1964), p. 20.

appeal to those who have committed violence to refuse to be a party to such indignities any longer and join the movement for justice. Deal patiently and fairly with dissidents.

• Consider dividing the action into a series of smaller actions, especially if arrests are likely. This allows for a longer period to build support for the campaign.

• During direct action campaigns an opponent's response often goes through the following stages: *

> *Indifference*—may be short-lived if problem is well presented and people personally confronted to change.
>
> *Active antagonism*—may include verbal or violent threats or retaliation. A lot of learning takes place here. It is especially important to have a strong educational component operating during this stage if persuasion is to work.
>
> *Disunity of opponent*—People in power structure will begin to question their own rightness, and reconsider your information.
>
> *Negotiation*—with reservation usually, but more sincerely than the first negotiation. Poor negotiation can mean the resuming of conflict. Prepare carefully. Describe results of *not* changing as MORE threatening. Describe results of change as *less* threatening than the opponent supposes. Use successes in other places. Give scenario of what will happen if changes are not made. Get public statements of opponent as in favor of "fairness, democracy, etc."

• Keep up efforts at persuasion. Keep major objectives before the public. Seek support from the uncommitted or uncertain. Especially seek to persuade one's adversaries, e.g.,

• Keep the initiative. The best defense is a good offense.
  —Respond creatively to acts of retaliation or reprisals.
  —Seek to widen the constituency of supporters and participants. Brainstorm continuing actions at every level of participation.
  —Develop new proposals and offers for negotiation. Be open to negotiation at every stage of the action.
  —Keep digging deeper into the problem. New information will surface that should be considered.

• If police behave improperly, follow up immediately (see information on Police, Courts, and Prisons in Part Nine: Practical Skills).

---

* Ibid, pp 22-25.

- Overcome violence of the power structure by:
  - —Expecting it and preparing for it.
  - —Maintaining a strong social organization. The best antidote to terror is community.
  - —Demonstrating that violence does not help achieve the opponent's objectives.
  - —Being friendly and understanding of the opponent's fears, and giving serious attention to their real problems.
  - —Keeping your own constituency informed regularly, especially of progress toward the objective, supporting actions, contributions made by participants, etc.
  - —Carrying on a continuous training, education, and organizing process within your own ranks.
  - —Day-by-day evaluation (essential). Are all participants operating at their highest level of creativity? Are people developing community? Are skills being learned and used? Is decision making shared? Is our analysis still accurate? Are the goals of the campaign being furthered?

6. Protracted Struggle

Goals:
- Sustain action until the injustice is eliminated.
- Build new institutions that replace inadequate or unjust ones.

Guidelines:
- Nonviolent action is most effective if part of a larger campaign and sustained or repeated until demands are met or until an alternative institution is formed.
- Nonviolent action can be escalated by using demonstrations, vigils, economic and political boycotts, or nonviolent intervention; by refusing to work with a group or an organization; by refusing to comply with a law, tax or social custom; by creating parallel institutions; or by taking over existing institutions (where appropriate).
- Constructive/alternative programs fuse with direct action to create new institutions. E.g., in the campaign for Indian independence, the creation of village industry, particularly the spinning and weaving of cotton, created economic independence for the movement as well as ongoing models for economic institutions for the country.

III
Examples of Organizing for Change

A. BLOCKADING UNITED STATES MILITARY SUPPORT OF PAKISTAN

In 1971 a small group of activists joined with others to attempt to block the shipment of military equipment from the United States to Pakistan. Their reasons, their actions and the results are vividly described below in a 1972 article by Richard Taylor, one of the organizers of the Overseas Impact Group and a full participant in the actions. For a fuller description of this event, read *Blockade*, by Richard Taylor (Orbis, NY, 1977), annotated in the bibliography below.

Blockading for Bangladesh *

For most Americans the India-Pakistan conflict [was] 12,000 miles away, but for a small group of us it was as close as a canoe bobbing in the Baltimore harbor, a sewer pipe refugee camp across from the White House, and the Miami convention of the International Longshoremen's Association.

Before last summer, we hardly knew where Pakistan was, much less what was happening there. But July 14 found us spending a warm evening carrying NO ARMS TO PAKISTAN signs and paddling a fleet of canoes and kyacks through the murky waters of Baltimore's harbor. Our goal: to try to block the docking of the *Padma*, a Pakistani ship which had been thwarted in picking up jet fighter parts in Montreal, and which was now bearing down on us, led by police and Coast Guard cutters.

"For your own safety, we're ordering you to get out of the way," shouted a police sergeant, leaning over the rail of a large police boat named *Intrepid*. "The wakes of these freighters are enormous—you can be flipped over and chopped up by their propellers."

"You have to do what you have to do," we shouted back, paddling toward the docking pier, "but we're here to block the *Padma*. We're concerned about the lives of twenty million Pakistanis who may die if we don't do something," we yelled,

---

* This article is reprinted by permission from *The Progressive*, where it appeared in the February 1972 issue. Some sections have been deleted to shorten it. Copyright © 1972, *The Progressive, Inc.*

paddling ahead doggedly and making the *Intrepid* gun its engine and come about.

Looking beyond the police boat and over the harbor waters, we could see silhouettes of freighters, docks, and cranes against the far shore and, just to their left, the smaller outline of the *Padma* and its escort steaming up the channel. Across the oil slicks in the other direction stroked the determined bunch who made up the fleet we had dubbed "The Francis Scott Key Armada," in honor of the Star Spangled Banner's author, who penned the anthem more then a century ago on the deck of a British ship in this same harbor. School employees, several teenagers, a doctor, a draft resister about to go to jail, a peace worker, a college student—we all wanted the United States to end its support of the Pakistani military dictatorship.

"You're violating harbor regulations by blocking a shipping lane," came a more impatient bullhorn voice. "You'll be arrested if you don't get out of the way."

A large white yacht, loaded with reporters and television cameras, roared up. A smaller inboard, steered by a television reporter with her camera crew in the back, sped in for a closer look. A second police boat closed in and two Coast Guard thirty-footers edged between us and the *Padma*, which had now moved to within 200 yards. The freighter's horn let loose a deafening blast and its tugboats added some piercing whistles of their own.

When a voice said, "O.K., arrest 'em," we knew that we wouldn't be able to accomplish the goal, but we kept threading our way between the boats, shouting things like: "We appeal to you to help prevent the death of millions of Pakistanis." Skillful Coast Guard piloting and the use of grappling hooks, however, soon had all of us loaded aboard the larger boats.

A city policeman politely but firmly escorted us into the front cabin of one of the craft, and we watched the *Padma*, now towering above us, slip into Pier 8. In the hot and crowded cabin, our only consolation came from the young Coast Guard steersman, who leaned over to whisper, "We have to do this job, but we're with you 100 per cent. You're doing the right thing." Soon we found ourselves in the Baltimore city jail, sharing narrow wooden bunks and reflecting on how we had gotten into this situation.

Many of us had spent the spring and early summer of 1971 working with peace activists in the Philadelphia area to help form "The Movement for a New Society," an organization emphasizing the role of nonviolent direct action in building a movement for fundamental change in the United States.

One MNS effort was a small study-action team called the "Overseas Impact Group," whose members tried to understand the actual effect on other nations of U.S. government policies and business relationships. Toward the middle of the summer this group began reading newspaper accounts of massacres in East Pakistan and the large-scale exodus of refugees into India. Knowing almost nothing about Pakistan, we began to study the country and the role of the United States in its development.

We found Pakistan to be ruled by a military dictatorship (with General Yaya Khan at the helm), that West Pakistan treated East Pakistan as a colony, and that capitalist-oriented development had created an immensely wealthy ownership class, while leaving the majority of the population in poverty.

The facade of Pakistani "democracy" came apart when General Khan, in response to the popular election won by East Pakistan's Awami League, ordered the military suppression of the East. The shockingly brutal military action which followed sent millions of refugees fleeing in terror to India.

With increasing study, the complicity of the United States in Pakistani events became evident. Although some of the Pakistani army's military equipment came from other countries, a major percentage came from the more than $1 billion of U.S. military aid—Sabrejet fighters, light tanks, bombers, C-130 transport planes, guns and ammunition—supplied to Pakistan since 1955. In April, the State Department admitted that U.S. tanks and F-86 fighters were being used in East Pakistan; it became clear that U.S. arms were helping to crush the Bengalis and that U.S. assistance would continue to flow.

Newspapers and contacts with Congressional offices indicated that Pakistani ships were plying our East Coast, picking up shipments of military and economic goods. One way to express our concern and to put the spotlight of publicity on the situation, we reasoned, would be to attempt to block these ships as they landed to pick up the material.

Knowing that some Philadelphians were already concerned about Pakistan, our team joined a local group called the Friends of East Bengal and became its Direct Action Committee. We were completely ignorant of port operations, but library research and telephone calls soon gave us a picture of the key sources of shipping information. In time we had a complete "intelligence apparatus," involving a nun who kept watch on newpaper reports of ship arrivals, sympathetic workers at the Longshoremen's and Bay Pilots' Associations, and, when necessary, spotters with binoculars along shipping lanes. A veil of secrecy suddenly closed over both governmental and private sources of information on the movements of Pakistani ships.

On July 8 we heard that the *Padma* had attempted to pick up spare parts for jet fighters in Montreal. *The Montreal Star* (June 28-30) reported that the shippers claimed only cobalt and foodstuffs were to be loaded, but, when demonstrators insisted that the cargo be inspected, forty-six crates of Sabrejet spare parts were discovered. The Canadian government suspended the shipper's license and the *Padma* headed for Baltimore, minus the jet parts. Thus the project, "The Pursuit of the *Padma*," which led to a night in Baltimore's jail and a sentence of thirty days probation on charges of "disorderly conduct" and "unlawfully casting loose, setting adrift or placing an object, to wit: a canoe, by obstructing navigation of the *S. S. Padma*."

Our discouragement at not being able to prevent docking of the *Padma* was more than counterbalanced by the elation we felt at the excellent nationwide coverage of the blockade on television, radio, and in the press. When the House Foreign Affairs Committee reported out a bill cutting off aid to Greece and Pakistan, a Congressional source and a well-known *New York Times* reporter told us that our Baltimore action was a major factor influencing the Committee to take this unprecedented action.

The need to work closely with the longshoremen was underscored by the Baltimore union's decision to load the ship, in spite of our appeals to the contrary. The Direct Action Committee therefore put together a team of two Bengalis and two Americans and rushed to the International Longshoremen's Association convention at Miami's DiLido hotel. There we explained our position to members of the ILA and, after meetings with top leaders and a speech on the convention floor, received a commitment that the ILA would not load military equipment bound for Pakistan.

Our most significant contact, it turned out, was Richard Askew, president of Philadelphia's ILA Local 1291. He expressed immediate sympathy for the Bengalis and stated his conviction that a small group was trying to suppress the majority. As a black leader, he understood the plight of downtrodden people who are victimized for simply trying to express their democratic rights.

While the small team worked in Miami, the rest of the Direct Action Committee urged groups in other port cities to encourage blockades there, and also began marches and picketing at the offices of the Philadelphia agents for Pakistani ships.

In early August, we learned that another Pakistani ship, the

Al Ahmadi, was headed for Philadelphia. On August 12 we set up a blockade at Philadelphia's Pier 80 to meet it, but it turned around in the Delaware River and went to Baltimore. We chased it there and met it with pickets on land and water, then found that it was heading back to Philadelphia.

On August 17 we arose at four in the morning to get our boats in the Delaware in time to meet the *Al Ahmadi*, which was expected at seven a.m. Four canoes and one kyack paddled about three miles to Pier 80 while thirty pickets formed in front of the gigantic warehouse on the dock side. We erected a thirty-foot mural depicting U.S. arms being shipped to Pakistan, and soon were embroiled in intense discussions and negotiations with longshoremen, teamsters (whose trucks were backed up by our pickets), and officials of the shipping company, who complained that we were shutting down their entire operation and causing the men to lose their pay. We finally agreed to leave one gate (where a Japanese ship was moored) free of pickets.

The tiny nonviolent fleet looked like five slivers of darkness on the glistening water, bouncing 200 yards away at the riverside entrance to the dock. Several police boats kept a close watch. In a few moments the enormous prow of the *Al Ahmadi* edged past the warehouse, nudged by two large tugs. Our small boats paddled straight for the bow, but the police, apparently with orders not to make arrests, pulled alongside, grabbed our boats, and dragged them across the mouth of the ship and out of the way. As soon as they released us, however, we paddled right back, fighting through tugboat wakes and turbulence to get in the freighter's path. For a good twenty minutes the fleet charged and was dragged back, while longshoremen, teamsters, demonstrators, newspaper reporters, television cameramen, and Pakistani crewmen leaning over the rail watched transfixedly. Finally, the *Al Ahmadi* was able to snag a hawser on the dock's mooring.

The longshoremen held the final card; we were in suspense to see if they would load or not. None had crossed the picket lines so far, and the next work gang was scheduled to pass through the gates at one p.m. At 12:30 they started coming and the picketing was intensified. At 12:45, Richard Askew drove a large black car into the middle of the growing crowd in front of the warehouse gate. He got out slowly and was immediately besieged with microphones and questions by reporters.

Speaking deliberately, he said: "I'm not here to tell the men what to do. I think they've already decided what to do. I'm here to express my own convictions. This company should be ashamed to have this ship tied up at its dock. West Pakistan is committing genocide on East Pakistan. If we load this ship, it would be as though we were helping to commit genocide.''

A reporter asked the question that had been thrown at the demonstrators all morning: "Mr. Askew, aren't your men losing money by not loading this ship?" Without the slightest hesitation he replied: "If I know in my heart that the money I'm earning is blood money, then I don't want to have anything to do with it,'' and he piled back into his car and drove off.

Not a single longshoreman crossed the picket line during the next twenty-eight hours, during which time a continuous day and night demonstration was organized. Fewer and fewer longshoremen responded to the shipping company's repeated calls for work crews, and the next afternoon the *Al Ahmadi* sailed away, leaving more than a thousand tons of equipment on the dock.

In October, we built eight replicas of sewer pipes (similar to those used for housing by Bengali refugees in India) and placed them in Lafayette Park, across from the White House. A team from the Direct Action Committee lived in them for more than a week, fasting or eating the meager diet of Bengali expatriates, to represent the plight of the refugees. From this base, we organized a march on the Pakistan Embassy, a lobbying day on Capitol Hill, an inter-faith religious service attended by Bangladesh representatives to the United Nations, and a refugee meal for government employees.

Because of the effective mass media coverage, these actions made an important contribution to public knowledge about the U.S. role in Pakistan. They also provided an example of how ordinary citizens can move beyond a sense of helplessness and into meaningful action to counter an obvious evil.

☆   ☆   ☆   ☆   ☆   ☆

Results:

It is difficult to weigh the effect of the actions described above on the ending of West Pakistan's brutal military actions a few months later. Many other people were speaking out, and eventually India went to war with Pakistan to try to end the problems caused by refugees fleeing across Indian borders.

But several things clearly resulted from the actions described above:

• The actions took the hidden *fact* of U.S. support of this massacre and turned it into daily *news*. They put pressure on Congress and the executive branch of government to either justify or change this support.

• In the fall of 1971 the U.S. government finally cut off all military aid to Pakistan. Many legislative assistants, in particular, felt the publicity from the actions helped build a constituency which gave them leverage to convince their congresspeople to support legislation to cut off military aid.

• The news reached the smallest villages of East Pakistan, through underground radios, to bring encouragement to the people there. On learning of the action, villagers were heard to say, "The American *government* is against us, but the American *people* are for us."

• Lives were saved by helping East Bengali sailors get off Pakistani ships on which they feared for their lives.

• Efforts and morale of the Pakistan government to continue the slaughter were undercut by preventing military supplies from getting to Pakistan, especially repair parts for large military equipment sent earlier by the U.S.

B. ORGANIZING A NEIGHBORHOOD FOR SAFETY

Early in the spring of 1972, there was a series of rapes, assaults and robberies in one section of West Philadelphia. A small group of people began to meet to discuss the most creative ways to respond to the problem. The information below is taken primarily from a description of the Neighborhood Safety Training Program of Philadelphia by Ross Flanagan, Ellie Wegener and Jim Williams, Project Trainers (Community Crime Prevention Letter, April 1974) and a handbook on Neighborhood Safety Organizing by Ross Flanagan. The balance is supplied by the authors of this manual, who participated in several aspects of the program.

The Problem:

Neighborhood Safety! Isolated and defensive reactions to crime increase victimization by promoting a climate of fear, heightening neighborhood instability and eroding the sense of community.

Purposes of the Program:

• To help neighborhood people develop a sense of community and mutual trust essential for effective crime prevention.

• To involve citizens in the prevention of crime in ways which overcome fear and help to improve the criminal justice system.

Component Parts:

A Loose Association of Neighboring Blocks . Each individual block is organized and meets as frequently as residents choose, usually 4-12 times a year. In addition, a representative for each block, usually a block captain, meets periodically with other block representatives to work on common problems.

Getting neighbors together in regularly scheduled block meetings is essential
- to reacquaint block residents with one another so they can distinguish between a neighbor and a stranger;
- to increase human contact, communication, and commitment to look out for each other;
- to pool information essential to detecting and interrupting crime patterns;
- to connect concern and energy required to secure adequate city services and correct deteriorating conditions on the block;
- to stabilize block community by giving residents increasing human incentive *not* to move.

Getting People Together

1. *You*, as a block resident, are the key to the successful organization of your block.

2. It is helpful to find someone who has lived on the block for a while and who may personally know people you don't. A block usually consists of all the houses which face each other from corner to corner.

3. In selecting a place for the first meeting, use the home of someone who is friendly, likes people and is genuinely interested in getting the block together. It isn't always the size or the decor of the room which counts. There doesn't have to be room for everyone to sit on a chair.

4. Select a date for the meeting in consultation with a minimum of two other residents and don't change the date or worry if not everybody can make it. A good time is a week day evening after 8:00 pm when small children are in bed. Avoid Fridays and holiday weekends.

5. Contact all block residents personally, face-to-face whenever possible, to notify them of the meeting. Weekends are generally the time you will find most folks home. Give people a minimum of one week's notice of the meeting date; too much time between your contact and the actual meeting date may allow people to forget or lose interest. You may want to call a few people the day before the meeting to remind them.

6. Keep any written announcement or mail-box reminder simple, like: *"Come Meet Your Neighbors/Let's Get Our Block Together."* If a recent crime incident has occurred or particular improvement of the block is proposed, it may be helpful to mention that in the notice, but don't list an agenda. Provide a phone number so people can call with their questions and so those who can't make the meeting can let you know of their interest. Don't place announcements in public places, since thefts have been known to occur in a block during a block meeting.

7. At subsequent meetings it may be helpful to invite residents who live in blocks adjacent to your block or someone from the block whose back yards adjoin yours.

Conducting the Meeting

1. The Block Meeting is primarily a time for connecting people. Allow plenty of time for informal conversation and sharing over coffee or punch.

2. Meetings should be kept free of pressure to think alike or manipulation for political purposes. Necessary business should be short and simple.

3. Since many people are motivated to come to block meetings out of a fear of crime, it is important to head off the tendency to trade horror stories. All too often the sharing of such stories develops a run-away momentum of its own which ends up reactivating a lot of fear, re-enforcing irrational behavior and generally depressing people.

4. *It is important* to help people understand from the very first meeting that they have a great deal more worth sharing than their common victimization. One good practice is to begin each meeting by asking everyone to share their name, street number and something good which has happened to them during the past week or since the last meeting. This helps keep some people from feeling that the only way they can get on the agenda and receive some human attention from others at the meeting is to share some bad or sad news.

5. After all residents of the block have introduced themselves in some such way, it is appropriate to introduce, but *not* turn the meeting over to, any visiting resource persons. Remember: such resource speakers will serve your block best if they are asked *to respond to* and not overwhelm the real concerns and good thinking of the people on your block.

6. The heart of every block meeting is the exchange of good information between neighbors, connecting up the needs and concerns of some with the resources and suggestions of others. Encourage *everyone* to participate, but try to keep the focus of

the discussion on matters directly affecting the safety and welfare of people on your immediate block.

7. It may be helpful to utilize a process like **Brainstorming** to assure you get as many people as possible to share their ideas without risking the sort of back and forth argument which wears people down. Remember that loud and insistent talkers are just people needing attention. Be firm in restricting their participation in meetings; but warm in conversation with them after the meeting in the informal coffee period and whenever you see them between meetings.

8. Ultimately it may be necessary to take a straw vote to decide on which concern the group wants to focus its problem-solving attention for the evening. Here is where a pre-arranged resource speaker can often be of help to your block meeting, or you can think the problem through yourself and agree to call in resource people later as needed.

9. Should the concern chosen require any follow-up between meetings, be sure to get two or three volunteers to share responsibility for working on it together. Make sure they know when and how to contact each other and ask one of them to serve as "spark plug" or convener of the group. Such between-meeting work groups can make a significant contribution towards helping your block develop a sense of community.

10. Be sure to arrange for the time, date, and place of the next meeting before adjourning. This can save considerable trouble and confusion. Meet at different homes or apartments on the block so people share hosting and hostessing responsibilities and get a chance to know one another better. It may also be helpful to vary the meeting time so that people with regular commitments can still make an occasional meeting.

Community Workshops to share information and learn new approaches.

Suggestions for conducting a workshop:

• *Registration*. Get name and address. Give name tag, alternating between two colors for introductions.

• *Getting to know each other* (20 min). Find someone you don't know with an opposite color tag and exchange introductions with them. Share something of what makes life good for you these days. Avoid talking about your roles (job, parent, titles, etc.). After 10 minutes the 2 of you find 2 others and introduce each other (not yourself) to the other pair.

• *What's going on around our neighborhood?* (15 min). Demonstrate some typical encounters with friends helping a crime victim, a fire or medical emergency victim, or a long-suffering "silent casualty." Audience/observers are asked to take notes of helpful and unhelpful approaches for use in later discussions.

- *Sharing personal experience* (20 min). In groups of 5-6, each person is asked to tell about one time s/he was supported by someone or was able to be of support to someone in time of need. Group appoints a time keeper to make sure each person has a chance to share an experience.

- *Identifying needs* (30 min). Brainstorm the kind of help you would like from others *and* hear brief reports as to where and how these needs are presently being met.

- *Pot-luck Lunch* (1 hr). Informally arranged to allow participants to get better acquainted.

- *Developing Resourcefulness* (1 hr). Divide into workshops on topics such as helping crime victims, helping fire and medical emergency victims, and helping silent casualties. Possible resource people are representatives from a community counseling center, Women Organized Against Rape, a local police district, the Red Cross Disaster Action Team, a local hospital emergency clinic, a fire rescue squad, a public health nurse and a senior citizens caseworker.

Each group has a facilitator involved in preworkshop planning. These groups generate information which is used to compile guidelines for "friends-in-need," neighborhood residents willing to offer support to one another. A recorder is appointed and a brief report is given by each group.

- *Where do we go from here?* (30 min). Programs, proposals and volunteer opportunities are listed and workshop participants encouraged to contact these groups to gain experience in victim counseling. Resource materials are distributed.

Persons with questions still unanswered at the end of the day are invited to write out their questions or comments and drop them in a question box with their name, address and phone. People interested in getting more involved in victim counseling work are encouraged to sign the available sheet.

Street Distress Alert System using freon horns to frighten off attackers and rally neighbors for assistance. Individuals carry horns when they feel fearful on the street and keep them in easily accessible places in their houses. Horns are sold to residents at cost and distributed through the block captains.

Neighborhood Walk to engage and encourage residents to use the streets, helping make them safer and friendlier. Men and women walk the streets of their neighborhood in groups of two or more, during high crime periods, armed only with freon horns, notebooks, and flashlights (if needed). They check out problems, offer assistance to persons in trouble, speak to everyone they meet, and use horns to sound alarm should they run into a problem in which additional human resources are needed.

For Further Information about this project and others like it, contact Ross Flanagan, 347 Independence Blvd., North Brunswick, NJ 08902, or Citizens Local Alliance for a Safer Philadelphia, 260 S 15th, Phila., PA 19102.

IV
Bibliographies

For manuals on organizing around police, courts, and prisons, see Part Nine: Practical Skills: Police, Courts, and Prisons.

STRATEGY AND ORGANIZING FOR NONVIOLENT SOCIAL CHANGE

Action Guide on Southern Africa (Peace Education, AFSC, 1501 Cherry, Phila., PA 19102, 52 pp, $1.00). Guide for organizing around Southern Africa issues.

Blockade, by Richard K. Taylor (Orbis Books, Maryknoll, NY 10545. Also available from MNS, 4722 Baltimore Ave., Phila., PA 19143, for $2.95 plus 50¢ postage.). Discusses action of nonviolent fleet which in 1971 blockaded Pakistani ships on the East Coast and engaged in other types of direct action to protest United States support for Pakistani dictatorship. Shows implications for challenging present unjust situations. The last chapter is a direct action manual that gives a detailed step-by-step method for developing a direct action campaign, including such essentials as press relations, fund raising, training and strategic thinking.

Civil Disobedience: Theory and Practice, by Christian Bay and Charles Walker (Black Rose Books, 3934 Rue, St. Urbain, Montreal, Quebec, $2.50). A handbook including a manual on organizing for civil disobedience.

"Conscientizing as a Way of Liberating," by LADOC (available from Philadelphia Macro-Analysis Collective, 4722 Baltimore Ave., Phila., PA 19143, $.55 postpaid).

"How to Commit Revolution," by William Domhoff (PMAC, 4722 Baltimore Ave., Philadelphia, PA 19143, $.50 postpaid). Describes a process for (1) analyzing the present American system, (2) developing, from the people, blueprints for a better society, and (3) using both psychic guerrilla warfare and a political organization to take power.

Moving Toward a New Society, by Susanne Gowan, et al. (MNS, 4722 Baltimore Ave., Phila., PA 19143, 1976, $3.50 plus 50¢ postage). A probing analysis of the U.S. political-economic system. Projections of what a new society could look like with helpful suggestions on how to develop a campaign for constructive change.

Neighborhood Power: The New Localism, by David Morris and Karl Hess (Beacon Press, Boston, 1975). Presents a strategy for urban rebirth based on political and economic neighborhood self-reliance. Includes discussion of neighborhood waste disposal and basement trout raising. An important book for urban organizers.

Nonviolent Action Manual, by William Moyer (MNS, 4722 Baltimore Ave., Phila., PA 19143, 1974, $1.25 plus 35¢ postage). How to develop a nonviolent direct action campaign. Written for a workshop on campaign organizing.

Organizers Manual, by the O. M. Collective (Bantam Books, 1971). Practical suggestions for small-group and grass roots organizing, political self-education, mass education and communications, alternate community services, mass actions, legal and medical self-defense. Strategies for organizing high schools, universities, radical groups, women, the military, labor, the professions. Includes a list of books and organizations.

Organizer's Manual, by War Resisters League (339 Lafayette, New York, NY 10012, 1974, $3.00). Sections on organizing skills, direct action, study guides and bibliographies, and resources. Being written piecemeal. Buyers get installments as they become available.

The Politics of Nonviolent Action, by Gene Sharp (Porter Sargent, 11 Beacon, Boston, MA 02108). Part One explains the technique of nonviolent action and its theory of power; Part Two gives examples of 198 methods of struggle; Part Three is a 350-page treatise on the dynamics of nonviolent action campaigns. Essential reading for the serious organizer.

Strategy for a Living Revolution, by George Lakey (W. H. Freeman, 1973. Available from MNS, 4722 Baltimore Ave., Phila., PA 19143, $7.50 postpaid). Focuses on strategies to transform a whole society, including stages needed. Historically well-documented argument for nonviolent revolution.

CONSTRUCTIVE PROGRAMS

The Community Land Trust: A Guide to a New Model for Land Tenure in America, by the International Independence Institute (available from Institute for Community Economics, 639 Massachusetts Ave., Cambridge, MA 02139, $5.00). A guide written for individuals or groups who intend to take some land out of private ownership and place it under a trusteeship committed to the idea of community. Large section on ways to confront the legal maze of landholding laws so as to control rather than be controlled. Gives examples and history too.

Communities Magazine, Box 426, Louisa, VA 23093. This is one of the best resources on new alternative communities. Check through back issues.

Constructive Programme: Its Meaning and Place, by M. K. Gandhi (Navajivan Publishing House: Ahmedabad, 1960). Gandhi on the relationship of constructive program to nonviolent direct action.

Finding Community: A Guide to Community Research and Action, by W. Ron Jones (James E. Freel and Associates, 577 College Ave., Palo Alto, CA 94306). This is a book about community organization, laid out by service area (e.g., health) and subdivided into: "indictment," "readings," "research," and "action alternatives."

Fire Under the Ashes: The Life of Danilo Dolci, by James Mac-Leish (Boston: Beacon Press, 1966). An excellent introduction to Danilo Dolci and the nonviolent ideas of constructive work he is experimenting with in Sicily.

Food Co-op Directory, 106 Girard SE, Albuquerque, NM 87106, 1978, $3.00. Lists 2300 food co-ops in the U.S. and Canada. Also lists food co-op warehouses and federations.

"Getting Together a People's Yellow Pages," (Vocations for Social Change, 353 Broadway, Cambridge, MA 02139, $1.00).

Gramdan: The Land Revolution of India, (War Resistance: London, No. 28 and 29, 1969). A report of a movement which seeks to lay the foundations of a new social order in India; a demonstration of Gandhian constructive work ideas.

No Bosses Here: A Manual on Working Collectively, by Vocations for Social Change (353 Broadway, Cambridge, MA

02139, 1976, $3.50). A "how to do it" manual which tells people how to start their own worker-controlled cooperative workplace. Describes the concept of a collective in which all members share decision making and tells how to form a collective. Topics covered include dealing with interpersonal problems, relation of co-ops to social change movement, bookkeeping, pricing, and incorporation.

People's Yellow Pages. Many cities now have people's yellow pages listing alternative institutions and constructive programs going on within the community. An example of one of the early people's yellow pages is Boston's. Write Vocations for Social Change, Cambridge (see above).

Sarvodaya: Its Principles and Programme, by M. K. Gandhi (Navajivan Publishing House: Ahmedabad, India, 1948). Available from American Vegan Society, Box H, Malaga, NJ 08328. Gandhi outlines his vision of a village-based society.

Workforce, Vocations for Social Change, 4911 Telegraph Ave., Oakland, CA 94609. Articles on analysis, alternatives, job opportunities. Inquire about subscription price.

A ROUND

Anonymous

Love, love, love, love, Peo-ple we are made for love.
Love each o-ther as our-selves, for we are all one.

Part Eight

Exercises and Other Tools

I
Analysis, Theory, and Vision

VIOLENCE/NONVIOLENCE SOCIAL GOOD CHART

Purpose/Uses: To think about definition of nonviolence and social good. To understand better others' perceptions of nonviolence and social value. To allow people to disagree with each other in areas of social change tactics or nonviolent philosophy and gain a clearer understanding of how they classify nonviolent actions.

Description:

1. The group chooses acts to place at the extremes of the horizontal and vertical axes—something violent with no redeeming social value, like sadistic torture, and some highly positive nonviolent act, like successful nonviolent intervention in an international conflict.

2. Participants place other things like robbery, rape, property destruction, income tax refusal, taking a life for an ideal, threat of non-injurious force to halt a crime, etc., at other points on the chart.

3. People will differ as to where they place acts on the chart. Discuss these disagreements. Consider how people decide where to place actions. Some of the bases for making judgments are: the situation, how the act is carried out, the intention of the doer, the effects of the act on the doer and on others.

Sample Chart:

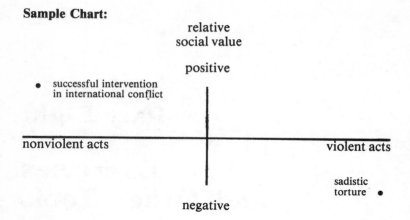

relative
social value

positive

● successful intervention
in international conflict

nonviolent acts | violent acts

sadistic
torture ●

negative

WEB CHART *

Purpose/Uses: To trace the general causes or effects of any specific problem, change or event. To locate the issue of concern in the center of a web of forces or events directly related to it. To get a larger perspective on the particular issue a group is working on. To investigate the causes of a problem by seeing the connections between personal problems and larger social forces. To trace results of an event or projected event; used to develop strategy or analysis, or to explore consequences of a vision.

Description:

1. Facilitator writes the issue of concern in the center of a chalkboard or wall chart, e.g., "American reliance on the automobile" (consequences of), "personal isolation" (causes), "elimination of automobile" (visionary consequences).

2. Group then lists around the central issue its immediate causes *or* consequences (not both). In a large group this should be done without discussion, but in a more thoughtful tempo than in a brainstorm. In a group of less than six people discussion is useful in keeping the chart simple and accurate.

3. The group then lists a few causes *or* consequences for each of the causes *or* consequences already listed, drawing lines of connection, arrows, etc. as appropriate. The facilitator needs

* The Web Chart is a modification of a "flow chart" exercise which originally came to our attention in 1972 through Jerry Glenn, a student at the Antioch Graduate School of Education. This description is taken in part from *Organizing Macro-Analysis Seminars: A Manual*, 3rd ed. (Phila. Macro-Analysis Collective, 4722 Baltimore Ave., Phila., PA 19143, $1.75).

to keep the group moving around the web to prevent focus on one avenue of cause or effect.

4. The group continues to list third and fourth level causes or effects as time allows. It is good to have some third level connections, at least.

Caution: The chart is useful to the extent that real thought goes into its creation. If it is difficult for your group to be calmly thoughtful when all are together, try breaking into groups of three or four for this process. Some report-back time needs to be allowed.

Variation #1: *Linking Personal Oppressions To Macro Forces** (2-3 hrs)

Purpose/Uses: To relate personal hurts to societal forces. To find personal motivation for social change work.

Description:

1. Participants begin by thinking for 3-5 minutes about what aspects of their lives really hurt. These might range from financial problems to the hurt at seeing others killed. Each person picks the three most important oppressions to report to the group, and these are listed on a wall chart.

2. The group then chooses one of these oppressions or groups several similar ones together and uses this as the basis for building a "web chart" of causes. It works best if the central issue is quite concrete. (See Web Chart Example #1.)

3. Continue with description under Web Chart, steps 1-4.

4. There are several ways of bringing this exercise to a useful finish. (a) When the Web Chart is complete, group members list items toward the edge of the web which are most important to them. The group selects from that list an item that might be changed by social action, and then each person says what s/he wishes could be true about the situation. The group then selects one of the wishes, and uses the *Vision to Project* exercise. (b) The group *Brainstorms* and discusses action projects to attack the causes of the central oppression. (c) Group Brainstorms questions for further research and analysis, to fill in holes in the web.

Since the overall process takes from 2-3 hours, it is unlikely that more than one theme can be followed through in a single meeting of a group.

---

* Taken from *Organizing Macro-Analysis Seminars: A Manual*, 3rd ed., p. 20 (see above).

Example: Web Chart

Theme: Lonelination

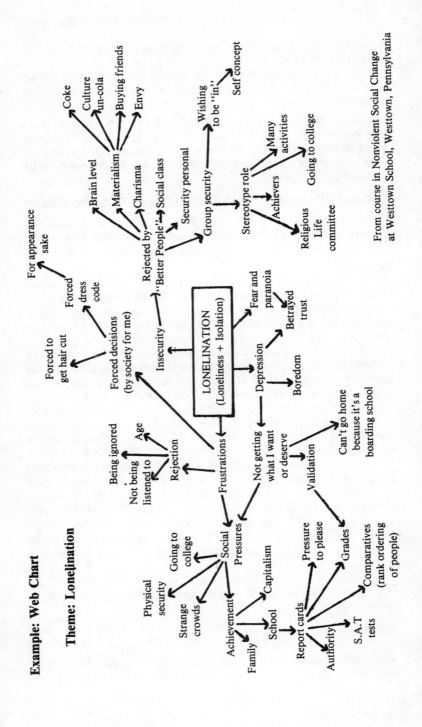

From course in Nonviolent Social Change
at Westtown School, Westtown, Pennsylvania

Variation #2: *Linking Personal Liberation to Macro Forces* (Pamela Haines)

Same process as in Variation #1, but think of three ways that you would like your life to be different (meaningful part-time job, knowing the people next door, etc.). Pick one of these for the center of the chart.

Think of the immediate things that would have to be true for that liberation to be possible, then the larger things that would be necessary. (The outer ring becomes societal visions rather than societal oppressions.)

SCENARIO WRITING

Purpose/Uses: To develop a time schedule for a social change project. To explore a number of possible strategies. To help people start to think strategically. To develop short or long-range visions.

Description:

1. People suggest areas needing change and select one.

2. Individuals write for 20 minutes to an hour or more a description of a series of events desired to bring about the change as if it had already happened. Set a clear time frame (week, month, decade). People can write as if they were witnesses to the events, reporters, participants who are writing to a friend about what happened, etc. In other words, have fun writing. Some people may want to make a *Time Line*: the first week this happened, the second this, etc. In any case the time element and a description of the actions of the opposition should be included. It is important to try to think in terms of optimistic reality.

3. People get into small groups, read their scenarios and combine them into a group scenario.

4. All the groups can come together and discuss the results, choosing a strategy to follow if appropriate.

Possible topics for a scenario:

• A poor family has just been evicted from its home. You are a church group that would like to have the family members live in the church building while you help them fight their eviction or find other housing. The property committee and many other members of the church are opposed.

• You are a group that is going to try to block the construction of a nuclear power plant because you feel that North Americans use too much energy and that nuclear energy is particularly dangerous to human life. The city government and the power company are going ahead without hearings.

• Your group is meeting to explore ways you and others in your town can cooperate more fully in living, study and action dimensions of social change. Scenario #1, Individual: "How I see myself in the struggle for social change the next 2-5 years." Scenario #2, Groups 3-5 each: "How we can work together more effectively to help each other and bring about social change."

VISION GALLERY

Purpose/Uses: To stretch people's imaginations in envisioning the kind of society they would like to create, going beyond vague values to specific features. To facilitate a group's development of a common vision and clarify the values its members share. To help people discover their own ideas and how much vision they have in common with others.

Materials: Large sheets of newsprint or construction paper, lots of markers, crayons, masking tape, and smooth floor or table space.

Description:

1. Select a topic, specific or general. People may want to work on many features of their vision simultaneously, such as government, defense, economic system, family structure and recreation; or they can focus on a specific question like "What might this community look like ten years from now if really good changes kept happening? What would my life look like? What would schools be like?" or "How will people defend themselves and/or their values?" Encourage each other to think creatively. Assume no constraints of money or power.

2. Questions could be **Brainstormed** at the beginning to trigger visionary thinking. Questions helpful to students might be: What would the goals of the "school" be? What kinds of decision-making processes would exist? How would learning take place? What kinds of social relationships would exist? What roles would students, faculty, administrators play? How would the physical plant be used?

3. For 15-30 minutes, individuals spend time alone, sketching their personal visions by writing, outlining, diagraming or drawing.

4. The next 30-45 minutes are spent in small clusters of 3-5 people, pooling their visions and expressing a common one on a large sheet of paper.

5. Each small group posts its composite utopia on the wall in the main meeting room, creating a vision gallery. People look, compare, discuss and question, informally.   (15-30 minutes)

6. The total group gathers to evaluate the vision exercise.

254

Questions to consider about process are: What are the areas of agreement revealed in the visions? What areas need the most work in developing a viable alternative to the status quo? What concepts do individuals agree or disagree with?

7. If the group wants to develop a full group vision, it can use *Small Group to Large Group Consensus*, adapted as needed.

VISIONARY PERSONAL PREFERENCES*
(20-60 min)

Purpose/Uses: Clarifies people's wishes for a new society and points up areas of conflict. Useful preparation for working together on a social change project.

Description:

1. Have each person think of (a) things they would never give up, (b) things they would be willing to share, and (c) things they would be willing to give up in order to achieve a society that met other needs.

2. List people's thoughts in three columns on a large chart.

3. Discuss.

II
Preparation for Action

INVENTORY OF SKILLS FOR THE ORGANIZER/TRAINER/PARTICIPANT

When preparing for an action campaign, it is valuable to take inventory of the skills possessed by the group, to know *who* has and *how many* have the necessary skills *and* to see if there are areas of skills which the group will need to acquire. Below is a sample format that could be used for this Inventory. It was developed by Lynne Shivers to help gather information from participants in a training program for social change at Pendle Hill.

---

* Adapted from *Organizing Macro-Analysis Seminars: A Manual*, 3rd ed., p. 19 (see above) which adapted it from an exercise in values clarification. For further information see *Values Clarification*, Sidney B. Simon, Leland W. Howe and Howard Kirschenbaum (Hart Publishing Co., 1972).

INVENTORY

_____

Name

• For skills/tools you are able to teach others
tell briefly in what situations you developed
or taught the skill/tool. Use another page
if necessary.

• Circle number of those skills you feel you want
to learn in the next _____.
                    (state period available)

| | Experience | | Can Teach |
| | None Some Extensive | | To Others |

Action Skills:
    1. street speaking
    2. leafleting
    3. etc.
Facilitation Tools:
    12. role play
    13. scenario writing
    14. evaluation
    15. etc.
Additional areas....

Skills not included above which
you would like to learn or teach.

_____
_____
_____

FORCE FIELD ANALYSIS

Purpose/Uses: To identify the forces and factors contributing to the success and failure of a particular action. To develop strategy. To organize information about an up-coming decision or dilemma in such a way as to clarify possible solutions and their implications. To help groups make decisions when they are in a mental bind. To analyze factors that go into societal conflict. To help groups examine the array of forces and see if negative forces can be reduced and positive forces increased. Useful for both individual and group problem solving.

Description:
    1. State the problem: "Will the campaign succeed?" "Shall I go to school?" "Shall we move?"
    2. Divide a piece of paper in half. List on one side the

positive forces and on the other side the negative forces. Often it is helpful to list the contradictory forces opposite each other.

Will the campaign succeed?

Forces contributing to its success (+)	Forces contributing to its failure (-)
The issue is of real concern to people in a wide spectrum of local groups	The police department is extremely repressive and paranoid.

3. Indicate the most important forces on the chart.

4. Draw a second chart indicating degree of force on a scale of 1-10 and place appropriately: 1 = weak forces, 10 = overwhelming forces.

+10	-	+1	-1	-	-10

5. Evaluate the balance of positive and negative forces. Can the effects of negative forces be reduced or eliminated?

Note: Much of the value of the Force Field Analysis is in shared thinking through of the factors to be put on the lists. The two lists, when completed and placed side-by-side, offer a holistic perspective to an extent not often produced by random discussions. The first chart may lead to a second one based on one of the items that appears on the first.

QUICK DECISION   (5-15 min)

Purpose/Uses: To generate a variety of possible options for a situation you may be facing soon. To prepare to respond creatively to situations that require instantaneous decisions. To help group gain cohesion and confidence. To prepare for demonstrations or theater exercises.

Description:

1. Divide the group into small groups of three or four people each.

2. Explain that you will present a number of situations that require quick responses. You might collect these situations from the group before starting by *Brainstorming*.

3. Present one situation and give a time limit, usually 30-60 seconds, to come up with a single solution. The group must reach consensus on its response.

257

4. Ask groups to report solutions.

5. Present additional situations as above. Later, solutions can be roleplayed or evaluated.

Examples of situations needing quick decision:

• You're in a nonviolent demonstration and someone in your ranks starts throwing stones at the police. What should you do? Take one minute.

• You are holding a difficult meeting and someone begins to cry. What should you do? Take 45 seconds.

• You're on the playground and some people start beating up one of your friends. What should you do? Take one minute.

• You and your friend have been sitting on the front steps of your house for 20 minutes waiting for a car pool driver to pick up your 3-year-old. A neighbor, black and in his early 20s, has been sitting across the street on his front steps for the same amount of time. A cruising police car suddenly stops and 2 policemen, both white, get out, rush to the neighbor, roughly force him against a wall and begin searching him. What should you do? Take one minute.

DECISION-MAKING STRUCTURE*

Purpose/Uses: To help groups decide which of their values are most basic and to sketch out general strategies according to them. To provide opportunity to relate values and philosophical ideas to practical courses of action. Good to use where people are considering actions.

Description:
1. Divide the group into small sections.

2. Propose an action problem and set *Time Limits* for each group to come up with a decision.   (10-20 min)

3. Return to the large group and report decisions. Evaluate the processes the groups used. How could each group have better facilitated its decision making?

Sample Situation: You are a group that hasn't been active for a while and have just received word that Wounded Knee has been seized by the American Indian Movement. Federal marshals have moved in and a second armed confrontation is in the offing. Your sympathies are with AIM. *Task:* You want to decide on a way to make this situation known publicly and to outline a strategy for nonviolent intervention between the two armed forces.

---

* Taken from materials prepared by Chuck Noell and Robert Levering.

NONVIOLENT AND VIOLENT REVOLUTION*
(3 hrs)

Purpose/Uses: To explore advantages and disadvantages of violent and nonviolent approaches to social change activities.

Description:

1. Explain tools and terms to be used. Tools: *Brainstorming, Extended Roleplay, Evaluation*. Terms: campaign, strategy, tactics.

2. *Brainstorm* elements of a new society, the goals of a revolution. (5 min) Review the brainstormed list, attempting to reach consensus on each item. Eliminate those not agreed upon. Questions of clarification can be asked of the person who listed the goal, but if consensus cannot be reached quickly (in less than 1 min), remove it from the list. (15-20 min)

3. Participants divide into two groups. One group takes the role of people who believe in violent revolution, the other group the role of those committed to nonviolent revolution. Each group is asked:

    a. to select an important visionary goal from the brainstormed list (5 min);

    b. to brainstorm possible campaigns concerning this goal and then choose one (15 min);

    c. to brainstorm possible tactics in that campaign and develop a strategy from that (30 min);

    d. to choose a reporter (1 min);

    e. to prepare a report, including a statement of the goal, campaign, and tactics chosen, and any additional statements needed (5 min).

4. The two groups then come together (facing each other).

    a. The violent revolutionaries outline their goal and campaign, including strategy and tactics to be used. (5 min)

    b. The nonviolent revolutionaries caucus to come up with challenges as to whether the other group's plans will produce the results desired. (2-3 min)

    c. The nonviolent group then asks challenging questions about relevance of strategy and tactics to goals *and* feasibility. (10 min)

5. In the same manner, the nonviolent revolutionaries present their plans and answer challenges from the other group. (18 min)

6. General discussion.

---

* With thanks to Blair Forlaw and P.J. Hoffman for their assistance in the development of this exercise.

7. *Evaluation*. Here are possible questions to be raised by the trainers: *The content:* How did you feel as violent and nonviolent revolutionaries? What did you feel was your source of power? Did you feel you had many options? How did you feel when you were challenged? Did good dialogue occur? How did each of you go about sorting out goals, campaigns, and tactics? Are there better ways? How did you make group decisions? *The tool:* Did it give you a better understanding of the various aspects of nonviolent and violent revolution? What were the most valuable parts of the exercise? the least valuable? What additions or changes would you make in the way the exercises were set up? How did you deal with domination or submission in your group?

DEVELOPING STRATEGIES*

Purpose/Uses: To learn to develop and analyze campaign proposals.

Description:

1. (A campaign has been selected to be analyzed.) Break into groups of 3-5 people each. *Brainstorm* maximum options for each element of the campaign. Discuss each idea in turn. Criticize, analyze and refine those considered most exciting.

2. Form one large group. Compare suggestions. Look for common ones. Further analyze any that are particularly exciting.

3. Break into small groups. Select suggestions from the list above and compare several possible strategies.

4. Write a campaign proposal for each, using a similar format for ease of comparison. A sample format might include possible goals, alternative institutions, constructive programs, negotiations with opponents, engagements of onlookers, and actions.

STRATEGY GAME**   (several hours)

Purpose/Uses: To gain information about the consequences of strategies developed. To point out the relationship between goals and strategy, strategy and tactics. To show in an involving way the development of a social change project. To introduce aspects of social change on a large scale. To provide the sense of a campaign. To test out before or during a campaign insights acquired through other training tools or experiences. To develop

---

* Taken from materials prepared by Chuck Noell and Robert Levering.
** Written in large part by Lynne Shivers.

an understanding of how the opponent may respond to your actions.

Note: A Strategy Game takes several hours to be effective. Where other exercises lead to similar insights, they should be considered as alternatives. The Strategy Game, however, is invaluable when preparing for a full-scale campaign or project.

Materials: Wall chart and felt pens or chalkboard and chalk for describing teams and situation. Paper and pencils for team members. If moves are to be written, carbon paper and typewriters (if available) for each team.

Physical arrangements: The best arrangement is usually for teams to be in one large room, at separate tables, far enough apart so as not to interfere with each other. If a large room is not available, teams can locate in small rooms near each other.

Setting Up the Game

A pre-strategy-game session, solely for trainers, is recommended. Trainers should write the scenario and list teams to be represented. The basic scenario and a brief description of all the teams are put on a wall chart, chalkboard or mimeographed sheet.

Trainers should go over rules carefully in the beginning. Each aspect of the structure should be explained. A brief time should be allowed for questions and clarification.

Each participant then decides what team s/he wants to be on, or whether s/he wants to function as a screener. When participants are clear about rules, the game begins (and time is kept), with the first move due about 20 minutes later and the others at 10 minute intervals after that. *Note:* Communications and decision making will necessarily be hurried, fragmented, and beset by pressures created by the game structure. But there is no good way to avoid this, and the pressure adds a note of reality. *Trainers should inform participants of this fact before the game begins.*

Sample schedule of a Strategy Game:

Tuesday evening: Trainers write the basic scenario and decide what teams will be represented.

Wednesday:
10:00 a.m. Trainers explain what a strategy game is, the scenario, rules, teams, structure of the game. Participants volunteer for teams. Questions are answered.

10:45 Participants form into teams.

261

11:05	First move due (spoken moves may take 10-15 minutes to report).
11:25	Second move due.
11:45	Third move due.
11:55	Additional moves, roleplay, etc.
2:00 p.m.	End of the game. Lunch.
3:00	Evaluation. (Break could be longer with evaluation in the evening.)

Structure

1. Teams: Six to sixty people can participate. Two to six teams designated, depending on (a) how many participants there are (each team should have 3-6 members) and (b) what sort of conflict people want to examine.

Two models of games are possible: *Two teams*, in which the conflict is narrowed and examined more closely, or *more than two*, which is sometimes called a "Population Game." The conflict here is more realistic since more groups are interacting. People should be asked to volunteer for the team they want to be on, unless too many want to play one team, in which case trainers should help equalize numbers.

The choice of teams to be represented depends on what the participants want to examine, for the number and nature of the teams will influence the results of the conflict situation. Trainers should keep the groups fairly well-defined so that learning can take place without much confusion; but groups should be representative to provide some semblance of reality.

2. Scenario: A background description of the conflict is provided to give some established facts and details. The scenario should be brief, at most one page—enough to give a skeletal background, but not so much as to be confusing or confining. It should define each participating group, who it is, its general politics, etc. It should build to a crisis point; this is where the game will begin. For example: the expulsion of a school teacher, the invasion of a country, or a critical situation of a present social change campaign.

An unfamiliar scenario can be used to introduce a new concept, like civilian defense. Generally speaking, the closer the scenario is to participants' experience, the more quickly they will become involved and learn.

Background information and preparation are *critical* to the success of strategy games. Trainers should explain the scenario carefully before the game begins.

3. Screeners: Select two or three screeners when there are 20-40

participants. In games with a large number of participants, allow one screener per group, and one overall screener. At least one person experienced in playing strategy games should be a screener. It is valuable to include less experienced people among screeners. Screeners function in the following ways:
- Keep time.
- Keep a log, with times, of all important moves for reference during the evaluation. The log is important, for it provides a more accurate account of moves than memory alone.
- Facilitate, *not* determine, the game.
- Function as a team: one to keep the log, another to observe the general interaction. Sometimes it is valuable for a screener to sit in on expecially difficult discussions one team is having. Near the end of the game, screeners should discuss among themselves the most important issues to raise during evaluation, based on what happened during the game.
- Rule on the reality of a move. For example, if one team moves that it organized 5,000 people to come to a rally, and the screeners think the team would not be capable of that organization, they can change and announce a total more "realistic" in their eyes. All screeners' rulings are final during the game, but can (and should) be questioned in the evaluation.
- See that teams make only moves of which they are capable. For example, a team representing "city government" cannot decide that a demonstration turned disruptive and people trashed windows, which justified mass arrests. It can move that city agents fomented trashing which thus resulted in mass arrests.
- Summarize the net effects of all the moves made at one time by the teams (optional; may be useful near the end of the game when moves are complex).
- Represent an important element which is not already represented by teams, for occasional moves. For example, they could produce a newspaper headline which might strongly affect the progress of the game; or, when a game is examining national strategy, they might want to announce the result of a poll of national public opinion. These moves should be interjected sparingly, however, lest the screeners become, in effect, another team, or come to dominate and control the game.

4. *Moves:* After the scenario has been presented and discussed, teams described, and teams formed by participants, the game begins. Screeners should allow 20 minutes for the first move and 10 minutes between moves thereafter. Teams make moves simultaneously. Once players have gotten into the game, times allotted for moves can be adjusted to provide longer or shorter

periods for deliberation. Screeners should be sensitive to the players' needs and the over-all time factor.

Written moves force people to be more exact about strategies they are developing. The game tends to have a more organized air about it. When moves are written, teams should make one copy for each team, plus one for screeners and one for themselves. *Spoken moves* tend to alter the game towards a marathon roleplay. People are more engaged than when they write moves. Both formats are valuable, but trainers should decide the format before the game and not mix them. For spoken moves, it is good to rotate which group reports first.

5. *Negotiations:* Any time during the game, teams can negotiate with each other without stopping the game or the time-keeping. Requests for negotiations should go through screeners, to provide more realism. For example, a response might be that the mayor is too busy to talk with anyone right now.

6. *Roleplaying:* Participants may decide that they want to roleplay a particular situation in the context of the game; for example, a crucial meeting of the school board with radical students, an arrest scene, or a critical demonstration. Screeners should call a temporary halt to the game, give teams time to prepare for the roleplay, run it through, take a break, briefly evaluate, and return to the game as before the roleplay. A mass roleplay, usually a public meeting of some sort in which it is appropriate for all teams to participate, is often a good culmination and final phase of a strategy game. You can end the roleplay at an appropriate point; e.g., city council calls in the police to arrest the social change advocates.

7. *Spying:* Spying is usually not allowed in the shorter, simpler games. Some view spying as useful, however, in marathon "population games." Spying on another team does provide a realistic way for teams to face the means-ends ethical question. If spying is permitted, don't allow it to dominate the game at the expense of searching for creative and open approaches to social problems.

Ending the Game

When screeners decide that the outcome seems determined, when trainers decide that the game has unearthed enough issues for discussion, or when people get tired, stop the game. Allow a break of at least an hour, for coffee, a run outside, a meal, or other tension-breakers. A break helps to get people out of their roles—necessary after a tense game. It also allows time for participants to assure people with whom they had heavy conflicts during the game that feelings are not carried over. If a long break is necessary, screeners should open the evaluation with a summary. To help simulate reality, screeners could present an in-depth broadcast, a newspaper, or a letter.

Evaluation

The evaluation can be broken into four parts: (a) initial feelings of participants (to help release tension), (b) strategy, (c) application of insights, and (d) evaluation of the game as a learning tool. The sample questions below are suggestions only; trainers should *not* feel compelled to use them all.

Evaluation is a very important part of a strategy game, for this is the time when people learn the effects of their strategies, get feedback, and assess the forces acting in a conflict situation. A good evaluation might take two hours; thus, a structure for the evaluation is encouraged.

Sample Evaluation Questions

Feelings:

• At what point did you/your team feel a great deal of tension?
• At what point did you/your team feel great frustration?
• What did you do about the tension/frustration?
• Can you isolate causes for the tension/frustration?
• At what point did you/your team feel "on top" of the situation?
• How well did your team members work together? Major problems?

Strategy:

• What was your strategy? Goal? Did other team(s) know what they were? Did your strategy change?
• What were the most/least effective moves?
• What moves by other teams helped/hindered your strategy and goals?
• What moves would you consider "nonviolent"? Did any of the teams have a consciously nonviolent strategy?
• Outline the escalation of the conflict and the resolution, if any.
• Were there outstanding actions by any team?
• At what point were ethical problems most acute? Did the team(s) with greater power have ethical problems with their moves?

Generalization and Application:

• How much power did your team really have? How much

were your moves dependent on the moves of other teams?
- What insights have you gained about conflict? Social change? Nonviolence?
- What did you learn from this game that you can apply to other conflict situations with which you identify?

Evaluation of the Game as A Learning Tool:
- Consider the role of the screeners. Did they rule realistically and fairly?
- How could the game be improved in the future?
- What do participants feel they did or didn't gain from the game?

Questions for Trainers:
- How did teams keep from getting bored while waiting for the others' moves?
- Was the pace brisk, but with enough time to involve people thoroughly?
- How did you keep screeners from becoming dictators?
- How did you keep things realistic?
- How did you decide when to stop the game?
- Did the position of the trainers interfere? Where, when or how?
- For what purpose did you use the strategy game?
- What were the main problems in the game? How did you attempt to solve them? What would you try next time?
- Did you discover any improvements for the structure of the game?
- Did you make innovations in the game? What were they?

Sample Situations:
The more relevant the situation to the issues people want to explore, the more learning will take place. It is usually best for trainers and a few participants to design the situations during the training session. If that is not possible, sample situations from below can be used as models. For the first two, a map of the city might help make them clearer.

1. *Ecology:* Citizens Against Pollution vs. International Refuse Company
- Purpose: To examine a conflict situation around the issue of local ecology.
- Teams: Citizens Against Pollution (CAP), International Refuse Company (IRC)

The location is in Eastchester County in suburban Greater Metropolis. Eastchester County has only one large town, the county seat of Eastchester (pop. 55,000), which is mixed in voting records, political opinions, etc. There is a thriving John Birch chapter and a growing New Democratic Coalition, both drawing heavily from professionals working in Greater Metropolis. The sole industry in Eastchester is IRC, which manufactures 1000 lb. garbage bombs to suffocate Viet Cong rice fields. As its by-product IRC pumps tons of pollution into the Eastchester River and the air each year. Being the county's only large industry, it holds great influence in the local media, country clubs, churches, etc. Fifteen to twenty-three percent of Eastchester's residents are employed either by IRC or by smaller companies which depend directly on its business for survival. IRC has also initiated the most progressive integrated-equal opportunity program in the area and has been highly praised by civil rights groups for its pioneering efforts in this field.

2. *Small Town:* Schwartztown
   • Purpose: To examine a conflict situation in a small town.
   • Teams: Collective of Local Unified Threadbare Students (CLUTS) activists, campus ministry of the local college, liberal townspeople, conservative and reactionary businessmen, school board.

Schwartztown is a small town with main industries of fruit-growing and light machinery. The local college has a population of 4,000, the town has 6,000. People have been moving into town from Mountainview, a larger city, because of a housing shortage there, and a trailer park has developed. Some blacks have moved in; before this, Schwartztown has had almost no blacks. The campus ministry has recently lost traditional money from local churches because it has opened a store-front, the "Gathering," where counseling on drugs, the draft, and abortion is offered. The campus ministry is also setting up a free school with CLUTS students, who congregate frequently at the Gathering. Drugs are an especially hot issue.

Housing is a problem at the college, and it has been traditional for local residents to rent rooms to college students. The college has announced that housing must be open to all students. Since the enrollment of blacks at the college, thirty percent of the residents have announced that they will refuse to rent rooms to blacks.

The only local high school has 300 students. Teacher Fred Morrison was threatened with dismissal when he agreed with CLUTS students that mandatory assemblies and pledging the flag were not necessary. When he gave permission to students to skip assemblies, he was dismissed. Sixty CLUTS students have

267

walked out of classes, announcing a boycott of school until Morrison is reinstated. First move: school board.

3. Coup d'Etat:

• Purpose: To examine nonviolent civilian defense and how it works.

• Teams: Liberals, supporters of William Marshall, advocates of nonviolent civilian defense, a loose alliance of minority groups, nonviolent activists. Military leaders, Joint Chiefs of Staff, FBI, CIA. Citizens living in major urban areas. Citizens living mainly in small towns and rural areas.

It is January 10, 1981. The United States has continued in ferment, with the revolutionary forces growing in size and strength. The have-nots, whether black, Chicano, Puerto Rican, young, or white, have all come to realize that a basic obstacle in the way of revolutionary change is the U.S. military. This, combined with the disillusionment with the military common among liberals, has swept William Marshall, who ran on a platform which included nonviolent civilian defense, into the Presidency in November 1980. The military, deciding that a coup d'etat is needed before the new president is inaugurated, launches one on January 10. The Joint Chiefs of Staff and most senior officers in active service are united on this, although some Pentagon officials and intellectuals are not expected to support the effort. Strongest non-military support comes from the FBI and CIA.

SIMULATION GAMES

Purpose/Uses: To develop strategies for change. To get a feel for real parties involved in a conflict situation and their strategies. To test out a projected long-range project.

Description:

A simulation game is much like a strategy game, except that participants physically act out the situation, such as an invasion, a coup, or imprisonment, instead of acting through oral or written moves. In a simulation game, one minute of action is one minute in real time; whereas in a strategy game, two weeks of action can occur in five minutes. A simulation game involves physical action, with intense emotional involvement and little time to reflect on the consequences of actions and strategies.

Clear rules and information should be supplied before the game begins. The situation may be fictitious or real. When it is real, participants may research the groups that they are going to represent in the game. Roles can be assigned to assure that major opinions or personalities within these groups are accurately portrayed. Some individuals may play themselves.

Note: There are many games now on the market that simulate the economy or international diplomacy. Our experience indicates that the scenario or game will be of greater practical use if it is designed with the help of the group.

Example: *The Oppression Game* * (approx 12 people)

Purpose/Uses: To simulate some roles in an oppressive society and to examine feelings about being in those roles. To examine the analogies between the game situation and real life. To examine participants' different reactions to the same situation.

Materials: String, scissors, blank cards, some cards with "defective" written on them.

Description:

1. Oppressors sit at one end of the room, supplier(s) at the other. The oppressed workers obtain cards from supplier(s) by "working" and bring them to oppressors who "pay" for cards by cutting off slices. The oppressed are physically and socially handicapped as described below. Oppressed persons who "earn" the equivalent of a whole card become free. Police enforce the rules.

2. *Suggestion to trainers:* Blank and defective cards are in the stack together. Don't mention to anyone, including suppliers, that "defective" cards are mixed in with the blank cards. What players do with them is unpredictable.

3. Roles usually include: 3 oppressors, 2 oppressed workers assigned to each oppressor, 2 police and 1 supplier. Numbers can vary. *Oppressed workers:* Physically limited—a string is tied around a wrist and an ankle so that the person must remain stooped over. Socially oppressed—may not speak aloud. Worker must stand quietly in line while waiting for a chance to work for a card. When his/her turn comes s/he must touch toes 5 times (or do other "work" which trainer chooses). Supplier then gives a card to the worker. Worker takes card to oppressor, bows 3 times and presents card. Holds out hand for payment. (No talking.) Then goes and stands in line again. *Oppressors:* Sit together at end of room. Recieve card after worker has bowed 3 times. Insist on this. Snip off a piece of card and give it to worker. Tell him/her to work faster. (Get as many cards as you can.) *Supplier(s):* Sit at other end of room. Give a card when

---

* By Martha Evans and Alan Tuttle.

work is done satisfactorily. *Police:* Make sure the "laws" are obeyed.

4. Allow a minute at the start to get into roles. Play 10-20 minutes.

5. Stop the game at an appropriate time. Free the workers, and sit in a circle. Feelings may be very strong during and after this game. You may want to talk about them together, in pairs or small groups. Consider: (a) What feelings did you have while playing your role? (b) How did you act? Did suppliers identify with oppressors? Did police? (c) Were you competitive, cooperative, defiant, other? (d) Did workers slow down, rebel, attempt to steal, other? (e) What are the analogies between this game and real life? e.g. physical restraint, rules, how oppressed workers treated each other, how oppressors treated workers, how oppressors treated each other, how supplier and police acted toward players.

COMBINING A CASE STUDY WITH STRATEGY GAME

Case studies can be selected from a variety of past actions. The procedure suggested here is best suited to examining case studies with a strong nonviolent action component. It can also be used for case studies having other theoretical frameworks, or a different process can be developed. In either case, using a strategy game to act out a case study is a good way to explore past efforts for change.

Purpose/Uses: To help people examine strategically various tactics as they have been used. To examine campaigns as whole pictures. To examine historical information in a non-lecture way. To further a long-term outlook on strategy. To compare actions. To become more conscious of one's own cultural heritage in nonviolent action. To add reality to the study of case histories.

Description:
1. Agree on a written case study. See section on Studying Case Histories for a bibliography on case studies of nonviolent actions.

2. Read case study materials and analyze the action under the following headings: (a) time, (b) duration, (c) place, (d) allies and supporters, (e) opponents and their allies, (f) goals, (g) preliminary events, actions, (h) reactions by opponents, and (i) results.*

* Adapted from Joan Bondurant's outline in *Conquest of Violence* (Univ. of California Press, 1965).

270

3. Trainers answer clarifying questions (no discussion).

4. Examine a list of Gene Sharp's methods of nonviolent action, discuss questions and give examples. (All 198 methods are listed and described with examples in *The Politics of Nonviolent Action:* Part Two, by Gene Sharp. A brochure of the table of contents, listing these methods, is available free from Porter Sargent, 11 Beacon, Boston, MA 02108.)

5. Using the case study as the scenario, try out tactics in *Roleplay*, strategy exercises or a *Strategy Game*.

Recommendation to trainers:

1. Choose case studies from participants' own culture, to help them better visualize themselves in action campaigns.

2. Select case studies carefully. Questions to ask yourself are: Is the case study dramatic? Does it have the ability to illustrate the dynamic of nonviolence, truth, suffering, success, or whatever you are hoping to examine? Is it simple enough to understand? Does it focus on a specific tactic? Does it stimulate further reading on a particular topic?

3. When participants ask for more formal information on nonviolent social change, in our experience, case studies are preferable to lectures. Discussions following presentation of case study material seem to be more involving and personal than those following lectures.

VISION TO PROJECT (30-40 min)

Purpose/Uses: To move from general, vague goals to specific practical projects. This can be used as a hope-building exercise or as a generator of practical ideas for an action project.

Description:

1. Bring together goals listed in previous discussions or *Brainstorm* a fresh list of positive wishes about a good society or goals for an action campaign.

2. Choose one goal or a synthesis of several that everyone is interested in pursuing further. Make sure the goal is stated clearly.

3. The group then Brainstorms a list of possible ways to achieve the goal.

4. The group picks one item from this newly Brainstormed list and Brainstorms again on specific ways the idea can be implemented.

5. If necessary, the group Brainstorms again, until ideas are specific enough to be worked on that week.

FLOW CHART

Purpose/Uses: To make choices about and evaluate the consequences of a particular tactic. To develop a time sequence for actions. To develop strategy in a campaign. To help select the lowest tension step or most socially acceptable action for use first.

Description:

1. Write down the problem being addressed.

2. In a column next to the problem list a number of actions that might be taken first. Write down the consequences of each action next to it.

3. Choose one or two actions and write down the actions that might follow it.

4. Continue until you have laid out as much as you need.

Example:

1st week	consequences

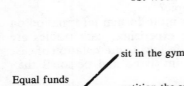

sit in the gym
- may lose support if first step
- will show we mean business
- may be arrested

Equal funds for women's athletics

petition the school
- probably won't bring change
- will raise consciousness
- will give chance to talk to people

bring a law suit
- we don't have much money
- will take a long time

(1st week)   *2nd week*   *consequences*

petition the school
- leaflet to let people know
- sit in
- Etc.

TIME LINE

Purpose/Uses: To set priorities among activities and events which must be completed within a given period of time. To develop a sequence of activities necessary to complete a task. Expecially useful in conference planning or in planning a campaign with a target date.

Description:

1. Draw a horizontal line on a piece of paper.

272

2. Graduate it into time blocks appropriate to the problem. First mark is NOW. Last mark would be completion date, conference date, etc.

3. Brainstorm all the tasks to be completed.

4. Place the tasks on the time line in the order of when they have to be done and which are most important to do at a particular time.

Example: *Time Line for a Conference*

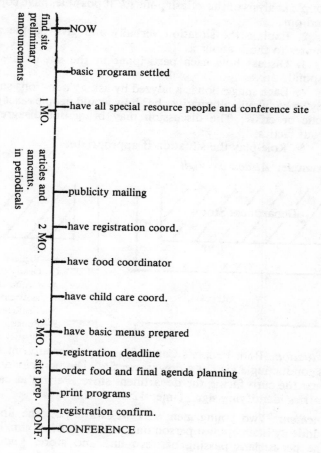

273

SITUATION ANALYSIS*

Purpose/Uses: To explore alternative tactics of a direct action situation. To familiarize participants with physical constraints of a particular action to be carried out. To think through possible creative responses, given crises which may arise.

Description:

1. Place on a wall chart or chalkboard the physical situation the group needs to examine. This will be based on the group's analysis of the "flash points." if possible, have copies to hand out.

2. Explain the situation verbally and give people a few minutes to think about it.

3. Discuss how each participant in the situation should respond.

4. Each suggestion is analyzed by asking questions such as: why? what would alternatives be? how would people react to this tactic or crisis? The discussion may bring out disagreement about tactics.

5. Role-play the situation if appropriate.

Example: *Attack on Vigil*

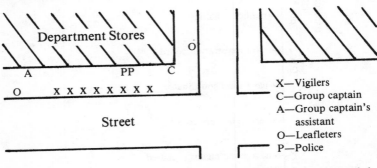

X—Vigilers
C—Group captain
A—Group captain's assistant
O—Leafleters
P—Police

Situation: Poor People's Campaign support group, interracial, is conducting a vigil at a downtown site. The participants stand near the curb facing the department store. Person at each end carries identifying sign. Time: 12:30 P.M.

Incident: Two young men walk westward past the line, then suddenly intercept last person on the line, shoving him/her into the pedestrians passing between line and store, knocking a pedestrian down. Attackers quickly run westward.

Task: Suggest responses: vigilers, captain, assistant, person next

---

* Developed by Charles C. Walker.

to one attacked. fallen pedestrian, leafleters, police. Analyze structure of the vigil for best responses. Evaluate effect after the incident has run its course.

Material for situation analysis is available in *A Manual for Direct Action*, by Martin Oppenheimer and George Lakey, Chapter 7 (Quadrangle, 1965, $2.45). Particularly useful are questions on p. 83 and the section on police tactics, p. 88. It is valuable to draw on the group's own past actions to see where it succeeded or failed. When a new action is contemplated, participants should scout the area of the demonstration and provide situation analysis charts based on actual logistics.

ROLEPLAYS*

A roleplay is an improvised drama in which the players take on roles in a stated situation as preparation for encountering a similar situation or evaluating a past one. The situation may be part of a carefully planned social change campaign or an experience encountered in a day-to-day living situation. Roleplay is a basic tool and can be used for many purposes. For this reason we include it with several variations.

Purpose/Uses: To help examine real problems on the level of theory, emotional responses, and physical social change. To try out and analyze situations, theories and tactics. To understand people and their roles. To develop insights into the thoughts and feelings of "opponents." To anticipate new situations. To reveal fears and anxieties and other feelings people have about an action. To gain more information. To develop group morale. To develop individual and group competence and confidence.

Description:

1. *Select a situation:* Participants need to be conscious of their reasons for wanting to do a roleplay so that relevant situations can be used. What do people want to examine? A trainer can suggest a situation, but it is usually better to have the group help design one. An irrelevant situation will result in boredom among participants. A simple situation is best. When used to demonstrate roleplaying, a problem should have a possible solution.

Caution: In choosing a situation, remember that a roleplay is *not* a *psychodrama*. A psychodrama is a form of therapy in which a person acts out with others situations related to his/her own problems, maintaining his/her own identity. In psycho-

---

* Thanks to Lynne Shivers, who did the initial writing for much of the 11 points explained here.

drama one is not asked to think about or create a role, but only to respond to one's feelings for the purpose of explaining the whole of one's personality. The goal is personal therapy for the participant. Psychodramas are not useful to prepare for a direct action of a social change nature.

A roleplay *is*, on the other hand, a *sociodrama*, which is the general term used for extemporaneously acting out roles in a social conflict situation, assuming an identity other than one's own. People are asked to draw on life experience (what they have seen or lived) to create a role. The purpose of sociodrama is to explore a conflict involving more than one person and containing social significance. Sociodramas are very useful in preparing people for direct action projects.

2. *Explain the situation:* To prevent confusion, the trainer explains carefully what groups are represented and the physical layout. In addition, the trainer or a participant explains enough of the background to make the situation clear so that roles will not be played solely from personal stereotypes. A roleplay is used to learn what to do in a situation *or* to study a particular role and reaction. Therefore, define carefully the situation *or* role to be examined, but not both, or spontaneity will suffer from over-programming.

3. *Cast roles:* Either people volunteer or the trainer urges people to take particular roles. It is good to cast people in roles that they do not identify with strongly. It is helpful if participants take fictitious names, whether they are to be used or not.

4. *Prepare roleplayers:* Allow a few minutes for people to get into their roles, decide on their general perspective and plan their strategy. Ask people to think of other aspects of their role lives (job, family, motivations) to make the roles real. The trainer can assist people if the roles are unfamiliar to them. If there are any special or secret instructions to be given to a roleplayer, they can be given at this time.

5. *Prepare observers:* Observation is as important as playing a role. Observers may be used when groups are too large for all to be in the roleplay or may be persons too shy to participate (though with additional roleplays reluctant persons often become more willing). Prepare observers by suggesting specific developments in the conflict for which they should watch. Instruct observers to be careful of language, comments, etc., which may distract players from their roles. If observers get tense, trainers need to ask them to share their feelings early in the evaluation.

6. *Set the scene:* The trainer establishes the scene, the

physical layout and any other relevant details. Participants should know beforehand what to watch for, based on the goals of the roleplay and critical incidents that occur, such as development of tension/hostility/violence, nonviolent aspects, tone of voice or elements which decrease hostility.

7. *The roleplay itself:* The trainer indicates when to begin. S/he may ask for 30 seconds of silence so participants can get into their roles.

8. *Cut:* The trainer cuts (or stops) the roleplay when enough issues have been uncovered, the action comes to a logical end, or people want to stop. Keep the goals of the roleplay clearly in mind. The trainer obviously should cut if someone is injured or the roleplay dissolves into laughter. If participants don't seem "into" their roles, the trainer should cut and redefine the situation or begin again. If a person over-identifies with a role (indicated by showing great tension), the roleplay should also be cut and the person helped to step out of the role. In this case, the trainer should stay with the group if possible and ask a co-trainer or participant to spend time with the tense individual.

9. *Short break:* It's generally a good idea to break the mood of the roleplay by providing a short break of a minute or less. Ask people to move out of the locations taken in the roleplay. If the experience was tense, the trainer should help release tension further by suggesting a quick game, stretch, song or *Attention Expander*, or mentioning the availability of refreshments.

10. *Evaluation:* This is an essential part of roleplaying, a time when people assimilate what took place. The tone of the evaluation is important; the trainer is responsible for setting and maintaining it. If the trainer sees him/herself as having all the answers, people will tend to rely on him/her rather than on themselves for learning. However, if the trainer is accepting of ideas, is able to say "I don't know" when that is so, is open to new ideas but has real contributions to make, then the learning process will be valuable and exciting.

Some trainers structure the evaluation to examine (a) feelings, tensions, (b) tactics, strategy, goals, and (c) theory and application. It is usually good to begin by asking the roleplayers how they felt in their roles: what was happening to them. If practical, give everybody a chance to speak. Ask observers for their impressions and then allow discussion. Ask participants to measure what they have learned against their goals for the roleplay. Encourage people to relate specific actions to their theory of change.

Refer to characters by the name used in the roleplay so the individual does not begin to feel hostility, anger, and criticism directed at him/her personally.

Discourage negative evaluation of participants which indicates what they *should* have done. This makes roleplaying feel like performing and it will make it difficult for people to participate in future roleplays. Mistakes made during roleplays are excellent sources for learning. People should be complimented for acting boldly in difficult situations regardless of the outcome. Language that encourages roleplayers is: "Another option that you might try is...," "Perhaps this would work...," "I learned _____ from your tactic and would like to try...," "From the response you got, _____ tactic might be used in the future."

Evaluation should not go on too long. If new insights come up, the group may wish to try them out in a new roleplay rather than talk about what might happen. When participants begin to lose interest, they are ready to go on to a new roleplay.

11. *Summation:* When the series of roleplays and evaluations is finished, a summation helps people achieve a sense of accomplishment. It is the trainer's role to help facilitate the summation. Ask participants to list new insights and new solutions which have occurred to them during the whole process. Pooling this information often reveals very creative and useful insights.

Variation #1: *Hassle Line*

Purpose/Uses: To get people to move around and warm up for more involved roleplays. To demonstrate roleplaying and get a whole group involved in a roleplay situation with limited variables. To isolate body language and study it. To prepare everyone rapidly for a particular negotiation, e.g., to talk with military police when expected in large numbers.

Description:

1. Ask people to form two lines facing each other: a line of Persons A and a line of Persons B. The person opposite you in the line is your partner for the hassle.

2. Set the scene. Give everyone a simple 2-role situation. Be specific if necessary: "Person A, you are..." "Person B, you are..." If helpful, give participants 30 seconds to get into their roles and ask them to play them out.

3. Tell people that when you yell "freeze" they should remain motionless. After a brief period of time you can continue that situation or propose a new situation, or evaluate.

4. In evaluating, first focus on body language: look at hands, eyes, power positions, height. Then focus on what happened in the various pairs during the action: tactics, resolutions, etc.

Sample two-role situations:

• Everyone in line A is a store owner, everyone in line B is a person cutting the chain on a bicycle in front of the owner's store.

• Everyone in line A is a policeman stopping a person for speeding or hitchhiking. Everyone in line B feels justified.

• Everyone in line A is making a pass at the person in line B.

• Person A is severely beating a child about the head. Person B is a passer-by.

• Get the group to come up with its own. Try brainstorming on "situations that paralyze me" or "frighten me" or "freak me out."

Variation #2: *Reverse Roleplay*

Purpose/Uses: To help people feel both positions in a conflict. To help people entrenched in one position think more flexibly about their position. Especially useful in dealing with conflict over power, sexism, ageism, etc.

Description:

1. Set up a situation involving two sides.

2. At an important point in the roleplay, have everyone freeze.

3. Have people take the opposite role and take up the conversation where it left off. The trainer may have to help people remember what the last lines of the dialogue were. It often helps if the trainer physically moves people to their new positions and says "You are now X, and you are now Y." Give people a minute to mentally shift to their new identities and resume the roleplay.

Example: Reverse Roleplay is particularly valuable for examining a critical incident that occurs repeatedly or is expected to occur and for developing a definition of acceptable behavior. It was used with Buffalo, NY, police in examining their most typical dangerous street incidents. (For more information on use of this technique and this particular project contact Ross Flanagan, 840 Edgewood Ave., Trenton, NJ 08618.)

What they did in Buffalo:

1st—Police and citizens played themselves.

2nd—Police and citizens took opposite roles. Each player

279

acted out his/her stereotypes of the other side as far more hostile than either had acted in 1st roleplay.

3rd—Staying in reversed roles, police and citizens acted out their conceptions of model conduct by their opposites.

Meanwhile other police, observing all three roleplays, evaluated and rated the actions of participants. Out of the roleplays and evaluation came definitions of acceptable behavior on the part of officers and new insights on how to handle these problems.

Variation #3: *Extended Roleplay*   (2 hrs-4 days)

Purpose/Uses: To study group behavior over a longer period of time. To allow people to explore a situation more fully. To study tactics of nonviolent (civilian) national defense or other theoretical problem.

Description:

1. Set up as a normal roleplay but choose an open-ended situation that involves a number of people.

2. Plan for an adequate period of time to evaluate (a few hours if necessary).

Variation #4: *Alter Ego*

Purpose/Uses: To reveal thoughts and feelings behind words or actions, especially stereotyped ones. To explore problems frequently arising in meetings.

Description:

1. Set up a normal roleplay in which each participant is paired with another person who is his/her alter ego.

2. The alter ego may say what ş/he believes a person is really feeling or thinking during the roleplay. Thus in a situation where a long-hair is asking the principal of a high school if a group might have a speaker come to talk on alternatives to the draft, the principal might say, "Thank you very much for coming to me with this question," while the alter ego might feel in the context that what was actually being felt was, "You long-hairs are a real pain in the neck."

3. An evaluation might include some reflection on nonverbal cues.

Variation #5: *Anger Tool*

Purpose/Uses: To start a discussion about personal nonviolence or the differences between anger, violence and aggression. To prepare for theater exercises. To have people simulate the difficult feeling of anger.

Description:

1. The trainer can ask a volunteer to help demonstrate the tool.

2. Explain that you are going to talk in nonsense syllables, starting with a low voice tone but continually raising it higher than the other person, who is doing the same. Demonstrate using a sound like "ra."

3. Have people pair up and try it. If people have a hard time making angry noises, suggest that they think of a person with whom they have been angry. Encourage experimentation: once reaching a peak, keep lowering your voice, or keep your voice constant, while the other person raises his/hers.

4. Evaluate what happened. Look for ways people kept themselves under control and how that affected the other person. Examine body language. What does anger have to do with violence?

5. This might be followed by sharing on "How I express my anger." Look at ways that anger might be gotten out without violence.

Note: Some people may become distressed if they allow themselves to feel anger. Be prepared to spend time bringing people out of their anger, back to the present situation. Possible ways of doing this are to use *Affirmation Exercises* or *Attention Expanders*.

III
Action

OBSERVATION OF AN EVENT

Purpose/Uses: To acquaint activists with the many forces at work in an event like a demonstration. To collect information for later analysis. If events continue or are repeated for a long duration, information collected can be used immediately to correct mistakes and improve desired results of the action. To allow timid or inexperienced people to fill a vital function while participating at a less threatening level.

Description:

Different observational techniques may be needed for different situations, and varying emphases may be given at different times. In most cases an observation sheet prepared in advance will maximize the gathering of useful information. It can list questions to be kept in mind so that the data gathered will be pertinent to the purpose of the observation.

To prepare an observation sheet, people familiar with the action or conflict to be observed should list the kinds of information needed to best evaluate the events. Then, design a mimeographed sheet with room to record this information.

Crowd observations

Demographic information can be determined by rough estimates. This can include approximate number of demonstrators, rough division of ages, percentages based on race or sex, etc. To count a moving crowd, estimate the rate of flow (number of persons per given period of time past a given point). For crowd situations, gain a high vantage point and count a square of 50 or 100 people, then estimate the number of such squares in the area observed. Check your estimate against the police and press estimates published later and extrapolate to get a basis of comparison for your own guess.

Note any or all of the following:

• Presence of police, reporters, and marshals.

• Counter-demonstrators: How many? Where are they in relation to demonstrators? Are they identified? Does their action seem a mob activity or organized? What type of disruption results, if any?

• Non-participating observers: Are they heckling, sympathetic, curious, etc.?

• Unusual persons: Any attention-getters, extraordinary in dress, action, or reputation?

• Groups represented: Might include schools or agencies. Are groups identifiable by appearance only or something more definite?

• Signs and ID: Which? How many in a particular group? Any repetitive themes? Are signs homemade or mass produced?

• Crowd-affecting factors: Do marshals seem effective? How is the tone set? What are the physical surroundings? What is the posture of the police? Any speakers? Where located?

• Crowd activity: Is it ordinary for the time of day? Any apparent commitment to either nonviolence or violence?

• Crowd atmosphere: How are people dressed? Is there any definable tone? How is it manifested? How is the atmosphere established?

• Outstanding incidents: Is there any event which changes or radically affects the demonstration? Try to be as objective and detailed as possible.

• Other observations: Keep your mind, eyes, and ears open for points not covered by the sheet and for suggestions from other observers.

Observation of conflicts:

Give a brief, factual description of the incident: where, when, number of people involved, onlookers, stated source of conflict.

• Describe body movements and nonverbal signs of individuals in the conflict: acts of aggression or attempted withdrawal, body posture, use of eyes, hands, arms, legs, and feet. Are any weapons in addition to the body used: knife, gun, rock, etc.?

Describe the use of language: verbal abuse, jokes, attempts to understand or reconcile the conflict.

If a third party intervenes, how? Is it needed? Does it help? Does it complicate matters?

Make suggestions for prevention or more creative resolution of the incident in the future.

Additional Resources:
Manual: "Training Observer Teams," by Charles C. Walker (Gandhi Institute, Box 92, Cheyney, PA 19319, 4 pp., $.50 postpaid, stamps acceptable). First used at anniversary observances, Kent State University, Kent, OH, May 1971.

LEAFLETING

Purpose/Uses: To make a demonstration more effective. To inform or educate the public about an issue. To clarify your position on an issue. To announce or publicize an event. To dramatize and generate enthusiasm for an issue. To counter or encourage prevailing public opinion. To win neutral people over to one side. To encourage participation in an event. To call people to action on an issue. To increase a group's membership or support.

Description:

How to Plan, Write and Reproduce a Leaflet:

1. Clearly think through the focus of the leaflet before beginning to write. (a) To what kind of audience is it directed (determines style and content)? (b) What are the purposes of the leaflet? Is it for one occasion or general use?

2. Use simple language, and limit the amount of information included. Quality is much more important than quantity.

3. Check facts thoroughly and use them carefully.

4. Take care for the tone, which often communicates as much as the text. The emotional effect of the words can vary widely: polite, annoying, dramatic, straight, screaming, low-key, threatening, arousing guilt, etc.

5. Clearly identify the sponsoring group on the leaflet. This legitimizes the leaflet, builds trust with an audience, and gives people a contact point. It may be a legal requirement. If participation by others is sought, include a return coupon for more information or follow-up.

6. Design it carefully.
- Arrange the content for simplicity and clarity.
- Vary the typography as much as possible, using different sizes of print, boxes, indentations, diagonals, arrows, etc.
- Pictures and political cartoons are effective for variety.
- Choose the size paper which fits the amount of information, and keep in mind various folding possibilities.
- Evaluate before making final.

7. There are several ways to reproduce a leaflet, varying in cost and quality:
- Ditto. Quantity from each master copy is limited.
- Mimeography. Quality depends on cleanly cut stencil and condition of the machine. Electro-stencils can be used for a variety of print types, illustrations, photographs, etc., but are difficult to manage, and occasionally 2 or 3 tries are needed before a desired product is obtained.
- Offset printing is modest in cost and can produce high quality leaflets. (Quality and price vary widely among printers. Ask around and check carefully.) It is recommended when large numbers of leaflets are to be produced.

Tips for Distributing Leaflets:

1. Carefully choose site and time to leaflet.

2. Roleplay leafleting situation to practice efficient ways to hand leaflets to people, ways of handling indifference, hostility, open interest, etc. (An experienced leafleter makes a friendly, positive comment with every leaflet, such as "This should interest you." Be persistent, not pushy. If leafleting leads to discussion, share what you know and admit what you don't know. Don't let people intimidate you.)

3. Attempt to speak to a store manager, minister, or whoever, in an attempt to establish rapport before you leaflet near his/her location. Tell the size of your group and where and for how long you intend to leaflet, and give him/her a sample leaflet. If the leaflet is not a protest against his/her activities, s/he may be supportive of your actions.

4. Be sure to clean up afterwards, so you can't be accused of littering or being insensitive to the needs of others.

RADICAL STREET THEATER   (Open-air, improvised)

Purpose/Uses: To create a message in a picture, and get people to stop and look at it. To challenge people to listen to and think about new issues in an imaginative way, or old ideas in new ways. To educate the public about public issues in a way that is fun. To develop individual self-confidence and group cohesion. To draw interest to a meeting or demonstration.

Description:

1. *Loosen up:* Use physical exercises or active *Attention Expanders*.

2. *Choose an issue: Brainstorm* a list of issues. Set time limits and narrow list down to a manageable issue. Focus on issues rather than personalities. Individuals come and go, but issues stay around.

3. *Develop a skit around the issue.* Keep the idea, and the actions and/or words to communicate it, as simple as possible, even to the point of overstatement, in order to attract and hold a crowd. Exaggeration often best conveys the reality. Street theater troupes often have to work against traffic noise and other distractions and their audiences are passers-by who have other things on their minds and thus have short attention spans. Tailor the message to the audience you want to reach.

Each time a play is done, it is a creative act. The idea is known, a general sequence of actions may be agreed upon, but lines need not be memorized, and people improvise. Skits should last three minutes or less, and can be repeated.

4. *Choose time and place* to perform, *and* plan *strategy* of presentation. Pick site and study it, so you know where you can enter, where you'll perform, and how you'll leave. Make sure people can stop and watch without blocking others. Mobility is very important. Design skit to be set up quickly.

Note: Street theater is legal as long as neither performers nor audience block sidewalks. Assign someone the task of talking to police if they should come around.

5. *Gather props:* Simple props, masks, costumes, and makeup can often add to the communicability and entertainment value of street theater. Signs are often useful to identify the group and to label or explain characters or situations in the skit. An understanding of the use of symbols is valuable here.

6. *Practice the skit:* A knowledge of basic stage techniques like projection of the voice and playing to an audience are valuable. Practicing in front of a small, friendly audience can give valuable criticism and suggestions. It's also good to roleplay various audience reactions, such as indifference, hostility,

285

obliviousness, "turned on-ness," etc. Practice until you feel ready to go out on the street.

7. *Perform and follow through:* Street theater is intended to provoke response, and it is important to follow up a performance. You might hand out leaflets right after the skit, or mingle with audience members and talk with them. You could encourage people to attend a street meeting or teach-in.

8. *Evaluate afterwards:* What did you learn? How could the skit be improved? What did you communicate to people? Was it what you intended to communicate? Could the site have been better chosen? Are there more effective techniques for following through with audiences?

Sample Skit: *Credibility*
Uncle Sam gets on the mike, welcomes everyone to the press conference. Behind him sit people holding signs reading Guatamala, Vietnam, Cambodia, etc. As Uncle Sam assures people we will not intervene in each country, a Strangler will strangle each. At the end, the Strangler gets Uncle Sam as he states we will never use atomic weapons or chemical-biological warfare to start World War III.

Pamphlets by Edward Myers Hayes, AFSC, 821 Euclid Ave., Syracuse, NY 13210.
"A Complete Klutz's Guide to Simple Prop and Costume Making," 18 pp, 25¢.
"A Cookbook of Theater Exercises," 19 pp, 25¢. Preparation for radical street theater development.
"The New, Improved, Better-Than-Ever Guerrilla Theater Manual," 40 pp, 50¢. All the basics.
"Make-up Made Easy," 7 pp, 25¢. More for radical street theater.
"A Political Puppetry Manual," 71 pp, 75¢. All you need to know to make the puppets and stage; includes sample texts.

STREET-SPEAKING

Purpose/Uses: To build self-confidence in one's ability to communicate ideas on controversial issues to an unknown audience, and to engage a crowd in dialogue. To learn to think on your feet; good preparation for radio and TV talk shows. To get or stay in touch with the thinking of other people and learn to convey your ideas in language understandable to most people. To learn about crowd dynamics and control. To motivate participants to study more about a topic. To provide experience in direct action on a small scale, a chance to participate in a conflict situation. To foster individual and group discipline.

A quick, lowcost training and recruiting technique which actively involves people. A good tool to end a workshop on training for action. Can be particularly useful for women and minority groups as a political act of reclaiming the streets.

Description:

1. Choose the topic, focusing on a list of questions you should be able to answer. Research the issue. Try to simplify the information to a few short points which can be said in a variety of ways.

2. Roleplay the street-speaking situation to test out your style of communication and to develop a sense of how to handle hecklers and other conflicts that may occur.

- Introduce self and explain who's conducting the meeting and why.
- Try to make short, concise points about the topic.
- Use concrete, vivid details to illustrate. Be personal.
- Keep a sense of humor.
- Repeat important points for newcomers.

3. Gather equipment: something to stand on, a sign identifying the group, and, where required by law, a U.S. flag. (Check local regulations.) Street meetings in public places are a legal right guaranteed by the First Amendment. A sound system should seldom be used, as it negates an atmosphere of dialogue.

4. Leaflets are a valuable addition to a street meeting, giving people more information and something to take away with them.

5. In selecting a location and time, be mindful of traffic, accessibility to people, and potential constituency, e.g., factory, school, business area, etc. People should be able to see and hear you without blocking traffic.

6. Decide discipline of the group ahead of time.

   a. Prearrange order of speakers, taking into account the importance of the attention-getting role and the need for variety. Be flexible when events necessitate a change in the order.

   b. Designate one or two persons to deal with reporters and police.

   c. Assign non-speakers the task of crowd tone-setters. These people should mingle with the crowd, listen attentively, ask leading questions, and engage bystanders in personal conversations. *There should be agreement to respond to all hecklers and trouble-makers nonviolently.*

   d. Dialogue is important, so speaker can, under circumstances usually agreed upon in advance, offer the stand to a bystander, perhaps setting a time limit for his/her remarks.

   e. Agree on a time to end and be sensitive to the mood of crowd.

   f. It is important to evaluate the whole experience as a learning experience, that is to consider it valuable in terms of what it has taught us, rather than to appraise it as a success or failure in itself.

For More Information:

"How to Conduct a Street Meeting," by George Lakey and David Richards, (Friends Peace Committee, 1515 Cherry, Phila., PA 19102, 1968, 12 pp, 50¢). Basic information about street speaking.

TEACH-IN

Purpose/Uses: To educate and stimulate new thinking by presenting differing points of view on a particular topic in a classroom or public forum. To further community awareness on a particular topic.

Description:

   1. Set up time and location and publicize well. It can be for any length of time, depending on number of speakers available and potential audience. It can be held in a home, a church, a usual group meeting place, a park, or on a sidewalk.

   2. Present background information and relevant facts. Take care to include various viewpoints among the speakers, ranging from high-level specialists to informed persons able to present their own personal viewpoints. The interaction of speakers with those attending furthers the information-sharing process. Confrontation of opposing viewpoints, questioning of speakers and discussion from the floor constitute important aspects of a teach-in.

DILEMMA DEMONSTRATION

Purpose/Uses: To place opponents in a position where they must either grant your demand or act in such as way as to harm their image in the public eye. Especially useful where demonstrators' immediate demand is considered reasonable and in harmony with widely accepted beliefs and principles.

Description:

   1. Focus on an injustice you wish to end. Research and analyze why that injustice continues. Locate specific people or institutions maintaining the injustice.

2. Issue a statement calling for an end to the injustice. Present your demands in writing and in person, if possible. Be specific about the source of the injustice and what you feel should be done to end it.

3. If the request is not responded to favorably, select a nonviolent action (usually a form of protest or intervention) in which the solution to the problem is acted out in a publicly visible way. Go into action taking great care to treat all people with respect and dignity even when you refuse to cooperate with unjust practices they may be enforcing.

Examples:

1. During the early 1960s, black citizens registering to vote put many white citizens in a dilemma. If blacks were allowed to register, they could remove from office politicians who were cruel and unresponsive to needs of black people, especially in places where black voters were a large percent of the population. If they were stopped from registering, those doing so appeared publicly to others as cruel and irresponsible by preventing an activity widely believed to be legitimate.

2. The voyage of the ship *Phoenix* with medical supplies for North Vietnam, sponsored by A Quaker Action Group, put the U.S. government into a dilemma. If the boat were allowed to reach its destination, a clear statement of opposition to the U.S.'s role in Vietnam would be made. If the government stopped its journey, publicity would result and a good opportunity for public education about the war and the government's position would be created.

CONDUCTING A VIGIL*

Vigils are often by-passed as ineffective by organizers of long-term social change projects; but when they are included in a carefully developed campaign for social change, vigils can convey information vital to the success of the campaign.

Purpose/Uses: To convey convictions strongly felt. To give information considered to be very important. To ask others by your example to give serious consideration to an issue.

Description:

A vigil at its best is a delicately wrought instrument for communication. Its notable features are patience, watchfulness and persistence.

---

* Most of this section is from "Conducting a Vigil" by Charles C. Walker (available from Gandhi Institute, Box 92, Cheyney, PA 19319, 25¢ postpaid).

Larger vigils require careful organization by a team of people. The larger the group, the more difficult is the start of the vigil. Avoid "herding" people, as sometimes results when situations are not planned carefully, or when plans go awry. In briefing sessions, discuss the plans and ask participants to help get things under way with patience and good humor.

Individual vigils reflect the style of the person doing it, usually emphasizing the opportunity to talk with those who show interest. Silence may be appropriate if the vigil is protracted or well publicized. Otherwise, talking seems more useful.

There are several types of *group vigils*. One occurs by just being there. Wives and relatives who gather at a mine entrance when disaster strikes don't organize themselves. They can do little except stay there. Another common form is the religious observance, often accompanied by special disciplines such as fasting, reading aloud or staying awake for protracted times. Both of these types of vigils *may* have political implications. A third form *is* a political act. The vigil at the germ warfare research center at Fort Detrick, Frederick, Maryland, lasted for 22 months. For one full year the vigil was kept every day from 7 AM to 5 PM. Persistence, reflection, and self-discipline were the hallmarks of this action.

The following suggestions can be adapted to any size group for any occasion or length of time:

1. Establish the pattern, possibly a line or circle, where the vigil can be readily seen and not easily disrupted by passers-by.

2. Stand far enough apart to extend the line as far as is practical. An easy way to test distances is to extend arms and touch finger tips with the person on each side. This increases the visual impact of the group, and minimizes temptations to socialize.

3. Use signs sparingly. Many feel that signs detract from the tone of the vigil. One or two signs identifying the group and the reason for the vigil are important.

4. Try to maintain silence and composure while on vigil. Those who talk with each other on line will be perceived by observers as more interested in each other than in them. Vigilers absorbed in talking cannot acknowledge signs of support from those who pass by, nor can they respond creatively to those who show hostility.

5. If a passer-by wants to talk, suggest that the two of you go aside to do so, while the vigil continues uninterrupted. Answer brief questions on the spot.

6. To talk, eat, smoke, or rest, leave the line and go to one

side. Choose a special spot where coats, equipment, and other items can be left and kept under observation. Otherwise, the clutter around a vigil can assume distracting, even amusing, proportions.

7. A vigil intently kept can become tiring. Individuals may withdraw for a time. At approximately half hour intervals the whole line can walk around in an orderly fashion, such as an oval, for a few minutes. Do this more often in cold or rainy weather. This should not be considered as a "break" in the vigil but as part of it.

8. Monitors should avoid scurrying about, or giving loud instructions to distant parts of the line. If geography permits, stay behind the line. Minimize the need to give instructions by holding advance briefings and/or giving a leaflet to participants.

9. Those at each end of the line can do much to set the tone, by their demeanor and by faithfully maintaining the inner spirit of the vigil. They are usually the first to be seen, and instantly communicate something about the group. Example is by far the best way for participants to help each other remember and maintain their purpose.

10. Participants will carry out their part in various ways. This brings a welcome diversity into the workings of the vigil. Some like to concentrate on "eye contact" with those who pass by. Others will consider it a religious observance to which they are called, carrying it out in any way that suits them and expresses their inner promptings. Still others will think, or reflect. Thus the silent line can be not an imposed structure to present a certain image, but a design providing a wide range of opportunities for expression for the participants.

11. Individuals might keep a diary of thoughts, conversations, and follow-up opportunities. The group might keep a log, in which individuals are encouraged to write. This material can be used later as a basis for a special publication, reports, and interpretive material.

12. Concentrate on the *quality* of the vigil. Numbers help but are not decisive.

IV
Evaluation*

Most of us are products of educational systems that discouraged us from being conscious about the learning process

---

* Thanks to Lynne Shivers for writing the first draft of this section.

and that stopped us from thinking that we could control what and how we learned. Evaluation encourages us to become more in control of our learning.

We evaluate what is happening all the time, whether we know it or not. Spending a regular amount of time in evaluation raises the importance of that process and helps us put it to fruitful use.

Many people and groups engaged in social change forget about evaluation. They are harried by time: "We have to save the world now!" or "I have so little time and all this information to pass out." They feel it would be a waste of time to examine their own experience. But in building institutions in which people are in charge of their own lives and learning, there is no substitute for honest feedback on the process and content of their activities.

Evaluation is not an answer to all problems which arise in training workshops and activities. It cannot redeem a poorly planned and run workshop, meeting, class, or campaign; nor tell us finally and definitively what to do the next time. But it is a necessary beginning.

The guidelines here are for evaluating extended workshops, campaigns, actions, or meetings with serious problems. For the regular evaluation of the process of a single session or meeting we generally use, *Brief Evaluation of a Meeting* in Part Two.

For further information on evaluation techniques, see Blumberg and Walker, "Self-Evaluation by Training Groups," in *Training for Nonviolent Action, Some History, Analysis, Reports of Surveys,* by Charles C. Walker, ed. (available from Gandhi Institute, Box 92, Cheyney, PA 19319, $2.00).

PURPOSES OF EVALUATION

• To allow all participants to learn from each other.

• To appreciate the successful and enjoyable aspects of the experience.

• To release whatever anxiety is still present. To allow time for participants to check back with each other, to clear up small or large confusions.

• To analyze and understand what happened and how various elements caused certain events.

• To bring to the surface unconscious knowledge, discover mistakes, share observations, experiment, bring out differences in areas.

• To integrate and consolidate learning, to bridge from smaller to larger scope, to reflect and summarize, to tie together loose ends.

- To check the relevance of techniques, tools, procedures.
- To measure results achieved against goals set.
- To allow people filling certain roles (facilitator, proposal maker, communicator with police, etc.) to get feedback concerning specific ways they did and did not fulfill their functions.
- To point out those elements that make for leadership so that less experienced people can learn to share in leadership responsibilities.
- To plan for the future.

GUIDELINES FOR EVALUATIONS

- The style of the evaluation should be geared to the purposes, feelings, and experiences of the participants.
- When planning each workshop or session, set aside appropriate amounts of time for evaluation of each session as well as of the entire workshop.
- Everyone who participated in an event should be encouraged to take part in its evaluation.
- The structure of the evaluation should be planned carefully. This may involve the exact phrasing of questions, time allotted to each item, size of groups, use of visual aids, etc. Decide what it is most important to learn from the evaluation and plan how you will draw out that type of information.
- Evaluations of the process and of the content of events should be kept separate. For instance, the choice of exercises and subject matter at a workshop should be examined separately from the conduct of facilitators and participants. Likewise, the relationship among the participants in a demonstration should be examined separately from the choice of a location or the type of signs used.
- There will be considerable difference of opinion among participants about which times are most enjoyable, important, boring, etc. These feelings are important data, but remember that no one reaction is the correct one, nor is it necessary for the group to come to agreement on the matter.
- To avoid getting depressed, it is important to point out what was successful as well as what went wrong. Begin with positive evaluations wherever possible. If events occurred of which all are not aware, a few anecdotes can be useful, especially positive ones.
- Evaluation should stress the continuation of learning, not competition for the right answer. Questions such as "What do I understand now that I did not understand before?" may be helpful.

- Where a participant facilitator might be defensive, an outside facilitator (someone not involved in the event) may be useful.

COMPONENTS OF AN EVALUATION

- *A discussion of the process can be structured* by listing on a chart aspects of the experience, e.g., events, kitchen work, child care, preparation, physical layout, etc.
- *Criteria for evaluation are needed.* To what degree was the group successful in meeting its goals? There are three bases for measurement:
  1. An absolute standard; e.g., did we meet our goals/ expectations?
  2. A relative comparison; e.g., how close did we come to meeting our expectations, given other forces at work?
  3. Self-comparison; e.g., what do I/we know now that I/we did not know before, and is this where I/we wanted to be?
- *Evaluation of the nonverbal aspects is important.* Ask two people to be aware of the statements people make with their bodies during the event. Questions to be aware of are: What degree of interest are people showing? To what degree is there full participation in the event? Are people staying to the end of an event, or are they leaving early? Are people encouraging an event to continue or be repeated, or to end early? Is there an informal, relaxed atmosphere? Is enthusiasm shown? Is there mild to heavy disruption, indicating varying degrees of dissatisfaction with the agenda? When there are a number of workshops or classes scheduled simultaneously, a rough evaluation is gained by counting the number of people in each workshop.

PROBLEMS AND CAUTIONS:

1. *Superficiality and irrelevancy:* Can be avoided by listing areas for evaluation and checking with all participants before actually beginning the evaluation process.

2. *Manipulation:* Avoid moralistic speeches. When processes are set up to help equalize participation, all should use them, including facilitators.

3. *Dumping:* Sometimes a legitimate criticism of an individual starts people dumping all their present and past upsets on that person. Stop this by pointing it out. Have people talk for themselves and of their own feelings, not analyzing or blaming others. Watch the emotional atmosphere. Keep it positive. pause for *Affirmations* or *Attention Expanders* if necessary.

4. *Spending too much time:* Be sensitive to the group's feelings and tiredness. If people feel evaluation is unimportant, remind them of the purposes of evaluation and encourage all who are willing to stay. If rediscussion of issues begins, terminate it. Remind people that evaluation is a time for reflection and feedback only.

5. *Fake evaluation:* Changes suggested need to be implemented or people will feel evaluation is unimportant. Ask for concrete solutions to generally felt problems and ways to implement them on a trial basis.

SPECIFIC STRUCTURES AND TECHNIQUES

Oral Evaluation:

Materials helpful: blackboard or flipchart paper, masking tape, crayons or felt pens, pencils, and scrap paper.

Structuring the group for evaluation: Small groups (4-8) allow everyone to feedback information and opinions better than a group of 30 plus. It is helpful to have a recorder in each small group to note general consensus. These records can be handed over to the organizers or evaluators for tabulation and further use.

Full group evaluations can follow small group evaluations. They are particularly useful when discussion of an issue would stimulate ideas in others or when the group is ready to think about future events.

Useful techniques:

• Ask everyone to say what two or three events were most important to him/her. Repeat with least important. Or ask for the high and low point for each person.

• List expectations as gathered at the beginning of the event, and have people discuss to what degree their expectations were satisfied or changed as the event progressed. Do the same with goals.

• Ask the question for general discussion: If a similar workshop were to be held, what could be changed or improved, and how? What was so good as to be repeated?

• Ask: What went right? what went wrong? what could have been improved? and list each response on a chart under the following headings:

Good aspects   Problems   Improvements

Make sure solutions are listed after each problem as it is brought up. Keep the tone optimistic. After completion, take a few minutes to decide on implementation of solutions. Apply this approach to specific areas or roles, e.g., the performances of the facilitators, trainers, and participants; the content; the physical facilities.

• Ask: What are you taking away from this session? This rapid review helps people notice what they have learned.

• Go through the list of events and ask for thumbs up for enjoyed, thumbs down for not enjoyed, and an umpire's safe signal if it was so-so. This is good with children who are reluctant to talk or for adults that talk too much. Repeat process using other phrases, such as "learned new things," "improved my skills," "accomplished group goals."

• The query approach is a rough way of evaluating some event. The query is a question posed to be pondered and gone back to over and over. It is not to be answered definitively or finally. Queries are meant to have people go home thinking and mulling over the event, and should be used sparingly. An example of a query: Are we following the most democratic process possible?

• Use a graph several yards long representing the entire event. Each participant, using a different colored crayon or chalk, draws a line from one end to the other, drawing it above or below a central line depending on how much s/he gained from each session, how much s/he enjoyed it, etc. The phrasing of the question is important. This exercise can be fun but must be interpreted carefully.

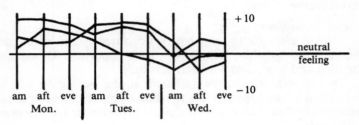

Written Evaluation:

Although oral evaluations don't need as much preparation time and are more spontaneous, written evaluations have the advantage of encouraging individual feedback that may otherwise be lost. There may be situations when there is not enough time for an oral evaluation or people may be more comfortable with a written one. Though small group oral evaluation is sufficient for most purposes, sometimes a combination oral and written evaluation provides fuller feedback.

Carefully word questions on a written evaluation. Sample questions are:

1. Evaluate the parts of the workshop by circling the term to the right which most nearly indicates your feeling.

Roleplaying	valuable	interesting	lost my interest
Macro-analysis	"	"	"
Conflict resolution	"	"	"

2. Circle the position on the scale that most nearly corresponds to your evaluation:

poor climate (polite, superficial, anxious)	1 2 3 4 5 6 7	*good climate* (mutual trust, caring, and understanding).
participation lacking or dominated by a few.	1 2 3 4 5 6 7	*full participation*, all seeking, sharing, sensitive to others.
poor communication of ideas and feelings, no listening or sharing.	1 2 3 4 5 6 7	*good communication* of ideas and feelings, ideas clearly presented, feelings accepted and shared.
productivity low, seemed irrelevant.	1 2 3 4 5 6 7	*productivity high,* we created, learned, achieved and enjoyed.

3. What were the most valuable sessions for you? the least valuable?

4. What could have been improved? Suggestions for improvement?

5. Did any procedure strike you as particularly good or bad?

6. How was this workshop better or worse than others you've participated in?

7. Other comments?

8. Names and addresses of friends interested in this kind of workshop.

9. Your name, address and phone.

An Evaluation Committee:

When a conference or event is particularly large, an evaluation committee is often effective. At least one organizer and one member from every major sub-grouping should participate on the evaluation committee. These people can perform an observer-participant function. They can also facilitate periodic evaluations within their smaller groups and bring that information to sessions of the evaluation committee.

Part Nine
Practical Skills

Running the mimeo machine, cooking tasty, nutritious and inexpensive meals for large groups, raising funds for special projects, and holding a good press conference can be as important to the social change process as street speaking or conflict resolution.

Early in any social change activity it is important that participants think through the practical skills necessary to carry out the projects, take an inventory of skills they have and consider who, in or out of the group, can teach them the skills they will need. The skill level of a group can increase quickly if members make a conscious effort to work with and share skills with each other.

Widespread ability to carry out practical tasks in situations of tension, deadline pressure and threats to personal safety increases a movement's strength and flexibility. As a result, activities can be decentralized and people can create their own institutions.

While this section was being compiled, a number of practical skills were considered but not included: physical exercises, meditation, playing musical instruments, crafts, leading folk dancing and folk singing, running movie and slide projectors, operating tape recorders and video tape, typing, photography, interviewing, speaking second and third languages, and printing. We have not included them here because each is relatively complex and opportunities to learn them are readily available elsewhere.

BASIC FIRST AID AND MEDICAL CARE

Before engaging in actions where physical harm is possible, workshops offering training in basic first aid, *and* roleplaying and discussion of potential crisis situations are *highly recommended*. The potential for panic is lessened when people know what to expect and can rely on each other for medical assistance. Listed are sources useful for emergency medical training, general education about first aid, and a better understanding of how our bodies function.

Emergency Care and Other Good Ideas, by the Neighborhood Health Collective of West Philadelphia (Movement for a New Society, 4722 Baltimore Ave., Phila., PA 19143, $1.35). A concise manual covering medical and other emergencies that are of special interest to movement people. Sections on home nursing, patient advocacy, victim counseling and nutrition.

Emergency Care and Transportation of the Sick and Injured, by the American Academy of Orthopaedic Surgeons (430 N. Michigan Ave., Chicago, IL 60611, $4.95). An excellent book dealing with basic anatomy and physiology and traumatic injuries and illnesses. Has many fine pictures and illustrations.

Our Bodies, Our Selves: A Book By and For Women, by the Boston Women's Health Book Collective (Simon and Schuster, NY, $4.95). An excellent book dealing with anatomy, physiology, sexuality, VD, birth control, abortion, pregnancy, childbirth and the postpartum period.

The People's Handbook of Medical Care, by Drs. Arthur and Stewart Frank (Vintage Books, NY, 1972, $2.95). Good in helping us to realize that we can be informed and alert about what is happening with our bodies.

REPAIR AND MAINTENANCE OF HOUSE OR PROJECT HEADQUARTERS

Many resources are available to assist in the learning of basic plumbing, electrical, carpentry and masonry skills. The do-it-yourself sections of your local library or bookstore are good places to evaluate the best books for your particular needs. A few sources are listed which we have used frequently.

America's Handyman Book, Revised Edition, by the staff of *The Family Handyman* (Charles Scribner's Sons, NY, 1970).

Complete Do-It-Yourself Manual, Reader's Digest Association, (Pleasantville, NY, 1973). Includes extensive information on electricity, plumbing, heating and carpentry. Clear illustrations. Excellent in a variety of areas.

Modern Carpentry, Willis H. Wagner (Goodheart-Willcox, South Holland, IL, 1973).

Wiring Simplified, H.P. Richter (Park Publishing, Inc., Minneapolis, MN, 1971).

RESEARCHING COMMUNITIES AND INSTITUTIONS

National Action/Research on the Military-Industrial Complex (NARMIC). AFSC, 1501 Cherry, Phila., PA 19102. (215) 241-7175. Offers research materials in a variety of areas. For more information see Part Ten: Groups to Contact.

The NACLA Research Methodology Guide (North American Congress on Latin America, Box 226, Berkeley, CA or Box 57, Cathedral Station, NY, 10025). If you need specific information about suspicious activities of corporations or government agencies, but don't know how to find it, this guide tells how.

Scientific Social Surveys and Research, by Pauline V. Young (Prentice-Hall, Englewood Cliffs, NJ, 1956). Excellent compendium of almost every research method one would want to use. Specific enough to be a manual for beginners.

Studying Your Community, by Roland L. Warren (New York Free Press, 1965). A good breakdown of questions to help you get important information about the community you are studying.

FUND RAISING

Simple methods for raising funds are dues, collections from members, pledges, subscriptions to newsletters, tin cups on the street, bake sales and rummage sales, etc. Choose methods appropriate to your circumstances.

There is no secret to fund raising, although much information about where to go for larger contributions is carefully guarded. To find out about the more complex aspects of fund raising, work or consult with an experienced fund raiser.

Two major methods of fund raising are the personal appeal and the funding proposal.

The Personal Appeal

This is a fairly fast fund-raising method which may bring in results a few weeks after you launch the campaign to raise funds. The basis of this type of fund raising is the appeal letter.

Things to be considered:

1. The appeal letter should be personal, stating clearly what

you are doing, why you need the money, and what you will do with it. It is often helpful if people know how much you need to raise from them.

2. The letter should be neat. If it can be printed, that is best. Think of the people you are trying to reach when considering how official the letter should look. Sometimes a letterhead is helpful. If possible, all letters should be personally signed by someone who is known to the contributors. A return envelope is useful.

3. Select your general sending list carefully. A flood of letters isn't necessary if you get the right people. Large contributors from past appeals should be considered. You may, for instance, decide to send only to those who contributed more than $25 in the past. Special letters might be sent to people who make large contributions and to interested organizations such as churches and socially concerned groups.

4. Some people prefer to contribute to non-profit (tax-deductible) groups. Legally, contributions are deductible only to religious bodies or organizations that have been approved by the Internal Revenue Service. Often an appeal can be made through such a group, which acts as a "funnel" organization.

5. Careful records of contributions—contributor, date, amount—make for efficient fund-raising. Thank-you notes should be sent to large contributors.

6. Calculate how often you will need to raise funds. Co-ordinate appeals so that you don't repeat requests to the same people.

7. If this is an on-going way of financing, think about what seasons of the year are best for your constituency. In our experience, for example, summer has not been a good time for fund raising.

The Funding Proposal

Foundations and other funding organizations are attractive sources for large amounts of money. A small outlay of energy and money can yield considerably more than direct appeals or bake sales. But there is competition for such grants, and many funding agencies rule out grants to informally organized action groups. The suggestions below will minimize unnecessary work and frustration when seeking grants.

1. *Locate some likely foundations or agencies and study their requirements.*

• Find out from similar groups what foundations might be interested in your program.

• Check *Foundation News*, a bi-monthly publication of the

Council of Foundations. Look at the "Key Word In Context" insert. Use the key words that are in your program; for example, a foreign exchange program might look up "foreign," "exchange," or "students." Look up the foundations listed as having made contributions in this area in the past.

• Check the *Foundations Directory,* ed. 4 (Columbia University Press, 1971). Foundations are listed alphabetically by state.

• Call the foundations. Tell them that you looked them up and found that they have made grants to programs like yours in the past. Ask them is if this is still an area in which they have interest, and if so, to whom you should talk.

• Check out the annual or bi-annual report of the foundations you are considering. Look them up at the Foundation Center Library, 555 7th Ave., New York City, or at one of their branches in your area. If there is no report on the foundation, look in the library's *IRS aperture cards.* The information you gather about their approach, values and expectations will be valuable in writing the proposal. Find out the appropriate times to submit proposals.

• Many foundations can give only to officially tax-exempt organizations. If your group wants to go after this money, it can either enlist another tax-exempt group (church or organization) to act as a "funnel" organization, or it can apply for tax-exempt status (see below).

2. *Write up a funding proposal tailored to each funding organization.* The following information may be useful:
• Introduction: how your program relates to that foundation or group.
• Budget for the time period the grant will cover.
• History of your group and project.
• Your present situation.
• Where your project is going, with or without the money for which you are asking; e.g., will the project be self-sufficient by the time the grant money will be used up?
• Why you need the money.
• Any literature, newspaper clippings, etc. on your group or project.

3. *Adopt accounting procedures, etc., as required by the funding organization.*

Tax Exemption

Applying to the IRS for tax-exempt status can take up to six months, paper work, and money, but it can make many sources of funding available to an on-going group. We don't recommend this path to most project groups, but it can be important to long-term projects requiring major capital or staff.

This process requires legal information. The description here is brief. If money is available, get a non-profit tax lawyer to do the work or to advise you while you do the paperwork. Some cities have alternative funding agencies, people's legal services, etc., that can advise you on this process.

Pros
- Foundations grant mostly to tax-exempt organizations.
- Some foundations are reluctant to use "funnel" organizations.
- Contributions from individuals and corporations will be tax deductible, and therefore more likely.
- A tax-exempt organization can act as a "funnel" organization for other projects.

Cons
- Time and energy at outset.
- Money for incorporation ($75 in Pennsylvania, plus legal advertising).
- Money for legal advice (not always necessary).
- Annual financial reporting to the IRS.
- Organization may become dependent on tax-exempt status and avoid challenging the government so as not to endanger status. Legally, tax-exempt status is not permitted to organizations that devote a major part of their resources to political activity. "Major" means 3-5% or more, and "political" means electoral or legislative, but these words are not defined by law, and their interpretation varies.

Should You Become a Non-profit Corporation?

It is not a legal requirement that organizations seeking tax exemption incorporate, but most do. Articles of incorporation are filed at the state level. There are some advantages, e.g., the corporation can own property and get bulk mailing privileges.

1. Write up articles of incorporation. These need to conform with the requirements of the IRS for tax-exempt organizations. The easiest way to insure this is to copy the articles of another tax-exempt organization, with slight modifications to fit your group.

2. File articles of incorporation with the state. Check state requirements for legal advertising, fee, etc.

3. Write corporate by-laws. These also need to be appropriate for the IRS.

Applying for Tax Exemption

Some lawyers recommend waiting a year after forming the organization, so IRS can see how it really operates.

1. Get forms and instructions from the IRS. (No cost involved.)

2. Fill out forms and go over them with a lawyer specializing in non-profit tax law.

3. Go over forms informally with an IRS agent.

4. Send off forms to IRS.

5. Appeal, if necessary. Appeals are not often won, so do it right the first time.

Bibliography: The three books below can be obtained from the Organizers Book Center, P.O. Box 21066, Washington, DC 20009.

Action for A Change: A Student's Manual for Public Interest Organizing, by Ralph Nader and Donald Ross (Grossman Pub., NY, 1972, $1.75) pp. 33-39. Good for fundraising in schools.

The Bread Game, The Realities of Foundation Fundraising, (Glide Publ., 330 Ellis, San Francisco 94102, 1973, $2.95). Very good on all aspects of fund raising.

The Organizer's Manual, by the O.M. Collective (Bantam Books, 1971, $1.25) pp 19-26. Very good on general fund raising.

COOKING FOR LARGE GROUPS*

Unless a commitment to fast has been made by a group as part of its social change project, food is a major consideration. Cooperative cooking may be the easiest and most inexpensive way to feed participants. We have included information to help you plan nutritious and ecologically sound meals as well as avoid harmful chemicals, food spoilage, and the spreading of disease.

When all participants share in the planning, purchase, preparation and clean-up of meals according to a process agreed on in advance, fewer tensions are likely to occur around meals. Genuine sharing is encouraged, and participants are able to learn from each other.

Personal difficulties arising from sexism, lack of experience, or different tastes in food will usually disappear when needed information is shared and when reluctant people are teamed with those they feel comfortable working with.

* With thanks to Lillian P. Willoughby, who supplied much of the information used in this section.

Food Planning and Preparation

Menu Planning:

1. If cooking is to be shared by many people, it is important for a few to take general responsibility for the whole process. Menus should be prepared at least one day in advance. When a project is operating on a strict budget, complete advance menu planning is important; otherwise, some produce may spoil through oversight and cheese and eggs may be used up in the first few days.

2. Try vegetarian recipes. With careful planning, meals can be inexpensive, nutritious and appetizing.

3. Find a good quantity recipe book or take any good recipe for 4, 6 etc. and multiply it to get proper amounts. Increase time for cooking or baking. The larger the pans, the greater the time; using several small pans will decrease cooking time. Where recipes are based on controlled servings, increase quantities for self-serve lines, or food may not last to the end.

Purchasing:

A significant amount of money can be saved by purchasing food in bulk quantities. This is easier if your city has a food cooperative or cooperative warehouse. If not, find out where the small groceries or delicatessens get their supplies, since they too buy outside the closed chain store systems. You may need to make a trip to the various distributors—probably a trip for cheese, a trip for dry goods, a trip for fresh produce and a trip for meats. Some planning is clearly necessary to avoid spoilage of perishable foods.

Equipment:

Make a check list. It should include: large pots (several), large spoons, large pitchers or dippers (for soup and drinks), measuring cups and spoons, serving spoons and forks, sharp knives (large and small), hot pads, hot plates, towels, pot scrubbers, washcloths, sources of heat, a source of refrigeration, plates, bowls, cups, glasses, silverware or appropriate substitutes. You may want to ask participants to bring their own. If so, say so clearly in *bold* letters on *all* publicity and provide a few extras for those who forget or cannot.

Storing Food:

1. Food-keeping temperatures: If refrigeration source is old, recycled, etc., it is good to check temperature. Safe temperatures are:

refrigerator: 40°-45°F
ice cube compartment: 20°-30°F
freezer: 0°-15°F

2. Canning, freezing and drying of foods: If long term cooperative living is part of your social change efforts, growing and preserving of your own food may become desirable or necessary. Because improper preservation, especially of non-acid vegetables and meats, can result in serious illness or death, consult reliable information for safe methods. Especially note *Stocking Up* in the bibliography below.

Sharing the Cooking and Clean-up

1. One person or team should give oversight to the general process of cooking and clean-up and be available to deal with problems when they arise.

2. Post sign-up sheets specifying how many people are needed for each task, and ask each person to sign up the number of times needed to get the work done. Include times at which tasks should be started and/or finished.

3. If space allows, set up dish washing in a location where each person can do his/her own dishes and leave them to drain. This is possible for buffet-cafeteria type feedings. People signed up wash cooking utensils, wipe off tables and sweep floors only. One possible layout is shown below.

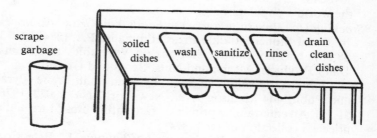

- Scrape food from dishes with rubber scraper.
- Wash.
- Sanitize with 1 teaspoon chlorine bleach for each 12 gallons of water. Sanitizing can also be accomplished by (a) washing by hand with soap and water at 110°-120°F, (b) rinsing and (c) immersing in clean hot water at 180°F for 30 seconds.
- Rinse.
- Let clean dishes drain.
- Put away, cover or turn upside down.

Bibliography of Recipes and Information

The Art of Vegetarian Cookery, by Betty Wason (ACE Publ. Corp., 1120 Ave. of the Americas, New York, NY 10036,

1970, $1.25). A basic with many succulent and flavorful recipes and menus. Features vegetables, grain foods, nuts, fruits and dairy products.

Diet for a Small Planet, by Frances M. Lappe (Ballantine Books, 101 5th Ave., New York, NY 10003, 1975, $1.95). Tells why you must have protein and how much, how to put protein rich meals together without the use of meat, and why it is important to stop eating off the top of the food chain.

The Natural Foods Cookbook, by Beatrice T. Hunter (Simon and Schuster, $2.95). 2000 recipes.

Quantity Recipes for 50, by Wood, Harris and Proud (New York State College of Home Economics, Cornell University, Ithaca, NY 14850, $1.00). A standard variety of recipes, general information on preparation of foods, conversion tables, etc.

Recipes for A Small Planet, by Ellen Buchman Ewald (Ballantine, NY, 1975, $1.95). Numerous vegetarian recipes that less experienced cooks can use successfully.

The Soybean Cookbook, by Mildred Lager and Dorothy Van Gundy Jones (Arc Books, 219 Park Ave. S, New York, NY 10003, 1968, $1.50). Almost as old as civilization itself, soybeans are today a useful way of providing protein for the world's population.

Stocking Up: How to preserve the Foods You Grow, Naturally, by Carol Stoner (Rodale Press, Emmaus, PA 10849, 1973, $8.95). Has informative sections on Vegetables and Fruits; Dairy Products; Meats; and Nuts, Seeds and Grains.

Uncle John's Original Bread Book, by John Rahn Braue (Pyramid Publ., 444 Madison Ave., New York, NY 10022, 1976 $1.25). An entertaining primer of fascinating bread lore and a priceless collection of recipes.

"48 Ways to Foil Food Infections" (Channing L. Bete Co., Greenfield, MA 01301, 1968, 15 pp). Cartoons and illustrations. Particularly good for children, but a friendly reminder for everyone on proper preparation, care and storage of food, before and after cooking.

KEEPING TRACK OF INFORMATION WITHIN THE GROUP

A Project Notebook

Organizers must keep track of many important details. Some jot notes to themselves on scraps of paper which tend to get lost, misplaced or scrunched up. A project notebook, individual or collective, is a more organized and permanent way to keep track of information.

Why keep a notebook?

• To provide access to the names and phone numbers of cooperating individuals and organizations.

• To record planning meetings and decisions made, so that memories can be refreshed and the group does not repeat old discussions.

• To record events. If there are legal hassles during the campaign, trials may not occur until months later. You may need to be a witness and will be asked for names, dates, times, places.

• To provide information for later evaluation of the project.

• To provide a measure of progress made over a period of time. To evaluate whether stated goals are being met.

What should go into a project notebook?

The easiest method is to separate a looseleaf notebook into sections with dividers. Possible areas to include:

• *Journal:* A day-by-day record of meetings, important contacts and events.

• *Support People:* A list of names, addresses and phone numbers of people, noting the type of support offered. List separately people and organizations you want to draw into the project.

• *Strategy:* Thoughts and plans on how to achieve the project's goals.

• *Responsibilities:* Commitments individuals or groups have made to carry out project tasks.

• *Police/Legal:* Information on police and local prison systems. Names and phones of lawyers who will help with court cases.

• *Press:* Phones of local and national newspapers, radio and TV, with the names of reporters and other helpful contacts.

Information Storage and Retrieval in the Office

Working in an office can be a real nightmare if information—letters addressed to the group, records of important phone calls, decisions made by the group—is not kept or is not easily retrievable.

Setting up a clear system for processing information will make it possible for:

• a group of people to share work in the same area, e.g., mailing literature to people requesting it;

- "drop-in" volunteers to find ways to be helpful even for short periods of time;
  - large amounts of information to be processed efficiently;
  - information to be transferred during a turnover in group membership.

The most important question to keep in mind when setting up a system of information storage and retrieval is: will a new person be able to recover and understand the information needed?

Suggestions:

1. *Filing:* Use a basic filing system for all information being stored. Usually it is best to have as few separate filing systems as possible. The three most common ways of organizing files are geographically (where the person lives), alphabetically by last name, and chronologically (in order of the time of the communication). The system you choose depends on your needs, but using chronology as the primary basis is less convenient because it is difficult to remember when things arrived. A good way to combine these systems is to divide first by geography (e.g., by state or by zip code), then alphabetically by last name within these geographical zones, and finally chronologically, putting the most recent communication in front of others from the same person.

2. *Telephone and letters:* So that all workers can find out what has happened in the past, it is important to make memos of important telephone conversations or face-to-face meetings, and make carbons of all letters sent. All memos and carbons should be filed in an agreed-upon location and order.

3. *Logs:* In offices where many people come in and out, a log book can be used to pass on important information, including phone messages. Entries are dated and signed. Every time an item is handled it is noted in the log. Other workers can then know what has happened by reading the log.

4. *Name boards:* Each regular office or group member can have a place on a board or a box where messages can be left.

5. *Computers:* For an office dealing with a large number of people (over 1000), there are advantages to computerized information storage. All kinds of information can be stored: contributions, degree of involvement, names, addresses, interests, etc. The main disadvantages are cost and reliance on specialized skills and equipment. For a simpler and inexpensive procedure incorporating some of the advantages of computerized storage, try the "knitting-needle" system for using key punch cards developed by Barry Greever.

310

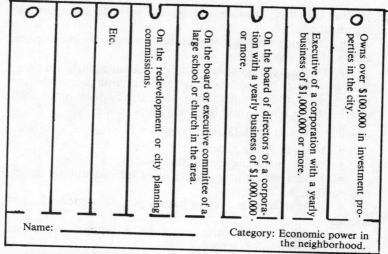

Name: _____ Category: Economic power in the neighborhood.

Card contents (punch-card labels):
- Owns over $100,000 in investment properties in the city.
- Executive of a corporation with a yearly business of $1,000,000 or more.
- On the board of directors of a corporation with a yearly business of $1,000,000 or more.
- On the board or executive committee of a large school or church in the area.
- On the redevelopment or city planning commissions.
- Etc.

1. Use card of any size
2. Place categories on card as desired.
3. For each category punch holes large enough to insert a knitting needle.
4. When information is added to the card in a specific category, cut away the space between the hole and the edge of the card. When the knitting needle is inserted cards containing information desired will fall out of the stack.

Simple Financial Records

1. Draw up a budget of anticipated income and expenses. In projecting expenses include a cushion; i.e., project the maximum needed or include a "miscellaneous and unexpected" category.

2. Open a special bank account if necessary. More than one signature is usually wise, since funds may need to be withdrawn when the check writer is out of town, in jail or ill.

3. Set up a simple bookkeeping system. It is important that financial records be kept so simple, clear and up to date that anyone in the group can look at them, get information needed or make entries. Regular rotation of financial responsibilities is recommended. Care should be taken to train each member of a group when s/he takes on financial obligations for the first time.

4. Select a treasurer and/or bookkeeper who has the time and persistence to keep records accurate and up to date.

5. Special care should be taken to note where donations come from and how they are spent. Exercise fanatical care on social-change oriented ventures. Charges of misuse of funds or

official IRS investigations are typical ways to discredit such organizations.

6. If funds become exceptionally large, periodic, public audits of the accounts are in order.

7. If you are seeking funding from outside your own group, draw up a rough budget. Indicate for which things contributions will be used and for which things you already have funds. Note where gifts in kind would be as useful as money.

Possible areas to include in projecting a budget:

- Office or living space;
- Phone, including long distance calls;
- Duplicating or printing expenses for educational materials, posters, leaflets, etc.;
- General supplies such as paper, pencils, stencils, folders, stamps;
- Equipment and furniture such as typewriters, tables, chairs, mimeograph machine;
- Repair work needed for building or equipment;
- Food;
- Transportation costs for people and materials;
- Emergency funds for lawyers and medical care, or support stipends to dependents if family supporters are expecting lengthy imprisonment;
- Stipends needed to free individuals at any point in the campaign;
- The unexpected or forgotten. This is *important* because it always happens.

8. There are many possible sources for meeting budget needs:

- Participants' own jobs—the best source, keeps non-participants from running the project. Even if funds are raised to finance specific parts of the campaign, we suggest that at some level the project be self-supporting, so that if outside funds are cut, the project can continue.
- Group's own local efforts: rummage or bake sales, flea markets, singing on the street.
- Alternative businesses such as cleaning and repair services (see economic alternatives).
- Gifts in kind: tables, chairs, etc., from attics and basements.
- Treasures from the streets on trash day. Excess paper from print shops, food from throw-away bins at large supermarkets.
- Second hand sources of furniture, office equipment.

Check local auction houses. Where possible, get a service contract on machines.

- Cash donations through special appeals and newsletters.
- Foundation grants with acceptable or no strings attached.

9. For frequent small expenses, a petty cash account is often adequate. A simple cash log might look like:

IN				OUT			
Date	From	Amount	Signed	Date	For	Amount	Signed

If mistakes are frequent, a built-in check system might be included. Problems are often the result of recording errors. A simple check-up system can help isolate problems. An example is:

Date	Person	Item	Amount	Balance	Does balance check with amt. remaining in envelope?

10. Example of financial records of a communal household:

		INCOME				EXPENSES →	
Date	Explanation	Food and expendables*	House and utilities*	Etc. *	√ # **	Food and expendables*→	→

→			MONEY ON HAND ***			
→	House and utilities*	Etc. *	Checks on hand +	Cash on hand +	Balance in check book ≈	Ledger balance
→						

* These are subheadings under Income and Expenses that should be changed and expanded to meet your needs. Example above is used by several communal households for running of house affairs.

** Symbol for "check number."

*** This budget assumes that a bank account is used. By counting amount of checks and cash not yet deposited, the ledger balance can be checked at any time. Simply add the bankbook balance and the checks and cash on hand; the total should equal the ledger balance.

313

Collective Office Work

Sensitivity and patience are required to avoid slipping into traditional hierarchical roles and relationships in an office. The pressures of work needing to be done, the differences in verbal and clerical skills, and degree of familiarity with the office are enough to kick people back into old ways of thinking and acting.

For a more extensive discussion of some areas mentioned here, see *No Bosses Here: A Manual on Working Collectively*, listed in the bibliography for Part Two.

The following suggestions can help to develop an atmosphere in which everyone feels accepted and capable of participating fully.

• Avoid having anyone do tasks on a regular basis for others working in the office, e.g., typing someone else's letters. Where this is not possible, make sure that members share in all levels of work.

• Write out clear descriptions of basic tasks like filling literature orders, filing, and answering certain kinds of letters. New people should be able to understand these directions clearly and not need to keep asking more experienced members of the work team.

• Have membership in the work team or collective based on work attitudes and willingness to put energy into the group's responsibilities, rather than on skills and experience. This opens avenues for those who are new but have energy and enthusiasm to learn needed skills and knowledge.

• Have regular collective meetings. Everyone should know that s/he will have an opportunity to bring new ideas or gripes to the group.

• Make decisions by consensus, so that those with the most experience or the most stake in a decision know they will be heard and yet everyone will have an opportunity for input. Record decisions so that previous decisions can be checked when necessary. Keep information in a place available to all collective members. (See Part Two: Working In Groups for more in this area.)

• Share with each other in ways that go beyond "business," daily office routine, and collective meetings. Have a retreat or playday together, share meals on a regular basis, start meetings by sharing excitement about things not connected to your common task.

• Create a humanized work environment with plants, pleasing colors, pictures and carpet. Set aside a room for meditation, releasing tension or reading. Encourage regular expressions of appreciation to the group as a whole and to individuals.

• Select one person to keep financial records. Rotate the responsibility every six to twelve months and be sure each new record keeper learns the skills required. Records should be set up in such a way that all members of the collective can look at records and get information needed. A financial statement should be prepared periodically for the collective, including reports on income and expenses and a comparison of projected and actual budgets.

HOW TO LOCATE ALLIES

1. Consider your constituency in this undertaking and how your program will affect its members.

2. Briefly put these thoughts in writing. Include your purpose, theory and background. Be concrete about suggestions and proposals. Sometimes it is good to include a scenario of what would happen if your proposal were to be implemented (see *Scenario Writing*).

3. Give the first draft to friends and critics willing to evaluate clarity of the proposal, accuracy of facts, style of communicating ideas, and correctness of your perceptions. Talk with people. Future allies may come from long and serious conversations.

4. Rewrite your proposal as often as is useful.

5. Begin active search for allies. You may decide to hold forums, leaflet, street-speak, etc. Go to places where allies are likely to be, such as movement groups, churches, bars, union meetings, factories, and community meetings.

6. Talk with people about your ideas. Actively listen to their ideas, frustrations, etc.

7. When you've got names of several people who've expressed interest, call an organizational meeting.

8. If appropriate, organize a public meeting or conference to find new allies and work with others interested in the same topic. Two good pamphlets available are "How to Organize a Conference," by Robert S. Vogel (Peace Literature Service, AFSC, 1501 Cherry, Phila., PA 19102), and "Defending a Public Meeting: A Manual for Planners," by Charles C. Walker (Gandhi Institute, Box 92, Cheyney, PA 19319, 1975-6, 9 pp, $1.00 postpaid).

LETTERS TO THE EDITOR, VISITS WITH PUBLIC OFFICIALS

Letter-writing and personal visits to newspapers and public officials will not, by themselves, transform society, but these activities can be an essential part of the continual dialogue and consciousness-raising that must accompany other efforts.

The following instructive flyers are available through Friends Committee on National Legislation, 245 Second St. NE, Washington, DC 20002 (5¢ each).

"How to Write Your Congressman and the President"
"How to Write a Letter to the Editor"
"How to Visit Your Congressman"
"How to Work for the Congressional Candidate of Your Choice"

POLICE, COURTS AND PRISONS

People committed to making basic changes in the society will eventually find themselves relating to police, courts and prisons. This could result from individual or group non-cooperation with unjust laws, or from advocacy of people currently caught in the criminal justice system. Certain information and related skills can make an arrest or confrontation with court or prison officials a positive experience. Good resources available are:

Arrested (American Civil Liberties Foundation of Pennsylvania, 260 S. 15th, Phila., PA 19102). Pamphlet. Good brief explanation of your rights and what might happen.

The County Jail—A Handbook for Citizen Action, by Vinton Deming, et al. (Friends Suburban Project, Box 462, Concordville, PA 19331, 1973 ($2.00 postpaid). Contains much useful information designed to assist those involved in a struggle for justice in their local communities.

A Court Action Handbook, by Betsy Leonard (Friends Suburban Project, Box 42, Concordville, PA 19331, 1971, $1.00). A manual on court monitoring and community action. Describes project in Chester, PA, with specifics on how to set up a court action program in your community. Includes a glossary of terms used in courts, and additional reading resources.

Instead of Prisons: A Handbook for Abolitionists, by the Prison Research Education Action Project (Safer Society Press, 3049 E Genesee, Syracuse, NY 13224, $6.50 + 50¢ postage and handling, bulk discounts). Spells out a variety of alternatives to prisons ranging from drastic reduction of the criminal law to the creation of nonpunitive responses to problems of criminality. Also available is a manual for weekend abolition workshops for $1.50 and $2.00 + 35¢ postage and handling.

MASS COMMUNICATION

Making Signs for Demonstrations

1. Signs should present one thought simply, clearly, and legibly. Avoid rhetoric. Sometimes blown-up photos are useful, though they may be expensive.

2. Before making the signs, brainstorm what should go on them and reach agreement among your group. It is often effective to have two or three basic messages repeated several times.

3. Use cardboard or other firm backing and waterproof lettering. Waterproof magic markers and crayons work well. *Remember* that red, orange, yellow and light blue will not show up on TV.

4. Care in lettering, spacing and size will make a difference in the value of the sign.

5. If rain is likely, waterproof your signs with plastic wrap or plastic bags.

6. Put care into making signs. A few well-made ones will have more positive impact that many sloppy and illegible ones.

Working With the Mass Media When Undertaking an Action

Advance Preparation:

1. As soon as an action is decided upon, at least two people should take responsibility for press contacts and coverage. One person should be at a press phone and one should bring in updated information. One week before the demonstration the phone should be covered continuously.

2. Get a list of all media contacts including newspapers, TV, radio and underground press. This should include names of friendly reporters, and editors of the news desk, religion desk, etc.

3. Get names of people (especially sympathetic ones) in each medium.

4. Check out the wire service in your area, UPI, AP and the smaller ones like Pacific News Service and Unicorn News Service. Wire services send out bulletins continually to most other media.

5. Log events and think of ways to write articles for periodicals, letters to the editor, etc.

6. Contact all local weekly and daily newspapers.

317

7. Write a press release. Give a written release in advance, especially if the action is in an out-of-the-way place or if camera crews might be sent.

8. Send copies to the news desk, city desk, special departments (women, religion, etc.) and specific reporters who have been friendly.

9. Sometimes specially written stories on the issue are welcome.

What to do the Day Before the Action:

1. Telephone all media. Give a brief run-down of the action (who, what, where, when, and why). Be enthusiastic and positive but not unrealistic. Stick to the purpose and underline the politics.

2. Contact radio "news" stations. Many will tape telephone interviews from people at the action site and send directly to the radio station. Some will also tape spots ½ minute or more in which you can read a prepared statement.

3. Put together a mini "press packet" for distribution on the day of the action. Include the press release sent to the media and your best leaflet.

4. Recruit amateur photographers. Pictures can be used in followup work.

The Day of the Action:

1. Call TV and radio stations early. Most coverage is assigned by 8:30 am. Ask them to come at least half an hour after the action is scheduled to start, so they aren't the first to arrive—a common problem.

2. Have written press releases available.

3. At the demonstration have one or more persons relate to the press and help them get good information and pictures. Keep a press log of information on who shows up.

Writing A Press Release

1. *Early* in the release include the time, date, place, participating groups and reasons for the action.

2. Don't exaggerate information. Make it interesting. Define the basic two or three points you want to make and avoid extraneous information.

3. Limit it to one page, if possible. Never exceed two pages. You can include additional pages of background material, if helpful, but they should be clearly separate from the press release.

4. Double-space and use large margins. Use one side of paper only.

5. Make clear who is releasing the statement. In the upper right-hand corner include names, addresses and phone numbers (day and night) of members of the group to be contacted for more information.

Holding a Press Conference

1. Figure out the two or three most important points you want to make and find ways of repeating them no matter what the question.

2. Hold the press conference at a time when reporters can come and meet their deadlines. Morning seems to be best.

3. It is often good to hold the conference at a significant location, e.g., at the mayor's office if you are refuting a statement by the mayor.

4. Be sure you are in a place where cameras are allowed and people can move in and out easily. Check availability of electric outlets for lighting equipment.

5. Send an announcement of the press conference to a contact person as well as someone on the city desk.

6. When announcing an action, don't pretend to have more people than you do. You are trying to build a good long-term relationship with press contacts.

7. Keep clearly in mind how you are going to end the conference. You might keep one good piece of information until the end and find a way to close with it.

8. Identify your information leaders and let the press know that questions can be asked of them. This keeps erroneous stories from getting out. Be sure your position is clear.

9. Have additional copies of your statement available. Print up and distribute any special messages you have received from noted persons.

Part Ten

Groups to Contact

Below are addresses of many groups and individuals, some of whom have been mentioned above. We or our co-workers have had personal experience, sometimes extensive, with each of them. The resources they offer, briefly mentioned here, are similar or complementary to those in this manual. Movement for a New Society/Life Center groups in the Philadelphia area have been listed in most detail.

This is not meant to be an exhaustive list, and no negative evaluation is implied if a group does not appear here.

"MNS," following the phone number, indicates that the group is part of the Movement for a New Society network and that you can find out more about MNS through it. *All* groups connected with MNS have *not* been listed, though an effort has been made to include groups from a variety of geographic areas. If you are looking for people in areas not included here you may write to the Network Service Collective, 4722 Baltimore Ave., Phila., PA 19143.

Groups listed in this manual vary widely as to person power and scope of resources and cannot be expected to make all services available in answer to every request. They are, however, all willing to be contacted and provide information when it is available.

We have found that people already involved in creative efforts for change are an excellent source of learning and support. We hope there will be groups on this list with which you will want to share information and skills or join in mutually supportive projects or campaigns for constructive change.

People and groups grow and change as rapidly as do the

events in which they are involved. For this reason some of these groups may soon cease to exist and others will change the resources they can offer. We are, however, including this section because we believe it can be of considerable value to you.

I
Inside the United States

ARIZONA

New West Trails Collective, 232 E Limberlost, Tucson, AZ 85705. (602) 888-6452. MNS. Printing and publishing, alternative economic institutions, training for nonviolent action, and group process skills.

CALIFORNIA

Fresno Friends of MNS, San Pablo House, 345 N San Pablo, Fresno, CA 93701. (209) 264-5803. MNS. Training for nonviolent action, work against nuclear power and for alternative energy systems.

David and Janet Hartsough, 2160 Lake, San Francisco, CA 94121. (415) 752-7766. MNS. Resources in simple living organizing, macro-analysis seminars and direct action training.

North American Congress on Latin America (NACLA), 464 19th, Oakland, CA 94612. (415) 835-0677. (See New York).

Northern California Land Trust, 2708 Sunset, Oakland, CA 94601. Newsletter and membership: $6/yr. low-income; $12/yr. regular.

COLORADO

American Friends Service Committee, Pam Solo, Art Warner, and Judy Danielson, 1428 Lafayette, Denver, CO 80218. (303) 832-1676. Workshops, consultation on nonviolent social change projects, conflict resolution and nonviolence training. Materials available in each of the areas above plus Chile, Indochina, Middle East, war/peace issues generally, and Third World literature and perspective. Good information on disarmament, the nature and dangers of plutonium, and the campaign against Rocky Flats, a nuclear weapons plant outside of Denver.

Paul Wehr, Institute of Behavioral Science, University of Colorado, Boulder, CO 80309. (303) 492-8093. Resources in conflict resolution theory and technique. Current focus is in area of environmental conflicts.

CONNECTICUT

P.R.E.A.P. (Prison Research Education Action Projects), 5 Daybreak Lane, Westport, CT 06880. (203) 227-7476. Designs and distributes education/action tools for use by those working for prison abolition. Facilitates workshops from 4 hours to full weekends.

DISTRICT OF COLUMBIA

Association for Selfmanagement, Larry Bonner, 1414 Spring Rd., NW, Washington, DC 20010. Encourages the study of self management and organizational democracy, and sponsors annual conferences. Publishes a quarterly reporting events, books and dissertations supportive of its goals. Subscription/membership $10 high income, $5 low income.

Community for Creative Nonviolence, 1335 N, NW, Washington, DC 20005. (202) 232-9533. A resource center in nonviolence. Peace studies. Involved in alternative institutions such as a soup kitchen, health clinic, pre-trial release and emergency shelter for people in need. Involved in direct action on social issues. Publishes a Catholic pacifist quarterly *Gamaliel* for $4/yr.

EPICA, 1500 Farragut, NW, Washington, DC 20001. (202) 723-8273. A Washington-based task force doing education and action on Central America and the Caribbean. EPICA has an ongoing publications program; leads workshops and programs; and maintains contact with base groups around the Caribbean. Publications are available on Panama, Puerto Rico, Jamaica and the Dominican Republic.

Institute for Local Self-Reliance, 1717 18th, NW, Washington, DC 20009. (202) 232-4108. A non-profit educational and research organization formed to counter tendencies toward over-centralization, over-bureaucratization and large-scale production systems isolated from the consumer. Purposes are to redefine urban neighborhoods and cities as increasingly self-reliant, productive systems; to teach people the tools of self-reliance; and to investigate the legal powers for municipal decentralization. Is investigating economic and technological alternatives for urban self-reliance; producing a series of pamphlets on aspects of urban decentralization; developing and testing models of small-scale, ecologically rational production and service systems. It provides technical assistance to communities, cities, and organizations concerned with issues of local initiative and independence. It maintains an information service on questions of urban development, economic alternatives, local production systems, and appropriate technology. Has a publications list. Publishes *Self-Reliance*, a ˙bi-monthly newsletter on research and achievement in technology, economics, and politics that is pertinent to self-reliant urban communities. Major projects being worked on by staff are urban food systems, energy generation and use, neighborhood economics, "waste" utilization, information, and community ownership.

LAOS, Inc., 4920 Piney Branch Rd., NW, Washington, DC 20011. (202) 723-8273. Places volunteers in religious and social change agencies mostly in the U.S. Special skills in health, carpentry, education, agriculture and community organizing often required, but "generalists" are sometimes needed. Conducts 3-7 day workshops on hunger and urban poverty.

GEORGIA

Atlanta Friends of MNS, PO Box 5434, Atlanta, GA 30307. (404) 523-2024. Have resources for simple living workshops, macro-analysis seminars, sexism workshops, men's and women's support groups, organizing around community issues. Training for direct action.

Savannah Friends of MNS, Box 9891, Savannah, GA 31402. MNS. Co-op organizing, macro-analysis, MNS literature, workshops on spiritual and personal growth and self-awareness. Anti-nuclear power organizing.

ILLINOIS

Midwest Trainers Network, c/o Omega Graphics, 711 S Dearborn, Chicago, IL 60605. MNS Group training skills in conflict resolution, nonviolent action, campaign building and group process. Printing and layout skills.

INDIANA

Charlie Springer, 217 N. 14th, Richmond, IN 47374. (317) 966-8529. Simple living workshops, work in criminal justice system, farmers markets. Good contact for information on things happening in the area.

KANSAS

Center for Democratic Process, Wendell Hendricks, 231 N Market, Wichita, KS 67202. (316) 262-6918. Democratic process for alternative economic institutions. Has information on social change efforts in the area.

Consortium on Peace Research, Education and Development (COPRED), William Keeney, Bethel College, North Newton, KS 67117. (316) 283-2500. An organization which collects and coordinates publications, course models, resource people, and research in the peace and conflict studies areas. The peace and education network for the high school and college levels has a variety of good contact people for those interested in teaching courses.

Stone Prairie Life Center, Stone Prairie, R 1, Marion, KS 66861. (316) 382-2057. Has information on social change efforts in the area. Can offer overnight hospitality at cost; please give adequate advance warning.

MAINE

Sam Ely Community Services, 183½ Water, PO Box 2762, Augusta, ME 04330. Organizing around a variety of economic alternatives, including land trusts and low-cost housing. Publishes bi-monthly journal, "The Maine Land Advocate" $3/yr. giving information on state-wide efforts on various activities.

MARYLAND

East Baltimore Neighborhood Housing Network, Jerry Locklee, 13 N Chester, Baltimore, MD 21231. (301) 342-1873. Generates capital to buy collectively owned and managed housing in East Baltimore.

Great Atlantic Radio Conspiracy, 2743 Maryland Ave., Baltimore, MD 21218. Produces 30-minute shows each week for stations across the country on a wide variety of subjects from current problems ("The Politics of Hunger"), alternatives ("Workers in Control"), and ideas for change ("The Social Anarchism of Murray Bookchin") to local organizing ("Socialism in a Small Town: Iowa City and the People's Alliance"), radical poetry and music, and the women's movement ("The Socialist-Feminist Conference of 1975"). Write for free catalog of over 100 programs.

Jonah House, 1933 Park Ave., Baltimore, MD 21217. (301)

669-6265. Organizes direct action on nuclear disarmament. Offers workshops.

Marvelous Toy Works, 2111 Eastern Ave., Baltimore MD 21231. (301) 276-5130. Worker managed, anarchist, toy-making business. Also: write for information on newly forming groups in the area offering resources in training and organizing for nonviolent action, macro-analysis seminars, literature and men's and women's support groups.

MASSACHUSETTS

AFSC Peace Education Program, 2161 Massachusetts Ave., Cambridge, MA 02140. (617) 661-6130. Staff and volunteers working on peace and nonviolence issues. Relates international with domestic oppression. Supports nonviolent alternatives and helps people take steps in changing their lives. Program focuses on: Southern Africa, Middle East, Human Rights, New International Economic Order, Disarmament and Nonviolence Training. Publishes *Peacework*, New England peace movement newsletter and *New England Briefs for Middle East Peacework* a monthly packet of briefs on events in the Middle East and discussion in the U.S. Middle East peace movement.

Boston Inreach/Outreach Collective, c/o Tania Hurie, 349 Broadway, Cambridge, MA 02139. (617) 547-1198. MNS. General contacts for workshops, literature and other resources related to nonviolent social change.

Boston Macro-Analysis Collective, c/o Martha Gordon, 9 Summit Rd., Wellesley, MA 02181. (617) 235-5213. Organizes macro-analysis seminars. Loans and sells literature used in seminars.

Institute for Community Economics, Bob Swann, Harold Shelton, 639 Massachusetts Ave., Cambridge, MA 02139. (617) 661-4661. Organizing for economic alternatives. Also information on community land trusts and appropriate technology and Community Investment Fund.

International Seminars on Training for Nonviolence (ISTNA), Beverly Woodward, 148 N Street, South Boston, MA 02127. (617) 269-5957. Organizes regional seminars in a variety of countries for people active in training and organizing for nonviolent social change.

New England Free Press, 60 Union Sq., Somerville, MA 02143. (617) 628-2450. Reprints of articles and pamphlets, very inexpensive, in a whole variety of areas including female liberation, the working class, imperialism and national liberation, the American political economy, early socialization, the university, black history and current struggles, China, movement history and perspectives, power structure research, health care, ecology, gay liberation. Free catalog. Also does printing for area community/movement groups.

MINNESOTA

North Country Macro-Analysis Collective, 1081 Laurel Ave., St. Paul, MN 55104. (612) 225-2089. Organizes macro-analysis seminars. Developing macro-seminar around worker self-management. Conducts workshops in group process and conflict resolution. Writes for local publication. Has slumber parties.

Plowshare Community/Twin Cities MNS, 3628 Park Ave. S, Minneapolis, MN 55407. (612) 825-8644. MNS. Printing skills, food co-op organizing, training programs for nonviolent action, simple living workshops, feminist organizing, workshops on children and nonviolence, organizing macro-analysis seminars, working with farmers on energy related issues.

MISSOURI

The Great Plains Prison Project and *St. George's House for Women,* Bob Mayer, 1600 E 58th, Kansas City, MO 64110. (816) 444-4750. Prison reform efforts. Halfway house for women.

Institute for Education in Peace and Justice, James McGinnis, 3700 W Pine, St. Louis, MO 63108. (314) 535-8884. Educational consultants for elementary and secondary school systems; developers of teachers' manuals and strategy guides in peace education; resource center for peace educators; summer programs in peace education; audio-visuals on racism, institutional violence, global economics, hunger, and women.

NEBRASKA

Omaha Friends of MNS, 518 N 40th, Omaha, NE 68131. MNS. Work on tax resistance, anti-militarism, simple living, feminist issues. Helps organize macro-analysis seminars.

NEW HAMPSHIRE

Clamshell Alliance, 62 Congress, Portsmouth, NH 03801. (603) 436-5414. Alliance of groups throughout New England organizing against nuclear power. Numerous resources available.

327

NEW JERSEY

Margaret DeMarco, 138 Atlantic, Bridgeton, NJ 08302. (609) 455-7779. Contact person for a growing community of people in southern New Jersey interested in alternative ways of organizing our lives and work. The community of women is the most active edge. Acquiring and passing on skill in mechanics and agriculture are Maggie's particular interests. Contact with farmworkers; work on community issues such as education and government. *Aqui se habla español.*

Ross Flanagan, 347 Independence Blvd., North Brunswick, NJ 08902. (201) 297-1773. Offers training/consultation to assist neighborhood residents in establishing community-based programs aimed at improving health, reducing stress, avoiding victimization, breaking crime patterns, organizing block meetings, street patrols, etc. Offers workshops on "Living Safe and Sound in Urban America," utilizing roleplaying and self-help techniques to instruct residents in effective methods of personal safety, victim counseling and health support.

NEW YORK

Alternatives to Violence Program, 15 Rutherford Place, New York, NY 10003. (212) 982-9288. Nonviolence training for Prison Residents (men and women) in New York State and northern New Jersey. Workshops, publications.

American Friends Service Committee, Upper NY state Area, 821 Euclid Ave., Syracuse, NY 13210. (315) 475-4822. Workshops in nonviolence, social change, and personal interaction. Assertive Conflict Resolution program for teachers to develop ways to help students handle interpersonal conflicts creatively. Middle East Peace Education and Action program. School Integration program. General peace education on current issues. Curriculum and nonviolence/social change libraries.

Children's Creative Response to Conflict, 15 Rutherford Place, New York, NY 10003. (212) 982-9288. Teacher and class training, facilitation in nonviolence techniques: Affirmation, Cooperation/Community Building, Communication, Conflict Resolution. Main publication: *Friendly Classroom for a Small Planet*. Affiliates in other parts of country.

Fellowship of Reconciliation (FOR), Box 271, Nyack, NY 10960. (212) LO8-8200. Runs a variety of programs related to nonviolent social change including training and direct action. Has contact with many church groups. Publishes *Fellowship* and has a literature service.

Al Moss, 326 Madison Ave., Albany, NY 12202. (518) 434-3813. Contact in Capital Area NYS for MNS, Aid to Battered Women group, resources for macro-analysis seminars and concerns for Native Americans.

Geoff Navias, Blake House, RD 1, Box 56, Oneonta, NY 13820. (518) 433-2367. Resource person for creative conflict resolution and children, teaching global concerns to children, and alternatives to violence. Has information on MNS.

North American Congress on Latin America (NACLA), Box 57, Cathedral Station, NY 10025. (212) 749-6513. Prepares excellent research report focusing on Latin America, *Report on the Americas*, 6 issues/yr. Subscription price: $11/yr. for individuals, $19/yr. for institutions. Occasional reports on special areas. Also available is *Research Methodology Guide*, a 70 page guide to researching local, national, and international power structures, $1.50.

Quaker Project on Community Conflict, 15 Rutherford Place, New York, NY 10003. (212) 982-9288. Major nonviolence training programs (publications, workshops, etc.) in schools (*Children's Creative Response to Conflict*) and in prisons (*Alternatives to Violence Program.*) Please see entries under these titles.

War Resisters League, 339 Lafayette, New York, NY 10012. (212) 228-0450. Pacifist group engaging in nonviolent actions; publishes and distributes related literature, has a resource packet on nonviolent action.

OHIO

Slim Bukofsky, 6013 Franklin, Cleveland, OH 44102. (216) 281-1922. Political action within the cooperative movement. Training for nonviolent action.

Next Step Collective, 903 Xenia Avenue, Yellow Springs, OH 45387. (513) 767-1633. Anti-nuclear power organizing, anti-militarism, training for nonviolent action and group process skills. Information on Re-evaluation Counseling.

OREGON

Charles and Leslie Gray, 1366 Lawrence, Eugene, OR 97401. (503) 344-0841. MNS. Involved in tax resistance, counseling and consultation on anti-nuclear power/weapons campaigns, non-violence training.

329

PENNSYLVANIA

Philadelphia Movement for a New Society/Life Center Community (MNS/LC)

For general literature and information contact the Network Service Collective. To participate in weekend orientation at the MNS/LC community contact the Orientation Weekend Coordinating Committee. Both are listed below.

An alternative educational environment for individuals and families wishing to learn and share skills and information useful in becoming long-term organizers for nonviolent social change. A minimum residence of one year is strongly encouraged. Offers long-term training in all aspects of nonviolent living and action; medium-term training programs in a variety of areas; macro-analysis seminars; alternative institutions; communal living; neighborhood safety organizing; action training in schools and colleges and on a variety of social issues; health care organizing; men's and women's liberation groups. Also: can make available literature, speakers, consultants and resources in most aspects of nonviolent social change included in this manual.

The following are parts of Philadelphia MNS/LC (write directly to addresses given):

Fatted Sprout, "The Food Service With a Conscience," 906 S 49th, Philadelphia, PA 19143. (215) SA6-0743. Provides nutritious, low cost food to organizations, groups, direct action campaigns, conferences. Does workshops on the politics of food/hunger, and the building of politically conscious alternative economic institutions. Willing to travel.

Medium-Term Training Organizing Collective, 4722 Baltimore Ave., Phila., PA 19143. (215) SA4-1464. MNS. Offers training opportunities for people interested in gaining or improving skills for organizing and nonviolent action in their own areas. The two-week general training programs include: group process skills, democratic decision making, macro-analysis, experience in community living, nonviolence theory and training, simple living, self empowerment, campaign-building and demonstrations. There are five 2-week training programs each year. Participants come to Philadelphia where they live in the MNS/LC community during training. Send for free brochure.

330

Network Service Collective, 4722 Baltimore Ave., Phila., PA 19143. (215) SA4-1464. MNS. Works to develop an MNS network of nonviolent social change activists by seeking out contacts to spread the word and by helping to develop groups that will join the network. Maintains a contact list for MNS organizers. Sends out MNS literature. Arranges and does outreach talks and trips.

Orientation Weekend Coordinating Collective, 4722 Baltimore Ave., Phila., PA 19143. (215) SA4-1464. MNS. Orientation Weekends are held the first full weekend of each month for folks who want to find out more about MNS, macro-analysis, training for nonviolent action, living in a political community, and related topics. The OWCC will send a flyer containing weekend dates, sample agenda, and application form.

Philadelphia Macro-Analysis Collective, 4722 Baltimore Ave., Phila., PA 19143. (215) SA4-1464. MNS. Helps groups start macro-analysis seminars and provides support to people and groups already involved in macro-analysis. *Organizing Macro-Analysis Seminars: A Manual* is available for $1.00 plus 25¢ postage. Special prices for bulk orders. Reprints literature needed by seminar groups. Has a newsletter to communicate with folks involved in macro-analysis. Has contacts throughout the U.S.A. and in Australia, Canada, England, New Zealand and West Germany. Write for name of person or group nearest you. Four very active contacts are Boston Macro-Analysis Collective (see Massachusetts), Janet Hartsough (see California), Norm Walsh (see New York), and North Country Macro-Analysis Collective (see Minnesota).

Philadelphia Namibia Action Group, 5021 Cedar Ave., Phila., PA 19143. (215) 474-9592. MNS. Organizes local and transnational direct action campaigns in support of Namibian independence. Has slide show for rent or for sale. Distributes literature.

Some of the Feminist Thinkers (SOFT), Amy Kietzman, 4819 Springfield Ave., Phila., PA 19143 (215) 729-5698. MNS. Offers women's workshops for personal and political change. Can design workshops on sexism, group process, conflict resolution, etc. to meet the needs of your group. Offers Feminist Macro-Analysis seminars.

Training Organizing Collective, 4722 Baltimore Ave., Phila., PA 19143. (215) SA4-1464. MNS. Organizes a 1-year training program designed to prepare people for long-term involvement in nonviolent social change and particularly to train organizers within the Movement for a New Society network. The training seeks to provide participants with the knowledge, skills, confidence, and sensitivity necessary to be effective change agents. An integrative learning experience through workshops and seminars, community living and field work. Areas included are: analysis of world society, visions of a new society, strategies for change, personal growth, nonviolent action, organizing and technical skills, consciousness raising, group dynamics, egalitarianism in groups, lifestyle, communities, alternative institutions, recreation and celebration.

Training/Action Affinity Group, Chris Moore, 4719 Springfield Ave., Phila., PA 19143. (215) SA9-7458. MNS. Offers training in democratic decision making for small or large groups, teacher training (high schools and universities) in nonviolent social change, conflict intervention/resolution in institutional and community conflicts, conflict resolution training in prisons, negotiation skills, and direct action. Will run workshops in other parts of the U.S. and other countries.

Transnational Collective, 4722 Baltimore Ave., Phila., PA 19143. (215) SA4-1464. MNS. Works to link radical nonviolent action groups through correspondence, exchange of people and literature, information evenings, newsletters, articles, support to relevant nonviolent direct action projects, and raise the consciousness level of other MNS-related collectives on various transnational issues.

WOW (Wonderful Older Women), 1014 S 47th, Phila., PA 19143. (215) SA4-5142. MNS. Offers workshops for older women for self-empowerment.

PENNSYLVANIA [Cont.]

Delaware Valley Community Land Trust, 980 Carver, Philadelphia, PA 19124. (215) PI4-6817. Accepts land into trust and leases trust land to people when available. Provides information about land trusts through monthly newsletter and meetings.

Friends Peace Committee, 1515 Cherry, Phila., PA 19102. (215) 241-7230. Has programs and resources in the areas of peace conversion and human security, disarmament, militarism and recruitment in high schools, nonviolence and children, foreign policy and legislation, and United Nations.

Friends Suburban Project, Box 462, Concordville, PA 19331. (215) GL9-4770. Deals with problems of police abuse and misconduct, organizing community mediation programs. Handbooks on county jails and court watching. Newsletter, *The Friendly Agitator*.

Gandhi Institute, Charles Walker, Box 92, Cheyney, PA 19319. (215) 399-0138. Manuals and other resources on training for direct action, international nonviolent action, peacekeeping, and history and theory of nonviolence. Associated with Gandhi Peace Foundation, India.

National Action/Research on the Military-Industrial Complex (NARMIC), AFSC, 1501 Cherry, Phila., PA 19102. (215) 241-7175. Produces educational resources in the area of disarmament and human rights, and answers requests for information about the military presence in local communities and the military work of particular companies. Publications include *The Military-Industrial Atlas of the U.S., The New Generation of Nuclear Weapons,* and *Meet your Local Merchant of Death.* Its latest slideshow, *Sharing Global Resources: Toward a New Economic Order*, explores complex issues of multinational corporations and U.S. trade relations with Third World countries.

North American Seminar for Training and Organizing in Nonviolent Action (NASTONA), Lynne Shivers, 4722 Baltimore Ave., Phila., PA 19143. (215) SA4-1464. The steering committee of NASTONA was formed at the North American seminar held at Iowa in May 1977. Its purposes are: (1) to create a national directory of trainers and organizers of nonviolent action, autumn 1978; (2) to disseminate information about training and organizing for nonviolent action through articles and a semi-annual newsletter; and (3) to encourage variety in training and organizing for nonviolent change through occasional conferences or workshops.

If you are a trainer or organizer for nonviolent action we'd like to hear from you. Ideas and suggestions are encouraged.

Pendle Hill, 338 Plush Mill Rd., Wallingford, PA 19086. (215) LO6-4507. Quaker center for religious and social study. Some nonviolent social change courses in both the nine months resident program and in weekend conferences, public lectures, summer sessions and courses open to persons unable to spend a term or year in residence. Good library.

Carl Zietlow, 423 W Nittany, State College, PA 16801. (814) 237-9223. Publisher of *A Reflective History of Training for Nonviolent Action in the Civil Rights and Peace Movements 1942-72*, a valuable resource for trainers. Also a trainer and organizer of nonviolent action.

RHODE ISLAND

American Friends Service Committee, 2 Stimson Ave., Providence, RI 02906. (401) 751-4488. Peace programs for schools, churches, community groups. Direct action and conflict resolution training.

Rhode Island Peace Education Project, 2 Stimson Ave., Providence, RI 02906. (401) 751-4488. Workshops/resources relating nonviolent social change to classroom education, elementary and high school.

SOUTH CAROLINA

Palmetto Alliance and *Grass Roots Organizing Workshop*, 18 Old Bluff Road, Columbia, SC 29201. (802) 254-8132. Organizing around poor people's issues and recently anti-nuclear activity.

VERMONT

Earth Bridge Community Land Trust, RD 1, Putney, VT 05346. (802) 387-5732. Working on projects in "Cooperative Self Reliance," land trusts, community garden projects and other economic alternatives.

Training/Action Affinity Group, c/o Movement for a New Society, R 2, St. Johnsbury, VT 05819. (802) 748-3512. Offers training in democratic decision making, teacher training for nonviolent social change, conflict intervention/resolution, direct action, and community building. Offers workshops in alternatives to prisons, and training in alternatives to violence for prison inmates. Provides outreach services including literature.

Claire Wilson, RFD 3, Putney, VT 05346. (802) 387-6635. Does training for nonviolent action. Involved in organizing around nuclear power and women's issues. Has information on MNS groups forming in the area.

WASHINGTON

Kenn Arning, 1425 E Prospect, Seattle, WA 98112. (206) 325-1945. Men's anti-sexism and consciousness-raising groups. Group dynamics workshops.

Re-evaluation Counseling Communities, 719 2nd Ave. N, Seattle, WA 98109. (206) 284-0311. Offers information on classes in your area in Re-evaluation Counseling, a peer-group, self-help approach to freeing oneself from distress which inhibits creative and flexible interaction with others and with the world. Has literature and information on workshops. (See Re-evaluation Counseling under Part Four.)

Tool Box, 337 17th Ave. E, Seattle, WA 98112. (206) 322-4962. Training resources in a variety of areas related to nonviolent social change, including group dynamics and process, facilitation, interpersonal communications, problem-solving, direct action, and strategy building; knowledge and skills in printing and publishing; and music.

WISCONSIN

Center for Conflict Resolution, 731 State, Madison, WI 53706. (608) 255-0488. Offers training in conflict resolution, group dynamics and facilitation, communication skills, egalitarian organizational skills, nonviolent theory and practice. Works with college, high school, elementary, and preschool programs for the purpose of applying conflict resolution, group, and communication skills in the classroom. Writes and distributes publications on the above areas.

II
Outside the United States

Building a successful movement for nonviolent social change often requires cooperative action across national boundaries. While working for change we have had the opportunity to work with people involved in social change in a number of places outside the U.S.

This is a list of groups and organizations outide the United States which are active in nonviolent social change organizing of various sorts. Many groups also are communities, but not all of them. A few organizations listed produce a newspaper or magazine as their main social change work. Many of these organizations are both organizing-oriented and produce their own newsletter.

This list is tentative and very incomplete. But a start in helping organizers in the U.S. connect with sisters and brothers outside the U.S. Due to our printing deadline we have been unable to confirm information directly so the list has been limited to people in contact with us. We hope to add more groups in future editions. Please excuse any inaccuracies which may appear.

For current information on additional contacts in these and other countries, write the Transnational Collective, 4722 Baltimore Avenue, Phila., PA 19143. If you know of other people or groups working for nonviolent social change outside of the United States the Transnational Collective would like to hear from you.

INTERNATIONAL

International Fellowship of Reconciliation (IFOR), Veerstraat 1, Alkmaar, Netherlands. Coordinating office for FOR groups, advocating nonviolent initiatives, analysis and action based on a religious perspective. Magazine by subscription ($6. US).

War Resisters International (WRI), van Elewyckstraat 35, Brussels 1050, Belgium. Groups in a number of countries involved in nonviolent initiatives, direct action, and analysis based on a radical political analysis. Monthly mailing by subscription.

CANADA

Norm Walsh, c/o Canadian Friends Service Committee, 60 Lowther Ave., Toronto, Ont. M5R 1C7. (416) 920-5213. Resource person for Macro Analysis, Native Peoples, Peace Education, how to make slide shows, and Re-evaluation Counselling.

DENMARK

NOAH, Husat, Radhustrade 13, 1466 Copenhagen K, Denmark. Peace action with a special emphasis on ecology.

FRANCE

"Alternatives Nonviolentes," 3 rue Lemont, 69001 Lyon, France. Quarterly magazine.

Antonie van As-Aruibu, Barlonges, 77320 La Terte, Gaucher, France. Community Arts and Research in Nonviolence. Antonie lived for a time at the Philadelphia Life Center and is an MNS contact in Europe.

Centre Quaker International, 114 Rue de Vaugirard, 75006,

Paris 6e, France. A clearing house for information on nonviolent actions in France; not a residential center.

Community of the Ark, La Borie Noble, 34960 Le Bosquet d'Orb, France. Gandhian community founded by Lanza del Vasto; active and vigorous community. Newsletter available by subscription.

GREAT BRITAIN

Campaign Against the Arms Trade (CAAT), 5 Caledonian Road, London N.1, Great Britain. Carries on research, public information education, and action around Britain's arms trade industry. Sandy Merritt, staff. Monthly mailing by subscription.

Friends Peace and International Relations Committee, Friends House, Euston Road, London NW1 2BJ, Great Britain. Peace committee for London Yearly Meeting; quarterly magazine subscription. Peace education and action.

Housman's Bookstore, 5 Caledonian Road, King's Cross, London N1, Great Britain. Well-known movement bookstore with wide selection. Will send book orders abroad.

Martin Jelfs, Some Friends Community, 128 Bethnal Green Road, London ER 6D6, Great Britain. Small community in East London. Martin is an MNS contact in Britain and is especially interested in training.

Peace News, 8 Elm Ave., Nottingham, Great Britain. Bi-weekly movement magazine advocating nonviolent revolution ($11. US subscription).

INDIA

Atheist Centre, Patamata, Vijawada 520006, India. Educational and medical work; nonviolent action; long standing campaigns to break down class barriers and challenge religious superstitions.

Gandhi Peace Foundation, 221-223 Deen Dayal Upadhyaya Marg, New Delhi 110001, India. Secretary is Radhakrishna. Major national peace organization carrying on Gandhian peace initiatives. Several offices. Newsletter by subscription, ''Gandhi Marg.''

Sarva Seva Sangh, Gopuri, Warda, India. Secretary is T. Bang. Gandhian peace organization which includes alternative social work (constructive work) and a peace ''army.''

ITALY

Centro Studie Iniziative, Largo Scalia 5, Partinico 90047, Italy. The work of Danilo Dolci and his staff in Sicily to challenge Mafia control. Developed a mass movement to help create a dam in 1971 to help farmers control their own water supply. The new educational center focuses on the quality of education in Sicily. Focuses on peace education and community development, combined with nonviolent direct action.

JAPAN

Yukio Aki, 4-2, 3-chome, Asahi-cho, Akishima-si, Tokyo, Japan. Nonviolent activist and experienced trainer; lived at the Philadelphia MNS/LC community in West Philadelphia. Good contact for simple living, ecology concerns and organizing for direct action.

"AMPO," Japan-Asia Quarterly Review, P.O. Box 5250, Tokyo Int., Japan. Quarterly magazine with a detailed radical analysis of East Asia social change issues ($12 US subscription).

Friendship Center, 1544 Midori-machi, Hiroshima-shi, 734 Hiroshima, Japan. Peace education and hospitality; jointly run by Japanese and Americans. Has a quarterly magazine in English.

Susume Ishitani, 8-19, Mita 4 chome, Minato ku, Tokyo, Japan. (03) 451 0804. Quaker Nonviolent Study group, WRI, IFOR. Group of about ten people. Good resource for training and direct action. National coordinating point for tax resistance.

Kazuo and Kuniko Iwatani, 10 6 Asahi 1 chome, Hiroshima, Japan. Group of about ten people with much direct action experience. Some training experience. Special concerns cooperative and simple living, Korea. Operate small alternative industry (coffeehouse).

NETHERLANDS

Center for Nonviolence, Postbus 4098, Amsterdam, Netherlands. Monthly magazine, "Geweldloos Aktief" (nonviolent action). Available in Dutch.

NORTHERN IRELAND

Community of the Peace People, 224 Lisburn Road, Belfast 9, Northern Ireland. Nobel Prize winning peace organization founded by Betty Williams and Mairead Corrigan. "Peace by Peace" bi-weekly newspaper by subscription.

"Dawn," 331 Ormeau Road, Belfast 7, Northern Ireland. Contact Rob Mitchell. Irish journal of nonviolence ($7 US subscription).

NORWAY

Paxhuset, Goteborgata 8, Oslo, Norway. Peace and liberation groups, peace press headquarters, coffeehouse.

SCOTLAND

Iona Community, 91 Prince George's Street, Glasgow, Scotland. Religious community associated with the Church of Scotland. Strong peace emphasis and affiliated with the Mobilization for Survival.

WEST GERMANY

"Graswurzel Revolution" (Grass Roots Revolution), Speckstrasse 8, 3400 Goettingen, West Germany. Monthly newspaper full of information and analysis about radical actions. Its editorial policy advocates nonviolent action.

Nonviolent Action Training Program (of the International FOR), Eric Bachman, Bismarkstr. 121, D-4900 Herford, West Germany. Peace education, training for nonviolent action, especially for anti-nukes campaigns.

FRIEND, COME AND SING

Words and music by Sarah Gowan and Susanne Terry Gowan
©1976 Susanne Terry Gowan

We'll sing a song of hope and joy. (X3)
A new day it's gonna be.

We'll end the song of death and war. (X3)
A new day...

We'll raze the prisons to the ground. (X3)
A new day...

Strong men and women side by side. (X3)
A new day...

Friend, come and sing and dance with me. (X3)
A new day...

Index

List of exercises and tools described in the manual

Bibliographies

COME ALIVE!

Words and music by P.J. Hoffman
© P.J. Hoffman 1976

CH: Come alive! we are the revolution.
Come alive! we are the revolution.
And everything is coming, yes,
everything is going all right.

1. We're gonna plant some seeds. We are the seeds. (X2)

2. We need some sunshine. We are the sunshine. (X2)

3. We need some spirit. We are the spirit. (X2)

4. We need some changes. We are the changes. (X2)

351